W9-BYV-337

BISHOP'S UNIVERSITY
LIBRARY
LENNOXVILLE

British Policy Towards Wartime Resistance in Yugoslavia and Greece

British Policy Towards Wartime Resistance in Yugoslavia and Greece

Edited by
PHYLLIS AUTY
Professor of Modern History and Chairman of the History Department, Simon Fraser University, British Columbia. Formerly Reader in the History of the South Slavs, School of Slavonic and East European Studies, University of London

and

RICHARD CLOGG
Lecturer in Modern Greek History, School of Slavonic and East European Studies and King's College, University of London

BOOKS
10 East 53d St., New York 10022
(a division of Harper & Row Publishers, Inc.)

in association with the School of Slavonic and East European Studies
University of London

© The Macmillan Press Ltd 1975

All rights reserved. No part of this publication may be reproduced or
transmitted, in any form or by any means, without permission.

First published 1975 by
THE MACMILLAN PRESS LTD
London and Basingstoke

Published in the U.S.A. 1975 by
HARPER & ROW PUBLISHERS, INC.
BARNES & NOBLE IMPORT DIVISION

ISBN–0–06–490249–8

Printed in Great Britain

Contents

Editors' Preface

This book is based on material delivered at a conference organised by the History Department of the School of Slavonic and East European Studies of the University of London in July 1973. The purpose of the conference was to reconsider official British attitudes towards wartime resistance in Yugoslavia and Greece in the light both of the official records (available for public inspection since January 1972) and of the recollections of some of those who participated in the formulation and execution of British policies. Attention is concentrated on British policy decisions, especially in 1943. No attempt is made to give a coherent picture of events in Yugoslavia and Greece between 1941 and 1945, though of course many of these events are mentioned, and some are discussed more fully. A short list of publications in English, from which interested readers can obtain such a picture, is appended. There is also no attempt to consider systematically the policies of the two other major Allies, or of the two governments-in-exile, or to relate events in Yugoslavia and Greece to those in neighbouring countries (Italy, Albania, Hungary, Rumania and Bulgaria) or to the overall strategic situation in the Mediterranean. These important subjects still await their historians.

The revelations contained in the documents, amplified by the material contributed in the discussion following the papers, elucidate a substantial number of points that are unclear in previously published accounts. These relate mainly to the relations between the various British institutions concerned with the war in the Balkans: the Foreign Office, the Special Operations Executive, General Headquarters Middle East, and to some extent the Political Warfare Executive and the British Broadcasting Corporation. None the less the picture that emerges, confused as it is, lacks a crucial dimension. This is occasioned by the withholding of a few key documents in the

Foreign Office papers and of the records of the Special Operations Executive in their entirety (with the exception of some S.O.E. papers passed to the Foreign Office, the War Cabinet and the Chiefs of Staff). It should be stressed however that in comparison with all other countries (with the exception of the United States) a generous policy has been adopted in making the official British papers available, while it is clear that even after thirty years some documents cannot yet be released.

In conclusion we should like to thank most warmly the contributors to this book – those that took part in the conference, the Council of the School of Slavonic and East European Studies which underwrote much of the cost of the conference, and the Nuffield Foundation which also made a generous contribution. We should also like to thank the many people who helped to make the conference a success or who helped in the preparation of this book, and particularly Nicholas Bugg and Anne Pilcher of King's College, University of London, Hilda Chan of the School of Slavonic and East European Studies, and Mary Jo Clogg, who compiled the index. A special debt of gratitude is owed to Jeanne Clissold who played a major part in the preparatory work for the conference, in the transcription of the discussion, and in typing the text of the book. Extracts from documents in the Public Record Office and the extract from J. Ehrman, *Grand Strategy*, Vol. v, are published by permission of the Controller of H.M. Stationery Office.

London   Phyllis Auty
March 1974   Richard Clogg

In the year which has elapsed between the conference and the final preparation of the book for the press, we have to note with distress the deaths of two who took part in it and, with great distinction, in the events themselves: Colonel Sir John Stevens, K.C.M.G., D.S.O., O.B.E. and Colonel S. W. Bailey, O.B.E. Both were men of unusual quality, very different yet sharing two outstanding gifts. The first was the curiosity and imagination which enabled them to understand other peoples and to feel as they did, to penetrate deeply into languages and cultures. The second was the power to win and inspire friendship and to get the best efforts out of them.

John Stevens came to S.O.E. Cairo in 1942 after serving in
the army in France and the Middle East. He went on two
missions to occupied Greece, in the north in 1943 and in the
Peloponnese in 1944, as well as to occupied North Italy in
1944–5. After the war he joined the Bank of England (in 1946)
and made a brilliant career in banking and financial diplomacy,
including service as Economic Minister at the British Embassy
in Washington from 1965 to 1967.

Bill Bailey, as a scientific expert at the Trepča mines in the
1930s, acquired a solid knowledge of Serbian, Yugoslav and
Balkan politics. A member of S.O.E. from 1939, he held posts of
responsibility in Istanbul, in the Middle East, and for a time in
the United States. He headed the British mission to General
Mihailović's headquarters in 1942–3. He was a member of the
British military component in the Allied Control Commission
in Bulgaria in 1945, and then served in the British Embassy in
Ankara. After the war he was for many years an official of the
United Nations in Geneva.

G. H. N. Seton-Watson

Notes on Contributors

Auty, Phyllis. B.B.C. Yugoslav Section, European Division, 1940–3. Political Intelligence Centre, Middle East, 1943–1944.

Bailey, S. W., O.B.E. (d. June 1974). S.O.E., 1939–41 (Belgrade, Cairo and U.S.A.). Senior Liaison Officer with Mihailović, 1942–4.

Barker, Elisabeth. Head of Balkan Region, Political Warfare Executive, 1942–5.

Bolsover, G. H. Attaché and First Secretary, H.M. Embassy, Moscow, 1943–7. Director, School of Slavonic and East European Studies, University of London.

Clissold, Stephen. Political Intelligence Centre, Middle East, 1943–4. British Military Mission to Yugoslavia, 1944–5

Clogg, Richard. Lecturer in Modern Greek History, School of Slavonic and East European Studies and King's College, University of London.

Davidson, Basil, M.C. S.O.E., Budapest, 1939–41, Istanbul, 1941–2, Cairo, 1942. British Liaison Officer in Yugoslavia, 1943–4.

Deakin, F. W. D., D.S.O. S.O.E., 1942–5. First British Liaison Officer at Tito's Headquarters, 1943.

Glen, Sir Alexander, K.B.E., D.S.C. Assistant Naval Attaché Belgrade 1939–41. Admiralty Representative in Albania, 1941–2. Personal Representative to Yugoslavia of Commander-in-Chief, Mediterranean, 1943–5.

Gubbins, Major-General Sir Colin, K.C.M.G., D.S.O., M.C. Director of Operations and Training, S.O.E., 1940–3. From 1943 Head of S.O.E.

Hammond, Professor N. G. L., D.S.O., F.B.A. British Liaison Officer in Greece, 1943–4.

Henniker-Major, The Hon. Sir John, K.C.M.G., C.V.O., M.C. British Liaison Officer, Yugoslavia, 1943–4.

Hornsby-Smith, The Rt Hon. Dame Patricia, D.B.E. Personal

Assistant to Lord Selborne, Minister of Economic Warfare responsible for Special Operations Executive.

Johnstone, Kenneth R., C.B., C.M.G. P.W.E. Cairo, 1941–2, 1943–4. Allied Greek Information Service, 1943–5.

Maclean, Brigadier Sir Fitzroy, Bt, C.B.E. Commander of Allied Mission to Tito, 1943–5.

Myers, Brigadier E. C. W., C.B.E., D.S.O. Commander of the British Military Mission to the Greek Resistance, 1942–3.

Pawson, David. S.O.E. in Greece, 1940–1, Istanbul, Izmir, 1941–3.

Pawson, Mrs Pamela. S.O.E. in Greece, 1940–1, Istanbul and Izmir, 1941–4.

Seton-Watson, Professor G. H. N., F.B.A. S.O.E. in Rumania, 1940, Yugoslavia, 1941, Cairo and Istanbul, 1942–4.

Stevens, Sir John, K.C.M.G., D.S.O., O.B.E. (d. November 1973). S.O.E. in Cairo, 1942. British Liaison Officer in Greece, 1943–4.

Sweet-Escott, B. A. C. Staff of S.O.E. Headquarters, London. Engaged on missions to Cairo and elsewhere.

Taylor, George F., C.B.E. Chief of Staff (1940–2) to Sir Frank Nelson and Sir Charles Hambro, Heads of S.O.E. Special Emissary to S.O.E. Overseas Missions in 1943.

Woodhouse, The Hon. C. M., D.S.O., O.B.E., Commander of the Allied Military Mission to the Greek Resistance, 1943–4.

PART ONE

PAPERS

1   S.O.E. in the Balkans

BICKHAM SWEET-ESCOTT

INTRODUCTION BY MAJOR GENERAL SIR COLIN GUBBINS

I would like to refer to one general aspect of our operations in the Balkans which has always seemed strange to me – that is why it took so long for General Headquarters in the Middle East to realise that they had on their hands in their own theatre a major war in which they were really taking no interest at all. By this war I mean the activities of resistance forces and the operations in the Balkans of the Special Operations Executive (S.O.E.).[1] I would suggest tentatively two reasons for this lack of interest: the first is that in retrospect I do not believe that theatre commanders, as they came to be called, or even Resident Ministers, were ever informed officially by the War Cabinet of the creation of S.O.E. in July 1940; and secondly they were not given any inkling of the charter upon which it was founded. From the beginning quite excessive secrecy was enjoined on S.O.E. itself from above, and I can now begin to understand why General Headquarters Middle East felt that resistance activities in distant countries (not even on their shores) though within their theatre, were not their direct concern. In this connection I cannot at the same time find anybody who was ever informed officially or in writing of what the charter of S.O.E. was. I think that S.O.E. was looked upon as a sort of branch of the secret service, and of course a secret service with no written charter, but S.O.E. had one written down in the Cabinet minutes, though as far as I can make out it never got beyond that.[2] That may well be the reason why General Headquarters Middle East did not appreciate that it very much deserved their concern, to stimulate this major war going on within their theatre. I can think of no other reason.

One other relevant matter is the question of British interception and decoding of German wireless traffic. The intelligence so obtained has of course the highest degree of reliability and is thus invaluable, but the 'source' must be guarded against any possibility of disclosure otherwise the enemy would change his ciphers overnight and one would be left in the dark maybe for months. Hence the extremely tight restrictions on the circulation of this information in its original form: this must be accepted.

I would not therefore have expected S.O.E. in Cairo to have had access to these intercepts, but I understand that none of the intelligence so obtained from high-level German wireless transmission traffic in the Balkans was made available to it even in paraphrased form and as 'from a very reliable source' which would have guarded its origin adequately. I do not of course know if General Headquarters Middle East had this intelligence themselves.[3]

In this paper I must firstly comply with a specific request and summarise S.O.E.'s activities in Greece and Yugoslavia up to the end of 1942. After that, I think the most useful contribution I can make is to try to describe the surrounding atmosphere in which we had to work in S.O.E. during the spring and summer of 1943 and the problems which worried us most in London and Cairo.[4]

It is a commonplace that history written from documentary sources only can be grossly misleading unless you describe the background against which the people you are writing about had to work. In Ranke's famous but often misleading words, history has to show 'what it was really like' – the past, that is. This is particularly difficult if you are writing about war, the fog of which is proverbial, but no less dense for that. Like any other headquarters, or indeed any other wartime unit I knew, we in S.O.E. were often beset by muddle and confusion. But to this was added in the early days a feeling of frustration and even despair which was quite peculiar to a new and untried body.

The birth pangs of S.O.E. were prolonged. Although it did not see the light of day till the summer of 1940, the attempt to act against the enemy in the Balkans and elsewhere by means which could not be acknowledged by the British government, dates from a much earlier period, for Section D of M.I.6 was formed sometime in 1938. When in April 1940 I joined the Balkan desk in London, D was run by an imaginative and colourful professional soldier, now General Laurence Grand, but it seemed to have no written terms of reference whatever. However, it did have an active section in Belgrade. This was also a sort of tactical headquarters for D's work in the surround-

ing countries. It was commanded by a man we all knew as
Julius Caesar, though alas his Commentaries are not available.[5]

That spring D was very busy in Yugoslavia. It was actively
engaged in small-scale sabotage; for instance we had Slovenes
putting sand in the axle boxes of goods trains bound for Germany. It had ambitious plans to block the Danube to oil barges
coming up the river from Rumania to Ratisbon or Ulm, though
more success was achieved by bribing the pilots and buying up
the barges than by the strong-arm methods Caesar was working
on. But even then D was trying its hand at political subversion
by underground propaganda, and particularly by putting out
feelers to the Serb Peasant Party, and to others – though unfortunately not to the Croats – who opposed the policy of the
Royalist government. Even in the summer of 1940 that policy
looked like compromising with the Germans when the crunch
came. D was also toying with the idea of a revolt in Albania. In
April there was a meeting in London of His Majesty's representatives in the Balkans which reluctantly recognised the
importance of D in the area. One of the results was that we were
allowed to start up a base in Greece that May – only just in
time as the Italian declaration of war in June 1940 made
physical communications between London and the Balkans a
matter no longer of hours but of months. Fortunately, at the
same time we set up a headquarters in Cairo for work into the
Balkans.

With the fall of France, and the knowledge that we now had
to fight alone, Churchill decided in July 1940 to make an honest
woman of D by creating S.O.E. under a Minister of the Crown,
combining D with several other clandestine organisations, and
regularising all their activities by the issue of a formal charter.
So S.O.E. was no more than a hopeful improvisation devised in
a really desperate situation. As Professor Foot has said, special
operations are as old as war.[6] Action of an S.O.E. type had
been put in hand by us many times before – by the younger
Pitt against Napoleon, and also in the Kaiser's war of course.
But jobs like the Arab Bureau and the Zimmerman letter were
isolated *ad hoc* operations. What was new about S.O.E. was that
there had never been a body specifically formed to carry on
S.O.E. action in enemy or enemy-occupied territory and in
neutral countries; and that this body should be responsible to a

Minister with direct access to the Chiefs of Staff and to the
Prime Minister. [7]

From the moment of its birth, S.O.E. inevitably aroused the
suspicion, jealousy and scepticism of established professional
bodies such as M.I.5 and M.I.6, which had been in business
for decades, not to mention the Foreign Office. They all accused
us in those early years of amateurishness, unreliability, gulli-
bility and of generally making their life more difficult. The same
was true of the Services, whose meagre resources we would have
to use. We had no war book of precedent to work on. We had
to find our own way about, making our own rules in this new
kind of total war. We had to recruit people of a rather special
type in the middle of a war, when anyone who seemed to be
what we were after was usefully employed elsewhere, and it was
not always easy to explain why S.O.E. needed him. We were
lucky indeed to get as many first-class men and women as we
did, but we were only too often fobbed off with duds.

For obvious reasons we had to work on our own operations in
deep secrecy. But the need for security was only too often mis-
understood by others. Why for instance had so few of us seen
the charter of 1940? I never saw it, and Sir Colin Gubbins
himself has told me that he never saw it either. Why was it that
so few of us were told at the time of Churchill's parting words to
Dalton, when he appointed him to oversee S.O.E., that he had
to 'set Europe ablaze'? [8] Too often we found that high-ranking
officers who ought to have known something about S.O.E. had
never even heard of it; others seemed to think it was a dodge to
avoid the fighting and have a good time at the taxpayers'
expense. Above all, we were beset by the logical difficulty that,
without scarce facilities such as aircraft and wireless transmission communications, we could not get results, but that
unless we did get results, we were hardly likely to get the
facilities.

By forming S.O.E. the government had at least recognised its
potential to harm the enemy by helping the 150 million Euro-
peans now under Axis domination, even if the Chiefs of Staff
could not or would not give S.O.E. the tools to get on with the
job just yet. As a result, that winter our activities in the Balkans
were largely confined to underground propaganda, in which we
had a good deal of success, notably in Greece, and to making

such preparations as we could – for instance by laying down stores of sabotage material – against the growing probability that there would be a Balkan campaign.

The Italian invasion of Greece in October 1940 greatly intensified our activities there and our preparations for Albania, but at the same time it made it difficult for us to get on with what should have been one of our most important tasks. This was to leave behind an organisation to work into the Balkans if, in spite of all our hopes, they were occupied by the enemy. But you could not do this except in the deepest secrecy, because if you were found out, it would be seen as a vote of no confidence by our local allies in any overt military aid we might provide. In any case, what we needed if we were to prepare for an enemy occupation of the Balkans were secret communications. On this absolutely vital point not only S.O.E. but all the British secret organisations were totally unprepared. At the time M.I.6 had a monopoly of secret W/T sets and their use. That winter all S.O.E. could squeeze out of them for the whole of the Balkans was seven sets. In the end we had to make our own, but they did not come into production until 1942.

Our work in the Balkans became even more urgent with the British decision in February 1941 to help Greece by sending troops, in addition to the token R.A.F. units there since Mussolini's invasion. True, S.O.E. was entitled to take some credit for the pro-Allied *coup d'état* in Belgrade of 27 March 1941 because our Minister had encouraged our people to keep in touch with some dissatisfied officers and with the leaders of the Serb Peasant Party, which we had even been financing; but most of us thought the *coup* would have happened if S.O.E. had not existed at all.[9] In the event, the whole Balkan campaign was over in a matter of weeks; of the seven W/T sets we had bullied M.I.6 to produce, six never came on the air at all. The seventh was given by David Pawson, before leaving Greece, to Colonel Bakirdzis, who handed it over to the celebrated Prometheus 2, and when it came on the air in November 1941, it was to prove the means whereby we were able eventually to work back into Greece.[10] Many of the demolitions which the regular forces had omitted, particularly in Salonika, were carried out by S.O.E.'s people and by David Pawson in the Lake Copais district. The disaster in Crete in May was a real calamity because, like everyone else, we had been told that Crete would be held, and we had planned to work back into Greece from there. Now that it was gone, we had to begin working back into the Balkans all over again very nearly from scratch.

Given that we had no aircraft and still very few W/T sets, the progress that S.O.E. Cairo made in the rest of 1941 was remarkable. That summer Lt-Commander (Skipper) Poole, former manager of the Imperial Airways staging post in Crete, succeeded in getting to Crete by submarine and rescuing some 200 British and Commonwealth troops; and there were several other invasions of Crete by S.O.E. with this purpose, notably that of Colonel C. M. Woodhouse in December. But these exploits, though useful, did not tell us what was really happening in Greece. For this we had to rely on Greeks who could get out by rail or road to Istanbul or, even at that early date, by caique to Smyrna. The information we obtained from them pointed unmistakably to the intense and growing unpopularity of the monarchy and the government-in-exile, tarnished as they were by their connection with the Metaxas dictatorship and by their exclusion from holding command of so many Venizelist officers.

It certainly confirmed that the spirit of resistance was strong. And when Prometheus 2 came on the air, it told us that some of the friends S.O.E. had made before the occupation were active and anxious for help. However, that autumn counsel was very naturally obsessed by the famine. It was darkened too by the tendency of the Royalist government to imply to the British that any Greek who opposed the monarchy was a Communist. Further progress in finding out what was happening in the mountains was impeded for a time by the calamity at Antiparos in February 1942, when a British officer was landed by submarine but captured with an impeccable Staff College operation order headed, 'Information – own troops', followed by a list of people he was to contact in Greece, most of whom were promptly arrested.

In Yugoslavia, we learnt in August 1941 through the Royalist government-in-exile that guerrillas had taken to the mountains in Serbia under a Colonel Draža Mihailović. It was not long before the Royalists saw to it that many others, including Churchill, learnt of it too. It was to find out what was really going on that in September we persuaded the Navy to land two

Royalist officers in Montenegro with two W/T sets. At the last moment Captain D. T. Hudson, who then did not even know the name of Mihailović, joined the party with his own cipher but no set or operator of his own.[11] When I left Egypt in November 1941, the name of Mihailović was the symbol of resistance in the Balkans, and though such news as we did get from Hudson mentioned that his people were fighting with the 'Communists', the two sides had not yet broken irreparably with each other. It seemed that S.O.E. had made a start in Yugoslavia too. The problem of communication was one of immediate priority, for even then Hudson was off the air for long periods, as he had lost control of the two W/T sets landed with him. So the version of the train of events which was to prevail for many months was that of Mihailović and of the Royalist government behind him.

I got back to London from Cairo (where I had been since July) at the end of November 1941 and for fifteen months was put on to quite different work. So for this period I cannot speak from my own experience. But when fresh from Washington I took over the Balkan desk in London in March 1943, it was to find that S.O.E. had managed to get the confidence to some degree of the Chiefs of Staff in the Middle East. They were impressed by the blowing of the Gorgopotamos viaduct in Greece at the end of November 1942. They were impressed by our contact with resistance movements in Yugoslavia and Albania as well. In his official account of our grand strategy of the period Michael Howard quotes W. J. M. Mackenzie as saying in his unpublished *History of S.O.E.* that in the spring of 1943 we had ten missions in Greece, a dozen with Mihailović and five in Albania – twenty-seven in all.[12] When in February 1943 General Sir Henry Maitland Wilson took over as commander-in-chief Middle East, he arranged for S.O.E. Cairo to attend his daily conference, which was progress. But Maitland Wilson adds in his book that relations between S.O.E. and the Services had been 'sporadic', the Services 'fulfilling demands to the best of their ability when called on', and 'S.O.E. arranging to carry out attacks on strategical objectives when asked'. This is significant, because it looks as if it had never then crossed his mind that S.O.E. could be of more than marginal use to the Services.[13]

The main demand we had made on them had amounted to the use of long-range aircraft, and in the spring of 1942 we had been given the use of four Liberators.[14] In the light of other claims to long-range aircraft at that time, this was far from negligible, though other secret organisations had to use them too, and all four aircraft were rarely serviceable at any one time. Otherwise, all we had asked for was the occasional submarine sortie, for by now production of S.O.E.'s own W/T sets was beginning to come on stream. At the beginning of 1943, the relations between S.O.E. and the Services in Cairo were rather like those between two friendly but quite independent nation-states. For in the passage I have quoted from his book Maitland Wilson was careful to point out that S.O.E. reported not to him, but to a Minister in London, though this was not unusual because M.I.5 and M.I.6 in the Middle East also reported to Ministers in London, and Political Warfare Executive (P.W.E.) Cairo reported at one time to a trinity of Ministers in London.

In the first few months of 1943 all this was to change dramatically. The change was the result of what had been happening in Greece and Yugoslavia that winter. On this I will try to tell you how I personally saw things at the time in London and Cairo. As our activities in Greece were to move to crisis point before those in Yugoslavia, I will deal with them first.

From the occupation until September 1942, S.O.E. had been working on a directive confirmed formally by the Chiefs of Staff in May that, while carrying out small-scale sabotage whenever possible, its main aim was to engineer and supply a country-wide revolt when, but only when, the time was ripe. The difficulty was that the Greeks who seemed prepared to do this were more and more reluctant to serve under the Royalist government. These people were very numerous, and we had contact through Prometheus and through various escapees with many potential resisters, of whom the most promising was a so-called 'Popular Front'. By the spring of 1942 this 'Popular Front' had become E.A.M. (National Liberation Front) and of this London and all the commanders in the Middle East and the Minister of State were kept currently informed.[15] There was no suggestion whatever that at this time E.A.M. was dominated by the Communist Party of Greece, the K.K.E.

What was abundantly clear was that, if S.O.E. were to help these people, some of them might do what the British asked them to do, but the vast majority would not do what the government-in-exile asked them to do unless it changed its policy radically, for instance by getting the King to say that he would not return to the country before a plebiscite had been held – as of course he eventually did when it was too late. This information was highly unpopular with the government-in-exile. It was also highly unpopular with the Foreign Office which did not wish to press the King. But we thought that unless they did, we would be unlikely to have the coordinated action the military wanted. The matter was getting urgent by the spring of 1942, because already groups of guerrillas of various political complexions were taking to the mountains, though General Napoleon Zervas had to have his journey money from Athens to the mountains paid for by S.O.E. in advance, in sovereigns.[16]

This was roughly the point at which the first S.O.E. mission was being prepared to go to mainland Greece. It was a party of twelve parachuted in during the early autumn of 1942 with the object of blowing up the Gorgopotamos viaduct (the *Harling* operation). This had been expressly desired by Middle East Command, for the railway it carried was the only one which could bring enemy troops from the north to the Piraeus for the campaign in North Africa, then at its height. It would probably have not been on at all unless Prometheus 2 had been on the air, for it was still the only set in Greece with which we had two-way communications. In the operation we had been helped by Zervas's men and by what eventually turned out to have been an E.L.A.S. (National Popular Liberation Army – the military arm of E.A.M.) detachment. But in an article published in 1971, Colonel Woodhouse quotes the text of the operation order given to Brigadier E. C. W. Myers which, incredible though it may seem, makes no reference to E.A.M., and very little mention of Greek politics at all.[17] He goes on to say that Panayiotis Kanellopoulos, the Minister of War in the government-in-exile, who had escaped to the Middle East in April 1942, and whom Woodhouse saw before he left Cairo, never mentioned that the K.K.E. was an active force in the resistance. He says he first saw the initials E.L.A.S. in Greece on 7 November. But it was not till January 1943 that Myers thought it fair to say that E.A.M.

'had a close connection with K.K.E., even if it was not under its actual domination'.[18]

By February 1943 London and Washington were actively preparing the invasion of Sicily. They wished S.O.E. to create a diversion in Greece to make the enemy believe that the operation was to be directed at Greece, not Sicily. We thought we could not do this without a great deal of help from the local resistance. S.O.E. in London and Cairo now knew that E.L.A.S. was almost certainly controlled by the K.K.E. As for Zervas, we knew that, though a republican, he was prepared to accept the orders of the British, which E.L.A.S. was not. All this we pointed out to the Chiefs of Staff in London, with the result that Churchill himself ruled early in March 1943 that 'in helping the resistance in Greece we would favour the groups which were willing to support the King and his government', but with a saving clause that this was 'subject to operational necessity'.

We were afraid that unless we made full use of this saving clause there could be no diversion in Greece. As it happened the help we got from the resistance was, broadly speaking, confined to the passive but important role of allowing our people transit through their areas. The actual operations started in June 1943 and were almost entirely carried out by the British. They were immensely successful, for by this and other similar ploys the Germans were taken in, and diverted at least two divisions to Greece which might otherwise have been used in Sicily.[19] What S.O.E. had done, however, was enough to compromise the British government's relations with the King and the government-in-exile, who were after all formally our allies.

On Yugoslavia there are two things I want to say. The first is about the intelligence available at the time to S.O.E. in London and Cairo. Colonel F. W. D. Deakin's book has shown that, even at the beginning of 1943, helping the resistance meant to S.O.E. helping Mihailović, who had received Colonel S. W. Bailey's mission on Christmas Day 1942.[20] For in spite of Hudson's heroic existence shuttling between Mihailović and Tito which started in September 1941, and his references to fighting between Mihailović and the Communists, we knew very little indeed about the Partisans. Cairo had been out of touch with Hudson for months on end, and we often feared he must have been killed. We sent three parties to the country in the spring of 1942 to try to find him, two by submarine and one parachuted blind. They all failed. It was largely thanks to Deakin himself, working away in Cairo on the discouraging news now coming in from Bailey about Mihailović, and on the experiences of Hudson, who had since turned up with Bailey, that we in S.O.E. began to realise how important the Partisans might be. But this was not until early in 1943.

My point here is that the most cogent intelligence about the Partisans' activities at this time was that provided by intercepts of enemy messages. But their circulation was closely restricted, for fear that if we acted on them the enemy might realise we were reading his signals and change his ciphers, and the people who produced them regarded them rather like a birthday cake given to a child but with strict orders not to eat it. Even in April 1943 S.O.E. London knew nothing about these messages, and S.O.E. Cairo seemed to know very little.[21] In London S.O.E. would have been hard put to it on what we did know, to have made out a convincing case for switching our major effort, such as it was, to the Partisans. That April, two fact-finding missions were sent to them, the first dropped blind. It was on the strength of what they told us that the Chiefs of Staff in Cairo decided to send Deakin in as liaison officer to Partisan headquarters at the end of May. A few days later the head of S.O.E. Cairo flew to London to explain why.

My second point is the obvious one that, here again, it is hard in the middle of a war to throw over an ally, for this was what a decision to support the Partisans would eventually mean. On this, opinion in London was genuinely split, as Deakin points out.[22] But I would like to confirm what he says by my own experience. For I thought opinion was split, not only in S.O.E. and the Foreign Office and the Services, but among Ministers as well. In S.O.E. there were several who had known Royalists like General Ilić and Jovan Djonović very well for a long time, and their loyalties were clearly engaged, shocked as they were by Mihailović's inactivity and the collaboration of some of his officers with the enemy.[23]

In the Foreign Office it was the same story, though they had the advantage over S.O.E. London of receiving the intercepts, for there were many in the Foreign Office who could not bring themselves to recommend a break with Mihailović. There were others like Sir Orme Sargent, a deputy under-secretary, who, as Deakin says, were in favour of helping the Partisans, provided we continued to help their opponent Mihailović; and Sir Orme said to me, when we were discussing the ultimatum (not the last as it turned out) to Mihailović of 12 May 1943, that he could not see why we did not help the Partisans, though he said nothing to me about the evidence of the intercepts.[24] As for the Ministers, Lord Selborne, who was not in the War Cabinet but was a man of influence and determination, not to say obstinacy, is on record as writing that his 'sympathies were definitely with Mihailović'. This seems also to have been the view of Mr Eden, for Howard says that in June the Foreign Office 'strongly objected' to support for the Partisans. But by this time we had the advantage of direct information about them from Deakin on the spot. And the Chiefs of Staff in the Middle East had rapidly concluded that the Partisans were the 'most formidable anti-Axis element in Yugoslavia', as they tele-graphed to London on 8 June[25].

So there were two problems common to our work in both Yugoslavia and Greece – one the absence of reliable intelligence available to S.O.E., and the other the conflict between British short-term military objectives and what many of our masters thought to be our long-term political aims. On the first, there is one more general point I must make. It is sometimes suggested or implied, most recently perhaps by the reviewer of Deakin's *The Embattled Mountain* in the *Times Literary Supplement*, that S.O.E. had all the information it needed, but that the 'nabobs of S.O.E. London', most of whom 'were men of banking or commercial experience', suppressed it 'in the interests of res-toring the *status quo ante bellum*'.[26] This I consider is ill-informed and malicious rubbish. I personally had at the time no evidence whatsoever of it. In any case S.O.E. London had little enough information about the Partisans to suppress. As it happens the head of S.O.E. Cairo, who as I have said came home to London expressly to urge support to the Partisans, was himself a banker, and a merchant banker at that; and he found no difficulty in persuading the nabobs. But why have we not heard that the wicked banker nabobs suppressed the equally unpalatable in-formation coming out of Greece at that time? After all, our commercial interests in Greece were then far greater than they were in Yugoslavia.

The conflict between the government's short-term military aims and its long-term political needs is duly mentioned by Howard as applying particularly to Yugoslavia and Greece in 1943.[27] There are two important things he does not say, however. One is that S.O.E. was not a policy-making body. Strategy was of course the job of the Chiefs of Staff. Likewise political affairs were the job of the Foreign Office. But S.O.E., like any other military body, was bound to point out if it thought so that the policy of the Foreign Office conflicted with the job that S.O.E. had to do. This is all that S.O.E. did. But it is not an enormous step from saying that S.O.E. had recommendations to make on policy to saying that S.O.E. had a policy of its own. This is exactly what S.O.E.'s enemies said at the time. The truth was that the policy had to be settled by bodies outside S.O.E. altogether, and all S.O.E. could do was to say its say and to wait for others to settle the policy.

The other point Howard does not mention is that this conflict was something S.O.E. had to face in many parts of the world. Nor does he explain why it came to be a problem. Yet the reason was crucial to our work. For it was the people inside the occupied countries, not only in Yugoslavia and Greece, but also in France, Italy, Burma and elsewhere, on whom we had to rely for the action which the Services asked of us. These people were not necessarily, or even mainly, the people who hoped that when the war was won things would go back to being just what they were when it began. In other words, they were not a group of English ex-public schoolboys with sound seconds at Oxbridge who could be conned into putting everything else except the fighting behind them for the duration, in the interests of British war aims. They were risking their lives for war aims of their own, which differed in many important respects from ours. Rarely was this elementary truth grasped by the Foreign Office and more rarely still by the Services.

The fact was that S.O.E.'s masters could not have it both ways. Either they opted for the long-term view, in which case they would have to forego the advantages to the military of using the resistance. Or they could opt for the short-term view, and let the political consequences look after themselves when the war was over. The only possible compromise was that tried in the summer of 1943 in Greece, where Myers and Woodhouse were told to negotiate a joint guerrilla headquarters in which the various resistance groups sank their political differences and put themselves under the command of the British commander-in-chief in the Middle East. But as some of us feared at the time, this was a sadly short-lived affair and it contributed little to our political objectives when the country was liberated.

In the summer of 1943, with the information coming out of Yugoslavia about the Partisans, and with the success of the diversion created in Greece, the Commanders-in-Chief in Cairo felt that the contribution S.O.E. could make was no longer marginal, and they assumed full operational control of our work in the Balkans. At last the way ahead was clearer. I need hardly say any more about Greece because, in the purely strategic sense, S.O.E.'s part there was over, though I must just mention the brilliant exploits in Athens and the Piraeus of the late Yanni Peltekis which were to continue almost up to the liberation of the country. In Yugoslavia the newly revealed potential of the Partisans seemed enormously important. For although D-Day for the invasion of Sicily was 10 July, the planners in London and Washington and elsewhere were already working on the invasion of Italy. Churchill has written that on 23 June he told the British Chiefs of Staff, rightly or wrongly, that Yugoslavia was containing about thirty-three Axis divisions.[28] It was obviously imperative that Yugoslavia should continue to contain them, for otherwise some of them might be sent to Italy when we invaded it. The invasion of Italy was being handled not by our General Headquarters in Cairo but by Allied Forces Headquarters in Algiers, who had no idea of the importance of the Partisans. I had to be sent to Algiers to tell them, and my journey was certainly necessary.

More generally, the collapse of Italy enhanced the potential importance of S.O.E. operations all over the Balkans.[29] We know now that, long before this stage, Churchill had reluctantly agreed with the Americans that there would be no major campaign in the Balkans. But at the time this was not so clear to the Chiefs of Staff in the Middle East. For one thing, plans might change. If so, the Middle East command had to be ready, and so had S.O.E. If anybody thinks this is of no importance, I would ask him what would have been expected of S.O.E. in the Balkans if Salerno had been a pushover, if we *had* had landing craft to use in the Eastern Mediterranean, and the Dodecanese operation had been a success?

But as Howard has recorded, S.O.E.'s problem was not whom to support in Yugoslavia and Greece, but what to support them with. Between February and March 1943 Churchill got us ten Halifaxes to add to our four Liberators. But it was months before the ten Halifaxes were in use, as they had to be extensively altered, and they were not all there by July; Howard quotes Selborne as writing to Churchill in June that the Liberators were 'on their last legs'. He also records a minute of Churchill of 22 June 1943, saying that S.O.E.'s demand for more aircraft still 'had priority even over the bombing of Germany'.[30] But it was not till the end of July that the Chiefs of Staff agreed that the aircraft available to us would be increased to thirty-six. Soon we could use an airfield at Bari, which was much nearer to Yugoslavia and Greece than North Africa.[31] In the last half of 1943 we dropped an average of 150 tons of supplies a month to the two countries. This was not nearly enough, of course, but it was more than a token gesture.

Where S.O.E. may be fairly criticised, I think, was for not being ready for this tremendous expansion in its activities. About two years ago in reviewing Deakin's book, Sir Fitzroy Maclean implied that S.O.E. had too many people in Cairo.[32] The truth is that we had far too few. I mentioned earlier that we had twenty-seven missions in the Balkans that spring. Six months later the number had trebled. Communications were the very essence of our work, and a home operator had to be on watch for each set for something like four times every twenty-four hours. For a few months that summer we had not got nearly enough operators to handle the traffic, or nearly enough F.A.N.Y.s to code and decode the messages. No wonder important signals were delayed, or even lost altogether, and it was a miracle that this did not cause really irreparable damage, except to our reputation. Again, we had no proper planning staff. And you could not look up the history of several important missions in the field, as many files had been burnt for security reasons when Cairo had been partly evacuated to Jerusalem in the summer of 1942. Above all, there was a shortage of people who could be sent on operations. Even the key men handling Greece and Yugoslavia inside S.O.E. Cairo had had to go. This hardly made for continuity of control. So when we had to gear ourselves to trebling our activities, we came in for a lot of well-deserved criticism. But it certainly was not because S.O.E. Cairo was overstaffed.

One other important point on which S.O.E. Cairo had been at fault was in its set up, and I think this may well explain among other things the Antiparos disaster, and the quite remarkable lack of political information given to Myers and Woodhouse in September 1942. With unfailing regularity S.O.E. Cairo was reorganised, and the head of it sacked, in each August of the war – something to do with tempers rising with the rise of the Nile, I suppose. I was in Cairo on the occasion of the sackings of August 1941. At that time there was a para-military body there concerned with guerrilla warfare which had performed very well in Ethiopia, but now had nothing to do. It was full of professional soldiers who later became very distinguished. It was called GR. The Middle East Command induced the new head of S.O.E. Cairo to take it over, and Wavell shortly after said to me, 'S.O.E. think they've taken over GR, and GR think they've taken over S.O.E., so everybody's happy'. When the takeover took place, the head of S.O.E. Cairo broke up the nascent country sections which were responsible for all S.O.E. activity in their areas – a step which as his personal assistant I advised strongly against.

Instead he created an operations directorate embodying the professional soldiers, and a so-called political directorate which was supposed to deal with agents. This comprised the un-professionals, who had all the experience of our work in the Balkans. It was a functional, not a regional system. I left Cairo before it really got down to work. But as far as I could see the two directorates rarely spoke to each other. I suspect none of our Greek experts such as David Pawson and Ian Pirie were asked to brief Myers and Woodhouse before they left, simply because this was supposed to be an operational matter and therefore not their concern. In 1942 the annual change in the head of S.O.E. Cairo took place on 21 August, and the first thing the new head of S.O.E. Cairo did was to abolish the old system and create one based on country sections. But the victory of the regional system had hardly time to become effective before Myers was briefed. The whole history of S.O.E. elsewhere showed that the functional system of August 1941 was a fundamental mistake. The truth is that S.O.E. had to muddle through, and certainly some of the muddles were of our making.

In his book on S.O.E. in France, Professor Michael Foot has attempted a sort of cost/benefit analysis on the value of S.O.E. in that country, and says that in the opinion of German and Allied generals it shortened the war by about six months.[33] I do not know of any such attempt to analyse the value of our work in the Balkans, and I am certainly not going to attempt one. For a start it would raise the difficult question of whether it would have been preferable to make available more long-range supply-dropping aircraft earlier in the war for S.O.E. by bombing Germany a little less. But some things are reasonably clear to me at any rate. For instance in Yugoslavia, if we had done as some suggested and never helped the Partisans at all, it would not have saved the Royalist government. On the contrary a case may perhaps be made out for saying that the help we did give them was enough to prevent Tito being overwhelmed some time in 1943 or 1944. What seems to me beyond question is that to take the short-term military view and to help the Partisans was the only practical course; that with all its shortcomings S.O.E. was the only body organised to give that help; and that, last but not least, whatever the reasons may have been, the German troops in Yugoslavia were too tied up there to be used against us when we invaded Italy. How much did this shorten the Italian campaign?

As for Greece, I am sure Woodhouse is right in thinking that if S.O.E. had sent no missions there, E.A.M. would have taken the country over on the liberation, as it very nearly did.[34] What difference it would have made to us if they had is quite another question. But the question is irrelevant to the reason why we sent the original missions in, for this was solely to gain a short-term military advantage. Here S.O.E. was conspicuously successful, by wrecking Rommel's lines of communication at a critical stage of the desert war in November 1942, and by sending at least two German divisions to the wrong address just before the invasion of Sicily. I have always felt that what S.O.E. achieved in the summer of 1943 in Yugoslavia and Greece amply justified our existence and was exactly the sort of thing that what we knew of our charter required us to do.

NOTES

1. The official papers of S.O.E. have not been released to the public. However, a considerable amount of information about S.O.E. and its activities can be gleaned from official papers (Foreign Office, Cabinet Office, War Office, etc.) that are available for public inspection at the Public Record Office. Other information, additional to that in Bickham Sweet-Escott, *Baker Street Irregular* (London, 1965), can be found in Hugh Dalton, *The Fateful Years* (London, 1957), M. R. D. Foot, *S.O.E. in France* (London, 1966), Winston Churchill *The Second World War*, v (London, 1952).

2. Dalton, op. cit. p. 366.

3. See below pp. 210–14 for references to intelligence based on intercepts.

4. Except where otherwise stated the author has relied on his memory fortified by the account given in his book, *Baker Street Irregular*. The book was written in 1953–4 but held up for eleven years before publication because of the delay in obtaining permission under the Official Secrets Act.

5. Julius Caesar was (Colonel) Julius Hanau; see Sweet-Escott, op. cit., p. 22.

6. M. R. D. Foot, in *The Fourth Dimension of Warfare* (London, 1970) ed. M. Elliott-Bateman, p. 21.

7. Sweet-Escott, pp. 40 et seq; Foot, *S.O.E. in France*, pp. 7, 8.

8. Details but not the text of the charter are given in J. R. M. Butler, *History of the Second World War, Grand Strategy*, II (London, 1957) p. 261.

9. Churchill, op. cit., III 148.

10. His name was Captain Koutsogiannopoulos, a captain in the Greek navy; see C. M. Woodhouse, 'Early British Contacts with the Greek Resistance', *Balkan Studies*, XII (1971) 348.

11. One W/T set had been taken over by Mihailović, and the other Hudson had left behind in Montenegro as being too heavy to carry during his arduous journey through the mountains on his way to join Mihailović. F. W. D. Deakin, *The Embattled Mountain* (London, 1971) pp. 131, 133.

12. M. Howard, *Grand Strategy*, IV (London, 1972) p. 481.

13. Field Marshal Lord Wilson, *Eight Years Overseas* (London, 1948) p. 164.

14. It has not been possible to ascertain the precise date on which these aircraft became available.

15. At that time there was in Cairo no British Ambassador to the Greek government-in-exile as that government was still in London.

16. On Zervas see Sweet-Escott, p. 160, and below, Chapters 5 and 6.

17. Woodhouse, op. cit., pp. 350–4.

18. E. C. W. Myers, *Greek Entanglement* (London, 1955) p. 102.

19. Churchill, op. cit., V, pp. 472–3. M. Howard, op. cit., pp. 370, 463, attaches much importance to operation 'Mincemeat' (The Man Who Never

Was), the cover plan for the invasion of Sicily. This operation took place in May 1943.

20. Deakin, op. cit., pp. 195–201.

21. See below pp. 210–14. It seems that Brigadier Keble (about whom see Sweet-Escott, p. 170), who was assistant to the head of S.O.E. Cairo, was, because of a previous post, still on the circulation list for some of the top secret intercepts.

22. Deakin, p. 185.

23. General Bogoljub Ilić was Minister of War in the Yugoslav government-in-exile in 1941 and Jovan Djonović was, towards the end of that year, appointed official representative in Cairo of that government. Both had known members of S.O.E. in Belgrade in the early years of the war.

24. Deakin, op. cit., pp. 181, 187–8.

25. M. Howard, op. cit., p. 482. No date for Selborne's minute is given.

26. *Times Literary Supplement*, 22 Oct 1971, 1306.

27. M. Howard, op. cit., pp. 484–5.

28. Churchill, op. cit., v, p. 410.

29. M. Howard, op. cit., pp. 433–4.

30. *Ibid.*, pp. 485–6.

31. There was an intermediate move to Protville in Tunisia before Bari became available and it was from this airfield that the Maclean Mission to Yugoslavia was despatched. See D. Hamilton-Hill, *S.O.E. Assignment* (London, 1973) pp. 54–61.

32. *Sunday Times*, 17 Oct 1971.

33. Foot, *S.O.E. in France*, p. ix.

34. Woodhouse, op. cit., p. 362.

2 Some Factors in British Decision-making over Yugoslavia 1941-4

ELISABETH BARKER

The Foreign Office papers on Yugoslavia released in 1972 provide an enormous mass of material, particularly for the years 1943-4. Besides Foreign Office telegrams, correspondence, minutes and memoranda, there is a certain amount of S.O.E. material, including very interesting reports from Hudson, Bailey and Armstrong,[1] the Maclean[2] report of November 1943, and a good many messages from the field. There are however no intercepts; and I take it that the reason why certain documents have been withheld from the public is that they referred to intercepts. On the other hand there are appreciations originating in the War Office, the Joint Intelligence Committee or elsewhere, which refer to Most Secret sources and obviously take account of intercepts. Finally, there are extracts from War Cabinet minutes and Chiefs of Staff minutes and the Prime Minister's minutes to the Foreign Secretary and others.

Out of this vast and tangled mass of material, there emerges some sort of picture of the complicated and laborious process of decision-making, as seen mainly from the Foreign Office angle. The picture may be distorted, if only because some important documents are missing; how much, it is difficult to tell.

There were four main factors in British decision-making: the Foreign Office, S.O.E. under its various names, the military (that is, the Chiefs of Staff, the Commanders-in-Chief, Middle East and the Supreme Commander, Mediterranean) and finally Churchill himself. There were also two or three jokers in the pack – by which I mean, quite respectfully, Brigadier Fitzroy Maclean, Colonel F. W. D. Deakin[3] and also, at one point,

Randolph Churchill[4] – who influenced decisions as individuals rather than members of organisations. On the fringe of decision-making there were two other organisations – the B.B.C. and P.W.E.[5] P.W.E.'s functions were ill-defined and its influence was small; it had no Minister of its own and a director[6] who carried amiability to the length of being perhaps excessively peace-loving. The B.B.C. was regarded as an instrument of policy, not a policy-maker, but it was a very unmanageable instrument and for this reason did have a certain influence on the policies it was supposed to serve.

Between the various organisations there were bound to be tensions and frictions. The Foreign Office were the mandarins – at least in theory, the professional experts in political decision-making. The Foreign Secretary, Anthony Eden, was very much a Foreign Office man and a believer in Office methods and wisdom. He minuted on a Southern Department record of a meeting with S.O.E. in April 1943: 'this is all thoroughly unsatisfactory. The Department writes...as if it was for S.O.E. to decide these matters. It is not, it is for the Department to advise me...I am responsible for all this to War Cabinet....'[7]

But the other organisations plunged into the business of political decision-making with great gusto. The Special Operations Executive (S.O.E.), coming into this field from banking and the City, showed particular enthusiasm. As early as November 1941, Lord Glenconner[8] was writing to the Foreign Office: 'to back the partisans would be tantamount to the repudiation of the Yugoslav Government...If the revolt is to prosper, its inspiration must be that it is a fight taken up by all Yugoslavs for Yugoslavia, and not a revolt...engineered by Moscow and led by Communists who are fighting for Russia....'[9] S.O.E.'s Minister during the crucial period, Lord Selborne,[10] does not seem from the documents to have played a very important part, but from the start he pinned his colours to the mast of anti-Communism and fought for the cause so fanatically that he was left behind by events, stranded like an unhappy whale. As late as May 1944 he was warning Churchill against the political perils of overestimating the Partisans' contribution to the war effort.[11]

The military also liked to have their say on the political aspects of decision-making. Of the Chiefs of Staff, Mountbatten[12] obviously enjoyed sticking pins into Eden or, as Eden saw it, trespassing on his ground. For instance on 6 May 1943 Mountbatten criticised the continuation of aid to Mihailović partly on the ground that it could imperil relations with Russia, and suggested that this should be brought to the notice of the Foreign Office. This was well calculated to annoy Eden who minuted: 'curiously enough, we had thought of this'.[13]

On the other hand the military also tended, with some justice, to suspect the Foreign Office of obstructing military requirements for inadequate political reasons. Mountbatten presented a memorandum to the Chiefs of Staff in June 1943 charging the Foreign Office with making the avoidance of 'political issues' – the quotation marks are his – with the Yugoslav government the paramount consideration, adding that the military disadvantages of this were obvious.[14]

Another cause of friction was Foreign Office mistrust of S.O.E. and suspicion that S.O.E. were suppressing information. This shows strongly in the documents of early 1943, though the cause of this suspicion is not revealed. In the documents for 1942 there are vague references to messages from Hudson (in S.O.E letters or appreciations from July onwards), used to explain away Mihailović's inactivity or reported collaboration with Nedić[15] or the Italians; but there are no actual texts of Hudson's messages until September 1942; this may perhaps have been relevant to the Foreign Office suspicions. In any case it is clear that when Bailey went in to Mihailović at the end of 1942, the Foreign Office was on the watch. On 22 January 1943 Lord Selborne wrote to Eden that he hoped soon to get an interim report from Bailey of which 'the portions of interest to the Foreign Office' would be communicated immediately.[16] On this, Eden minuted: 'surely we should see Bailey's telegrams. S.O.E. treat us like irresponsible children,' adding sarcastically, 'perhaps they did not know that the P.M. considers me fit to see operational telegrams *almost* as important as these.'[17] Selborne wrote again on 4 February, 'there is nothing which I wish to hide from you, as I have often told you, in regard to S.O.E. matters, but it has not occurred to me that your people would wish to be troubled with a mass of detail...I have impressed upon my people the importance of not leaving out anything which might be of interest to the Foreign Office.'[18] On this a junior member of the Southern Department minuted: 'personally, I think this should be enough. There is no earthly way of preventing S.O.E. from concealing telegrams from us if they really have a mind to, unless we take over their communications system.'[19] However Eden wrote back to Selborne asking for 'the actual text of Bailey's telegrams, that is, his own views and words, rather than a paraphrase'.[20]

The other side of the picture was that the Foreign Office – in its higher reaches, at least – showed signs of being unable to digest messages from the field when these *were* supplied by S.O.E. On 18 January 1943 Sir Orme Sargent[21] minuted on the first Bailey telegram which he saw – a fairly simple one – 'this report conveys nothing to me without further analysis and elucidation.'[22] When in February Eden saw a telegram from Bailey on the arrangements between the Italians and Četniks in Bosnia and reported German disapproval of them, he minuted merely: 'an unsatisfactory tangle'[23] – which does not suggest great understanding of the situation.

When Deakin was dropped to the Partisans in May 1943, there is no sign that the Foreign Office made any special effort to see the text of his telegrams, as they had done in Bailey's case. So far as I can see the public files contain no messages from Deakin until the latter part of July, when they begin to appear either embedded in weekly situation reports or singly. However, the old suspicions were displayed again when Maclean went to Cairo in August 1943 on his way to Tito, with the determination that his reports should reach the right destination quickly. Douglas Howard, the Head of the Southern Department, minuted on 1 September: 'It is a well-known fact that S.O.E.'s military interests in the Balkans have not always coincided with the Foreign Office political interests... The Foreign Office feel most strongly that arrangements should be made for the establishment of direct communications between their political agents and His Majesty's representatives thereby disposing of the necessity of passing political reports... through S.O.E. channels.'[24] Sargent minuted that General Wilson was going to suggest certain measures – as he put it – 'to see that S.O.E. play the game in future', but he did not think much of them: 'we are all agreed that this is not good enough'[25] – a view which was personally endorsed by Eden with the one word 'Yes'. However, Maclean's reports seem to have got through without any difficulty, although normally passing through S.O.E. channels.

If the Foreign Office were suspicious of S.O.E., they themselves were not above trying to withhold information on occasion. There was an odd incident early in June 1943 when, after Churchill had tried unsuccessfully to see Deakin in North Africa, the Minister of State, Cairo, sent him two reports on the Yugoslav situation. When these reached No. 10, they were read by Major Desmond Morton, who concluded that they were 'very contrary to H.M.G.'s policy as laid down by the F.O.' and passed them to Sargent. Sargent discussed them with S.O.E. and agreed that they were 'tendentious and incorrect' and that it was most undesirable that the Prime Minister should see them. Desmond Morton said he could not suppress them but would try to dissuade Churchill from reading them by covering them with a note saying that the whole matter was now again under consideration and new recommendations were to be made.[26]

The files do not show whether this device succeeded, but it seems unlikely. John Colville – who presumably knew – has written that Churchill had no love for the Foreign Office, 'one of the very few Departments of which he had never been head', suspecting them of pursuing their own policy irrespective of what the government might wish, and mistrusting their judgement.[27] Certainly, once Churchill had become interested in the Yugoslav problem, he was determined to lay on his own sources of information. That was obviously why he had wanted to see Deakin in May 1943; why he then arranged that the Minister of State, Cairo, should send him private fortnightly appreciations of the situation in the Balkans – which the Foreign Office did not discover until the following October;[28] probably, too, why he personally decreed that Fitzroy Maclean should head the mission to Tito instead of being its political adviser responsible to the Foreign Office;[29] and why he grilled both Maclean and Deakin in Cairo in December 1943.

But even if Churchill mistrusted the Foreign Office, it is clear that he had considerable respect and liking for Eden and was extremely reluctant to overrule him when they were at loggerheads. Eden on his side showed remarkable firmness – at times extreme stubbornness – in holding his ground in the face of heavy pressure from Churchill, though sometimes it looks to be less from conviction than from determination to uphold the independence and prestige of the Foreign Office and to retain the respect of his permanent officials. One small incident shows this – the argument between the two over King Peter's wish to get married against the advice of his Serb Ministers – and of Nedić – and in the face of an equivocal attitude on Mihailović's part. The Foreign Office thought the King should delay the marriage. Churchill thought otherwise. His minute to Eden of 12 July 1943 – which appears in Volume v of his war history[30] – was half funny and half bullying. He accused Eden of chopping and changing, said that the Foreign Office should discard eighteenth-century politics, and went on: 'we might be back in the refinements of Louis XIV instead of the lusty squalor of the twentieth century... My advice to the King will be to go to the nearest Registry Office and take a chance. So what?' Eden did not take this altogether as a joke; in his reply he denied that the King was in a hurry to get married; 'my sole interest in this business', he wrote, 'is that King Peter should keep his throne for only thus can Yugoslavia continue to live as a unit, perhaps.' And Eden wound up: 'if you think me incapable of handling even this minor Balkan domestic imbroglio the remedy is in your hands. So what.'[31] It is possible to see this as a half humorous reminder to Churchill that Eden had already resigned once – under Chamberlain – and if pushed too far might do it again, which would be very unpleasant for Churchill. In any case, the relationship between these two men was a surprisingly equal one – a factor which at one juncture virtually paralysed the process of British decision-making over Yugoslavia.

The relationship between the Foreign Office and the military, in the same way, contained the danger of paralysis: the military could block political decisions on military grounds, as happened between November 1941 and the spring of 1943, and the Foreign Office could hold up military decisions on political grounds, as happened after that. Incidentally the War Cabinet as such does not appear to have played an important role, at least so far as Yugoslavia is concerned.

Between P.W.E. and the B.B.C. on one side, and the Foreign Office and still more S.O.E. on the other, there was at times a good deal of friction. This was because the Foreign Office and

S.O.E. – anyhow up to May 1943 – did not seem to think it mattered, from the point of view of propaganda and broadcasting, what was actually happening inside Yugoslavia, or what was being said about events in Yugoslavia in the rest of Europe or in Yugoslavia itself. They seemed to assume that somewhere in the B.B.C. there were two taps, one labelled Mihailović and the other labelled Partisans – or Patriots – and all you had to do was to give the word, through P.W.E., and one tap or the other could be turned on or off at a moment's notice, or else both could be turned on in exactly the right mixture. P.W.E., recruited largely from journalists or broadcasters, and the B.B.C. itself, took a different view – roughly, that successful propaganda must be closely related to hard facts and that hard facts cannot be successfully concealed over a long period. They were unlikely to share the rather happy-go-lucky attitude sometimes shown by S.O.E. and the Foreign Office. In July 1942, for instance, Lord Glenconner wrote to the Southern Department: 'as we know...any activity in Yugoslavia should really be attributed to the Partisans, but, for public consumption, we can see no harm in a certain amount of this going to the credit of Mihailović.'[32] Or again, in early March 1943, Douglas Howard of the Southern Department wrote to P.W.E. suggesting that a more even balance should be kept between the two sides, either by suppressing some of the messages about the Partisans or by inventing news about Mihailović: 'we do not really mind which course you adopt,' he wrote.[33]

In the eyes of P.W.E. – even more, of the B.B.C, if they had known about it – this sort of attitude was quite unrealistic and, in the long term, very harmful to British propaganda and British credibility. The same goes for S.O.E.'s belief in myth-building – there was for instance a letter from Sir Charles Hambro to Sargent early in 1943, enclosing a memorandum on S.O.E. policy which asserted: 'great men are largely myths but once they have been created they are a power in the land...It is within our power to build up Mihailović into such a figure....'[34] In this case, however, even the Foreign Office jibbed. Howard minuted: 'I am not at all sure we want (even if we could) to build up a new Dictator.'[35]

One disadvantage for P.W.E. was that they got only a limited amount of secret information – an *ad hoc* sprinkle of S.O.E.

material and of course no intercepts. But they tried to make up for this by studying all other sources – that is, the open and public sources of which no one else took much notice. At a time of very heavy pressure from S.O.E. in March 1943, I myself wrote a rather pompous letter to Douglas Howard saying that a ban on mention of the Partisans would lay British propaganda open to the charge of deliberate obscurantism and concealment of news of anti-Axis operations which were being regularly reported not only by the Russians and other Communist organs but also by the Swiss, Swedes, Germans, and Hungarians and by Zagreb press and radio; it might moreover increase the danger of civil war in Yugoslavia.[36]

I can see that to the man in the field – to Colonel Bailey wrestling with Mihailović – this kind of attitude must have seemed bloody-minded. But for the B.B.C. or P.W.E. it was professionally inevitable.

Finally, P.W.E. was in no position to compel or trick the B.B.C. into putting out phony stories about Yugoslavia. The B.B.C., in spite of the war, still cherished its professional integrity; and Harrison,[37] the Balkans editor, who had been Reuter correspondent in Belgrade for years, was a fairly formidable character. Sir George Rendel,[38] as Ambassador to the Yugoslavs, labelled him 'Leftist'[39] – just as he labelled P.W.E. anti-Mihailović and pro-Partisan and Hudson as 'very strong Leftist'.[40] I should have said rather that Harrison was a tough journalist used to working for a reputable news agency and that he thought, rightly, that he knew more about Yugoslavia than some of the people who were trying to prescribe policy to him (including myself). He was *not* a tap which could be turned on or off to order.

All these various frictions between the various organisations and individuals involved in British policy towards Yugoslavia may seem trivial and to mention them may seem a mild form of muck-raking. But I think they did have a certain influence on the evolution of policy; and the three key points in decision-making can perhaps be better understood in the light of these relationships.

Before looking at these, it is perhaps worth noting that the *coup* of 27 March 1941 confirmed the general British conviction that the Serbs were the only Yugoslavs who could be expected to resist the Germans, and that British involvement in it created, or strengthened, the conviction that resistance elements in Yugoslavia could be brought under British control and leadership – a sort of T. E. Lawrence complex. Both these beliefs influenced later developments.

After the *coup*, the first important point in policy-making was the decision towards the end of 1941 to give exclusive support to Mihailović at a time when it was already known that he had lapsed into inactivity, that he was at loggerheads with the Partisans who *were* fighting the Germans, and that he had had contact with Nedić. At this stage, the Foreign Office and S.O.E. were working closely together, backed by Churchill, but found themselves up against a half-hearted and very cautious attitude on the part of the military.

The problem of Mihailović's inactivity seems, from the documents, to have been known to the Foreign Office as early as the beginning of November 1941. It was at first seen as something which could be set right by getting the exiled government to send him the right instructions. The Prime Minister, Simović, told Eden on 29 October that he had instructed the insurgents to go slow.[41] S.O.E. in London had not known of this[42] and Gladwyn Jebb, at that time representing S.O.E. interests, disapproved of this policy.[43] Eden told the War Cabinet about the problem when he presented a memorandum on 31 October about the steps taken by S.O.E. and the Chiefs of Staff to help the insurgents, as he called them, but said that Simović would be brought into line.[44] (However on 15 November Simović broadcast instructions over the B.B.C. that sabotage and individual attacks should be discontinued: he had obviously paid no heed to British views.)[45]

The problem of the clash between Mihailović and the Communists became known in London during the first half of November. Before that, in the confusion over the first messages from Mihailović and Hudson, no clear line had been drawn between the Četniks and the Partisans. Eden, in his memorandum to the War Cabinet of 31 October, particularly stressed the revolt in Montenegro, apparently unaware of the Communists' role in it. It was not until after the Mihailović–Partisan clash had become known that Lord Glenconner, in a letter to the Foreign Office strongly opposing support to the

Partisans, pointed out that any supplies sent by submarine to Montenegro might fall into the hands of the Communists.[46]

It was on 13 November that the news of the clash reached London from the Middle East Command[47] and immediately influenced the argument that was going on between the Foreign Office and S.O.E. on one side and the military on the other, about the way to deal with the Yugoslav 'revolt'. Ten days earlier, at a Chiefs of Staff meeting on 4 November, both Churchill and Eden had urged that everything possible should be done to send arms to keep the rebellion going.[48] In spite of this, the Chiefs of Staff had drafted a telegram to the Middle East implying that the revolt had broken out prematurely and that help must be on a limited scale. The Foreign Office thought this was much too weak; the telegram which finally went on 8 November, and which was presumably a compromise, said: 'at present we are not in a position to give the Yugoslavs substantial military aid... Our policy... must be to do our utmost to provide rebels with supplies necessary to maintain movement in the hills' – but the movement should not, it was stated, spread to the towns.[49]

The news of the clash inevitably strengthened the military argument for caution. But the Foreign Office – and S.O.E. – fought back. On 16 November they asked the Chiefs of Staff – who agreed – to reply to Cairo: 'we recognize that so long as virtual civil war between the Communists and Mihailović continues, the difficulties of sending supplies are enormously increased...H.M.G. have decided that if the revolt is to prosper it is essential to persuade the Communists and Mihailović to sink their mutual differences.' For this purpose, an approach was to be made in Moscow and Mihailović was to be instructed not to retaliate.[50] (In a message of 9 November he had disclosed his intention of liquidating the Partisans.)[51]

Mihailović obviously grasped the situation very quickly and by 26 November Simović was able to give Eden the message from him saying: 'I have succeeded in ending the internal fighting provoked by the other side.' On the basis of this, Hugh Dalton (as the Minister responsible for S.O.E.) urged Eden to raise afresh the question of supplies to Mihailović.[52]

This faced the Foreign Office with what might be called its first moral dilemma. Was Mihailović's very brief message to be

taken as proof that the civil war was over? The Southern
Department minuted: 'we have only one message from Col.
Mihailović to show that he has come to terms with the Partisans... The Service Departments and Commander-in-Chief
Middle East may still feel rather reluctant, on the strength of
this single message, to send supplies to Yugoslavia.' But, the
Department argued, supplies *should* be sent, and not just on the
ground that the civil war had ended: 'what seems essential is
that the Partisans should be made to realize that Mihailović is
the man who is receiving support from H.M. Government, the
Yugoslav Government and the Soviet Government; that is, I
think, the real argument in favour of sending supplies...'[53]

But this was not the argument used when Eden raised the
matter in the War Cabinet on 27 November. He simply presented it as an unquestioned fact that 'the dispute between the
two parties taking part in the revolt' had been 'settled', and he
urged that supplies be sent as a matter of the utmost importance. The War Cabinet told him to take it up with the Chiefs
of Staff.[54] Churchill minuted on 28 November: 'everything in
human power should be done.'[55] The next day the Chiefs of
Staff concurred in a Foreign Office draft of a message sending
Mihailović 'heartiest congratulations on the understanding he
has reached with the Partisans' and promising help in material
and money within one week; continued help would however
depend on 'the maintenance of the united front between all
patriots in Yugoslavia under Colonel Mihailović's leadership.'[56]
(As things turned out, of course, this was a condition which
begged all the vital questions.)

It then appeared that no aircraft were available from operations in Libya; it was a question of getting the Air Ministry to
send out one Whitley and one Halifax to Malta. But Eden did
not leave the matter there. On 7 December he sent a minute to
Churchill proposing formation of a special operational squadron of long-range bombers to work exclusively for the Yugoslav
revolt.[57] And it seems that some sort of action must have been
taken, since a War Office report of a later date refers to a
squadron of special bombers, destined for this work, being
diverted to the defence of Ceylon against the Japanese in the
spring of 1942.[58]

As for the question of Mihailović's collaboration, it is not clear from the available documents what was in fact known in late 1941. In the files for October there is an American Most Secret report from Budapest mentioning Italian aid to the Četniks, but there is no Foreign Office minute on it.[59] What is odd is that when Stafford Cripps, the Ambassador in Moscow, made the promised approach to the Soviet Government on 18 November, he told A. Y. Vishinsky that the Yugoslav Government had urged Mihailović 'to lay down his arms' and that this was 'the probable reason for his reported contact with Nedić'.[60] When Cripps reported this to the Foreign Office, the Southern Department minuted that it was not clear where Cripps got his information from; and the Head of the Department, Douglas Howard, wrote: 'I don't know anything about Mihailović's reported contact with Nedić.'[61] So it looks as though Cripps got his information either from S.O.E. sources or else from Russian sources.

However this may be, on the basis of the available documents, it seems fair to say that the original decision to back Mihailović exclusively was taken by the Foreign Office and S.O.E., not for operational reasons, nor because they believed him to be the most effective resistance leader, but with the longer-term political aim of *establishing* him as sole leader and inducing the Communists to subordinate themselves to him, or at least of drawing off support from the Partisans.

The second important stage in the evolution of British policy was the decision to contact the Partisans while still maintaining support of Mihailović in spite of his increasingly obvious defects. This decision was reached gradually by a painful process which extended from about August 1942 until April 1943. It was also the period when the Foreign Office and S.O.E. diverged, with the Foreign Office showing increasing distrust and resentment of S.O.E. who, in London at least, put up a remarkably stiff resistance to contacting the Partisans.

The start of the process was probably a meeting held by Sargent in the Foreign Office on 8 August 1942. Two things were discussed. One was a document which the Soviet Ambassador had given Eden the day before, listing cases of collaboration between Četniks and Italians against the Partisans from March 1942 onwards, also one case of collaboration with Nedić.[62] The other appears to have been a most secret paper which is

withheld from the public files and which, according to a Southern
Department minute of 6 August, showed that 'General Mihailović is not playing the game.'[63] It cannot have been based on
messages from Hudson since the Foreign Office suggested that
Hudson should be asked for his view.[64] Although the record is
not available, the meeting of 8 August was clearly concerned
with the wider implications of Mihailović's reported collaboration.

Ten days later, on 19 August, Ralph Murray[65] of P.W.E.
sent the Foreign Office a paper on the Partisan–Mihailović
issue, analysing reports from the enemy and neutral press and
radio, reports received through Slovene and Croat exiled politicians, and such secret sources as were available to P.W.E.; all
showed that there was very little resistance in Serbia but a great
deal of resistance elsewhere in Yugoslavia, which had not been
claimed by Mihailović.[66] Of course, this can have told the
Foreign Office nothing which they did not already know, but it
did at least point out that the rest of the world knew it too, so
that it was no good pretending that the Partisans did not exist.
In September, the Foreign Office agreed that British propaganda could praise 'any anti-Axis activity', though without
specifying who were actively resisting[67] – this was the 'Patriots'
rather than 'Partisans' formula which was so unpopular with
both sides. Soon after, Murray raised with the Foreign Office
the inconsistency of this new propaganda line with the Yugoslav
Military Cabinet bulletins which the B.B.C. was obliged to put
out weekly;[68] but neither then nor in response to later P.W.E.
requests was the Foreign Office willing to make any move to
stop these broadcasts which were finally terminated by the
Yugoslav government themselves in May 1943; by then of
course they had done the B.B.C. and the British in general a
good deal of harm.

To go back to August 1942: by the end of the month S.O.E.
had agreed reluctantly with the Foreign Office on sending three
questions to Hudson. One of these was revealing: 'would you
say that the whole of Mihailović's military effort to date has
been directed against the Partisans until the latter submit or
have been exterminated?'[69]

The rather cryptic replies which came from Hudson obviously worried the Foreign Office seriously – particularly

perhaps one saying that the Partisans would only submit to Mihailović if he would promise post-war political freedom and allow them to go on fighting the Axis.[70] At one point in October the Southern Department suggested that Hudson might be mistaken.[71] The Foreign Office and S.O.E. decided to send in Colonel Bailey and await his views before answering the Russian charges against Mihailović, or modifying policy. It is interesting that Bailey, in one of his first messages after his arrival, said: 'our doubts regarding the authorship of Hudson's telegrams were unfounded. He has an excellent grasp of all aspects of the situation.'[72]

In spite of these doubts about Hudson's messages, the Foreign Office could not ignore them, and they became more and more outspoken on Mihailović's collaboration with the Italians; in mid-November Hudson gave the estimate: 'I consider him perfectly capable of coming to any understanding with either Italians or Germans, which he believes might serve his purpose without compromising him.'[73] Meanwhile, the Foreign Office was gradually reacting to these and other developments. On 9 October Dixon wrote: 'we still feel that we are bound to continue our support of Mihailović because of his potential value, both military and political at a later stage of the war.'[74] Two weeks later, Dixon minuted on a letter from Murray: 'are we going to continue our present policy...Or are we going to modify our policy to the extent of putting some of our money on the Partisan horse?'[75] A month later, towards the end of November, Howard minuted: 'we all recognize that we may be faced with the awkward dilemma – Mihailović or Partisans – but it would seem to me futile and fatal to try to back both horses at once.'[76]

In December, Sargent minuted on reports of Mihailović's collaboration with the Italians: 'I do not think the time has come to break with Mihailović and still less to give direct assistance to the Partisans,' but he added that pressure should be put on Mihailović to mend his ways and a direct message should be sent him for this purpose.[77] On 17 December Eden sent Churchill a minute on the reports of Mihailović's collaboration, quoting Hudson's estimate and adding that while it might be in our short-term interest to break with Mihailović, on a long view it was not; we must however make it clear to him that we expected him to carry out sabotage and establish a 'united front of resistance', and His Majesty's government should send him a message to this effect. Churchill agreed.[78]

By 1 January 1943, however, there had been a change: the Foreign Office officials were proposing that the message to Mihailović should *not* be sent until a new approach had been made to Moscow – if possible to Stalin personally – about unifying resistance.[79] This delay in tackling Mihailović provoked angry comment from Eden who attributed it to S.O.E. and the Commander-in-Chief Middle East, and minuted that he saw no sense in giving full backing to a man who was not fighting our enemies and was being publicly denounced by our Soviet ally.[80] However, Cadogan smoothed Eden down, saying that Bailey had just arrived in Yugoslavia;[81] and Eden agreed to wait for Bailey before doing anything. Presumably S.O.E. had been anxious that no warning should go to Mihailović until Bailey had had time to get on good terms with him.

A few weeks later, Bailey put forward a plan by which the Partisans were to withdraw to Croatia, leaving Bosnia to Mihailović[82] – the first of the various plans for a territorial division between the two. In the Foreign Office, Eden, Sargent and Cadogan opposed it and agreed that if the new British approach to Moscow failed, as seemed likely, an effort should be made to contact the Partisans, to bring them into line with Mihailović and to support them if possible and advisable. This, the Southern Department later minuted, 'constituted the first step in our policy towards the support of the Partisans.'[83] Around the same time, on 11 February, the Chiefs of Staff considered a paper produced in Cairo (presumably by S.O.E., with the aim of extracting Liberators from General Eisenhower) which advocated aid to resistance elements in Croatia and Slovenia, as well as Mihailović.[84]

A week later, on 18 February, Cadogan held a meeting with S.O.E. and other departments to discuss ways and means of contacting the Partisans. It was at this point that the trouble between the Foreign Office and S.O.E. which had been brewing up for some time got really serious. Howard, as head of the Southern Department, minuted later: 'quite naturally S.O.E. had put all their money on Mihailović...They had therefore consistently built him up...That policy coincided with our own, up to a point. But when it came to our suggesting getting into touch with the Partisans... they raised endless difficulties, due of course to their displeasure at the prospect of doing anything to upset Mihailović or make Bailey's position more difficult than it already was. As a result, they consistently belittled the Partisans' activities and utility as well as Mihailović's faults and failings; and it was with some difficulty that they were persuaded at Sir A. Cadogan's meeting to take steps to contact the Partisans... Eventually they came, rather half-heartedly, into line...'[85]

S.O.E. London certainly seem to have put up a stiff rearguard action. Early in March the Chiefs of Staff said that Liberators were not available and suggested that it would be a mistake to back both sides since there were hardly enough aircraft available to back one side effectively.[86] This gave S.O.E. a fresh weapon. Around this time Hambro sent Sargent a long memorandum from S.O.E. Cairo arguing yet again that 'in spite of Mihailović's drawbacks, he must be our choice,' and that 'the policy of the Partisans does not suit us, nor would it ever be easy for us to bring them under our control.'[87] Early in March Colonel Pearson of S.O.E. complained about P.W.E. – with whom S.O.E.'s relations were very strained at that moment – and wrote to the Foreign Office: 'we cannot have it both ways – at least when the war is on... When there are two or more opposing and irreconcileable forces, we must surely decide which one to support and build up.'[88]

In early April Lord Selborne wrote to Sargent to argue against backing both sides.[89] On 12 April Colonel Pearson wrote to Howard that the Partisan movement had infinitely less potentialities than that of the Četnik organisation and that there did not seem to be the slightest possibility of running the two in double harness.[90]

This was four days *after* the Foreign Office had sent a telegram to Cairo saying that – the Russians having refused to help – we were now considering whether it was practically possible to establish contact with the Partisans on our own.[91] However, the Chiefs of Staff finally decided the issue for S.O.E. by demanding a 'tuning-up' of guerrilla warfare in the Balkans.[92] S.O.E. could not ignore this; and at a meeting with the Foreign Office on 21 April, Hambro – in Foreign Office words – went so far as to hint that if Mihailović did not change his ways S.O.E. would be prepared to switch their support to some other resistance group. This, Howard minuted, was an innovation, since S.O.E. had never previously deviated one inch from their blind support of Mihailović.[93]

So, at least as far as the story emerges from the Foreign Office documents, it was the Foreign Office, with decisive last-minute backing from the military, who slowly pushed an extremely reluctant S.O.E. London into making contact with the Partisans.[94]

Very soon afterwards however there was a curious realignment of forces – or perhaps a shift back to a more natural pattern. A gap opened up between London and Cairo. In London the Foreign Office, though standing by the policy of contacting and later supporting the Partisans, became almost more devoted defenders of Mihailović than S.O.E. had so far been, insisting on showing the utmost patience and handling him with kid gloves, while more and more evidence piled up that he had no intention of doing what the British told him they wanted and was drifting steadily nearer to direct collaboration not only with the Italians but also the Germans in his struggle against the Partisans. S.O.E. London on the whole aligned themselves with the Foreign Office; Lord Selborne, at the end of July 1943, went right out on a limb by involving himself in a rather undignified row with Brendan Bracken because the B.B.C. had once again been upsetting Mihailović. But on this Howard minuted: 'the point I find most extraordinary is that Lord Selborne continues to tread his own path of out and out sympathy for Mihailović at complete variance with the views and policy of his own Department.'[95]

On the other side, once S.O.E. Cairo had successfully established missions with the Partisans, they began to move much too fast and too far for London's liking. Hence the prolonged row between London and Cairo – with the Chiefs of Staff inclining to the Cairo side – over the Ibar plan for dividing Tito's and Mihailović's forces. On this Howard minuted bitterly: 'S.O.E. [Cairo] have excelled themselves.'[96] Then there was Howard's discovery in late July that S.O.E. Cairo had been sending supplies to the Slovene Partisans without first obtaining the required formal assurances that they would not be used to attack other resistance groups. 'I suspected it all along,' he minuted.[97] Also in late July, when P.W.E. and S.O.E. Cairo jointly recommended that British propaganda should cautiously mention Tito, the Southern Department minuted: 'another case of Cairo rushing madly ahead'.[98]

It was about this time that Churchill openly and directly intervened, by insisting that Fitzroy Maclean should head the proposed high-level mission to Tito,[99] and by overruling all opposition, whether from Selborne and S.O.E. or, at first, from Eden.[100] Churchill thereby showed that he was going to play a personal part in Yugoslav affairs; and his intervention obviously gave Maclean a lot of extra weight in British decision-making. The Maclean report of 6 November 1943[101] had the effect of a blockbuster. It was immediately issued by the Foreign Office as a green print – even though they did not like its conclusions on Mihailović and the Serbs – so it hit the War Cabinet and the Chiefs of Staff with considerable impact;[102] Churchill himself minuted 'most interesting' on it. The report made it much more difficult for the Foreign Office to carry on its kid-glove policy towards Mihailović and gave a big shove to the movement towards dropping Mihailović which was gathering momentum throughout November and the first half of December 1943.

This movement must in fact have started some time before the Maclean report – perhaps with the document of 19 October drawn up by S.O.E. Cairo – or M.O.4 – on Mihailović's internal and external communications; this contained the sentence: 'it is known from at least two irrefutable and separate sources that both Mihailović's internal and external ciphers are cracked by the Germans, either in some cases because the ciphers are in their possession or in other cases because they are insufficiently secure.' The report drew the conclusion: 'any orders for operations or sabotage attacks which Mihailović passes to his commanders are blown from the start.'[103]

Another factor which had a big impact on the movement to drop Mihailović was, rather oddly, the report from Radeslav Djurić in mid-November that Mihailović was co-operating with Nedić and even, tacitly, with the Germans.[104] On this Howard minuted on 22 November that it could mean a radical alteration in our whole policy and make it impossible to continue to support Mihailović in any form whatever, whether military, political or moral.[105] This was odd in that Howard does not seem to have made any comment on – or taken any notice of – the reports from Deakin and others which S.O.E. London had been sending him from early August onwards about documents captured by the Partisans which proved Četnik collaboration;[106] in fact Michael Rose, the man in the Third Room dealing with Yugoslavia, wrote to S.O.E. in October that he had never seen any such reports from Deakin.[107]

Presumably as a result of these various factors, on 19 November S.O.E. Cairo – or Force 133 – formally stated the case for stopping aid to Mihailović and withdrawing the British Liaison Officers (B.L.O.s).[108] This course was also recommended by the Joint Intelligence Committee on 25 November, and from subsequent statements it emerges that supplies did virtually cease in November.[109] However, the Commander-in-Chief, General Wilson, took the view that Mihailović should be left to rot and fall off the branch rather than be pushed off – which seemed to mean that he did not see the point of getting King Peter to sack him publicly.[110]

Neither Eden nor Churchill took this view: both wanted to give the King a chance of keeping his throne by bringing him together with Tito. On 10 December Churchill saw the King and the Royal Yugoslav Prime Minister, Purić, in Cairo and gave a clear warning that the British were moving towards a break with Mihailović.[111] The Foreign Office too, at this point, thought that it was important for the King, in his own interest, to get rid of Mihailović quickly. On 11 December Sargent minuted: 'we cannot allow the present situation to drag on a moment longer than is necessary. Our hand is being forced by events and these events are going to make our present position increasingly anomalous and indefensible... The only way we can put ourselves right, is to free ourselves at once from our commitments in connexion with Mihailović for which we cannot possibly find any justification which we could put to the British public....'[112] On 14 December the Southern Department had reached the point of drafting a telegram to Cairo proposing that the Ambassador, Ralph Stevenson, should at once inform King Peter that we wanted him to dismiss Mihailović and, if possible, get him out of Yugoslavia by calling him to Cairo for consultation. This draft was initialled by both Sargent and Cadogan on the 15th; it was then held so that Eden could get Cabinet approval for the general policy advocated.[113]

At this point, the whole policy of breaking with Mihailović came to a sudden halt and the British decision-making machine ground to a stop. To understand just why, it is necessary to go outside the Foreign Office papers. As Dedijer disclosed in 1953, the Jajce resolutions of 29 November 1943 had been a gesture of independence by Tito; they had not been approved in advance by Stalin who, when news of them reached Moscow, was extremely angry.[114] As a result, when the Jajce resolutions were first broadcast by Free Yugoslavia on 3 December, they were severely censored by the Russians; the passages denouncing the Royal Government and forbidding King Peter to return to Yugoslavia were cut out and the claims of Tito's new National Committee were soft-pedalled.[115] The Foreign Office therefore at first took the news of the Jajce resolutions very calmly. In fact on 14 December Cadogan saw the Soviet Ambassador and, referring to the Free Yugoslavia reports about the National Committee, stated that the British government could understand the need for these administrative measures and did not consider that they need affect their policy towards Yugoslavia nor their relations with the Partisan movement.[116] On the same day, Eden made a speech in the House of Commons referring in the most friendly terms to Tito and the Partisans and mentioning the new committee in an off-hand way as purely provisional. He said nothing about Mihailović, but spoke protectively and sympathetically about King Peter.[117] Also on 14 December, Moscow newspapers carried the censored version of the Jajce resolutions.[118]

Three days later, on 17 December, Stevenson in Cairo informed his Soviet opposite number 'briefly' of the plans drawn up in General Headquarters for withdrawal of the B.L.O.s if Mihailović failed to carry out certain specified operations – the 'test operations' – by 29 December.[119]

On the same day, Free Yugoslavia started broadcasting the real version of the Jajce resolutions – 'deposing' the Royal Government and forbidding the King's return until the people had decided the issue. This news reached the Foreign Office on 18 December, first through P.W.E. London and then in a telegram from Stevenson in Cairo.[120] P.W.E. London unintentionally contributed to the ensuing confusion. When I sent the text of the broadcast as monitored here to the Foreign Office, I wrote that although the transmission was badly blurred, there appeared to be a sentence saying that 'our people desire in what concerns the King and the Monarchy that steps should be taken to ensure that the King and the Monarchy share in the struggle of national liberation.'[121]

This – presumably misheard – sentence seems to have stimulated the Foreign Office to adopt the policy which they thereafter clung to with such extraordinary tenacity – to try to strike a bargain with Tito, by postponing any move to break with Mihailović until Tito had agreed to co-operate with the King. In this they were at odds with Cairo, where Stevenson's immediate reaction to the full version of Jajce was to advise going ahead with withdrawal of B.L.O.s from Mihailović territory as planned, but dropping the idea of approaching the King to get him to sack Mihailović;[122] and Stevenson endorsed Maclean's view that the simplest thing would be to tell Tito that we were not going to recognise his National Committee but would go on recognising the King and the Royal Government while at the same time giving Tito all military aid.[123] This would of course have been in line with General Wilson's 'let Mihailović rot on the branch' view.

The Foreign Office, on the other hand, as they told Cairo on 20 December, basing themselves partly on the misheard sentence, wondered 'whether we cannot adopt a more drastic remedy' – 'if we could ascertain that Tito would accept him, could we advise King Peter to proceed to Tito's Headquarters?'[124]

The Foreign Office was encouraged in this policy by a memorandum which the Soviet Ambassador, F. T. Gusev, gave Eden on the same day, saying that the Soviet government shared the British view that efforts should be made to find a basis for collaboration between the two sides in Yugoslavia and was ready to do everything possible to find a compromise between the two with the purpose of uniting all the forces of the Yugoslav people.[125] This was the first time Moscow had shown the slightest willingness to go along with repeated British proposals for co-operation; and it is tempting to link this gesture – because it turned out to be only a gesture – with Stalin's anger with Tito over the Jajce resolutions.

Two days later, on 22 December, Eden sent a telegram to Churchill, then convalescing in Marrakesh, setting out the Foreign Office proposal and adding: 'the moment seems to have come... when we ought to make ourselves a direct proposal to Tito in order to bring the matter to a head.'[126]

So began the extraordinary correspondence between Eden in London and Churchill in Marrakesh, with Stevenson in Cairo dithering unhappily between the Maclean line and the wishes of his Foreign Office masters. The Foreign Office and Eden committed themselves more and more deeply to the position that *no* step should be taken towards breaking with Mihailović – not even the withdrawal of the B.L.O.s, which they seemed to regard as a highly spectacular and public act, to judge by one minute of Sargent's – *until* it had been ascertained whether Tito was willing to meet King Peter. On the other side, Stevenson was reporting the pressures from S.O.E. and General Headquarters Middle East for withdrawal of the B.L.O.s, both for their own safety and so as to get Tito's co-operation in introducing missions to the Partisans in Serbia.[127]

Churchill, in Marrakesh, enthusiastically adopted the Foreign Office idea of sending the King to join Tito in Yugoslavia, which obviously appealed to all the romantic and monarchist elements in his make-up; and up till Christmas Eve he seemed to approve Foreign Office policy without reserve.[128] However Randolph Churchill, who was waiting to be dropped to Tito, visited him at Christmas and wrote a 'note' dated Christmas Day pressing for the 'immediate repudiation of Mihailović by H.M.G. and if possible the King'.[129] Simultaneously Churchill must have seen Stevenson's telegrams reporting Maclean's strong opposition to any immediate approach to Tito about the King. By 29 December Churchill was insisting strongly in telegrams to Eden that King Peter should drop Mihailović first, before any approach was made to Tito. In this stand he was fortified a few days later by Randolph and Maclean jointly, when he summoned them from Bari where they were held up by bad weather;[130] and he continued to hold it stubbornly until early February.

At first, the argument between Eden and Churchill took place over the message which Churchill wanted to send Tito in reply to Tito's good wishes for his recovery. This letter, in its

final form, was a compromise between the two men: to please
Eden, Churchill said nothing about asking King Peter to sack
Mihailović, but he also refused to say anything about Tito
receiving the King in Yugoslavia.[131] So even after the letter had
gone, the argument continued. Eden drew support from General
Wilson, then visiting London, who repeated his 'rot on the
branch' theory,[132] and also from the War Cabinet, to whom
Eden presented the Foreign Office case on 11 January, and who
agreed that King Peter should not be approached about dropping Mihailović until Tito had reacted to Churchill's letter.[133]

At this point the main worry of the Foreign Office was that
Churchill, when sending off the letter, had given Maclean discretion over the timing of any subsequent approach to Tito
about the King – the Foreign Office assumed that this meant
never.[134] Eden took the matter up with Churchill when Churchill got back to London, on 18 January – but failed to move
him.[135] On 19 January each wrote a minute to the other, Eden
arguing that Maclean should be instructed to approach Tito
about the King, adding 'naturally to Maclean Tito is all white
and Mihailović all black. I have an impression that grey is a
more common Balkan colour.' Churchill argued for an immediate approach to the King to sack Mihailović: 'every day that
the poor little King has this Mihailović millstone hanging round
his neck, his chances of ever regaining his throne diminish.'[136]

So the Churchill–Eden deadlock seemed complete. Meanwhile, the position of the B.L.O.s with Mihailović was getting
very difficult. On 19 January the Foreign Office sent a telegram
to Cairo saying that no further supplies were to be sent to
Mihailović but that this did not mean that the B.L.O.s were to
be withdrawn.[137] On 22 January Eden minuted that if Mihailović actually carried out an operation the resumption of supplies
to him could be considered. On 23 January, the long-awaited
S.O.E. digest of documents on Mihailović's collaboration – the
documents brought out by Maclean in December – arrived in
London from Cairo; Eden, when he saw it, minuted 'it seems
pretty damning to me.'[138] But there was no immediate change
of policy.

At the beginning of February, Churchill wanted to try his
hand at a second letter to Tito, and in doing so made an important concession to Foreign Office views, in that he asked Tito

whether the King's dismissal of Mihailović would pave the way for friendly relations with Tito.[139] This enabled the Foreign Office to go on playing for time. But on 9 February the military intervened: the Commanders-in-Chief Middle East sent General Wilson, as Supreme Commander Mediterranean, a powerful document saying among other things: 'we ceased material support to Mihailović some three months ago. This policy now has the sanction of H.M.G. The logical implication...is to withdraw Allied missions with him...Hitherto the decision to withdraw has been held up on political grounds that withdrawal ...involves a revision of H.M.G.'s policy towards the Yugoslav Government and that this must await clarification of Tito's attitude towards the King. We consider however that there are the strongest military grounds for immediate withdrawal... Irrespective of future political developments, and even if H.M.G. continue to recognize Mihailović, there would still be no operational grounds for retaining their missions with Mihailović forces.'[140]

On this document, Churchill immediately minuted: 'I agree. Let us act now.' But in the Foreign Office, Howard minuted: 'I...cannot see the advantage in any circumstances of withdrawing Missions until we see from Tito's reply how the wind is blowing.' Sargent and Cadogan both agreed with Howard. Eden minuted that he was reluctant to disagree, but added that he was troubled about the safety of the B.L.O.s.[141] No action was taken, however, until Tito's reply to Churchill's second letter was received on 14 February, setting stiff political terms for any sort of co-operation with the King.[142] Churchill's immediate reaction was to propose to Eden that the B.L.O.s should be withdrawn at once, that Tito's terms should be accepted, and that on this basis he himself should send a further appeal to Tito about the King.[143]

Faced with Churchill's two-pronged attack, Eden at last gave way over the B.L.O.s, but only so that he could fight back over Tito's political terms.[144] On 17 February 1944 instructions went to Cairo, from the Foreign Office and the Chiefs of Staff, that the missions should be withdrawn forthwith.[145] Three days later Eden sent a long minute to Churchill urging that Tito's terms should not be accepted and that he should be pressed further over the return of the King.[146] After all, he wrote in a phrase coined by Sargent,[147] this is only the first move in the game, and no doubt Tito is sufficiently oriental to be a keen bargainer. And this was the beginning of the Šubašić story, which does not belong here.

In their rearguard action over the break with Mihailović, from 18 December 1943 to 17 February 1944, the Foreign Office had pitted themselves against the military (with the doubtful exception of General Wilson), S.O.E. both in Cairo and London, and Churchill himself, whom Eden had only kept in play by appealing to his monarchist feelings and by flattering him about his personal power to influence Tito.

There remains the question: exactly why did the Foreign Office fight so stubbornly, and what were their underlying motives both then and earlier?

It was certainly not devotion to the Royal Yugoslav Government. By the autumn of 1942 the Foreign Office had become so tired of the wranglings of the exiled politicians that they almost gave up hope of restoring a united Yugoslavia. When in August 1943 Rendel wrote his valedictory despatch, he was extremely scathing about the politicians and wrote: 'the Yugoslav Ministers know that we do not expect them to return to power in Yugoslavia...'[148] In the autumn of 1943 Foreign Office minutes several times contain the phrases 'we do not care a rap for the Purić government' or 'we do not care tuppence for Purić.' The formal obligation to an allied government seems to have worried them very little.[149]

King Peter was a different matter. When he first came to England in June 1941 Dixon minuted: 'there is a great opportunity to ensure that the King is thoroughly anglicized...';[150] and the Foreign Office set out to do this by sending him to study in Cambridge, by trying to free him from his mother's apronstrings, by attaching Major Dunlop Mackenzie to him, and by arranging for him to train with the R.A.F. – also by asking King George VI, who was of course his *kum**, to take him under his wing and give him good advice.[151] In spite of all this he remained under the thumb of the small group of Serb officers who exercised great power in Yugoslav affairs, until the British at last allowed him to marry in the spring of 1944, when he

* Akin to being Godfather, but implying a strong protective relationship.

immediately fell completely under the thumb of his Greek mother-in-law.[152] Everyone who met him remarked that he was exceptionally young for his age and he always seemed to agree with whoever was talking to him. Rendel, strongly prejudiced in his favour at the start, wrote in August 1943 that his instability and irresponsibility were disturbing.[153] How the Foreign Office – or Churchill – ever thought he was going to be able to keep his end up with Tito is a mystery – he would probably have fallen completely under Tito's thumb from the word go. Yet presumably the Foreign Office thought that through the King, Britain would be able to wield a certain influence in post-war Yugoslavia.

This seems to be the key to their thinking. It is true that in their day-to-day dealings with the Yugoslav problem, the Foreign Office were often influenced by the tactics of inter-departmental warfare or the determination to keep a grip on policy in the face of multiple pressures from S.O.E. or the military or Churchill. But they do seem to have had the long-term aim of trying to establish British influence in post-war Yugoslavia, in the face of a clearly-seen threat of Soviet domination in the Balkans.

Eden's first Moscow visit and his talk with Stalin at the end of 1941 deeply implanted a fear of Soviet aims. Dixon minuted in January 1942: 'although it was not stated in Moscow, the Soviet plan may well be the constitution of a greater Yugoslavia not only as a counterweight to Italy but also as a channel for Soviet penetration on to the Adriatic via Rumania and Bulgaria.'[154] At the end of 1942, when the Foreign Office was moving towards the decision to contact the Partisans, Eden minuted to Churchill that although it might be in our short-term interest to transfer our support to the Partisans, 'on a long view...we should be wise to go on supporting Mihailović in order to prevent anarchy and Communist chaos after the war.'[155] Howard minuted on 1 January 1943: 'it was precisely in view of this (Russian) danger, not out of excessive love of Mihailović, that we recently decided that...we must continue to support Mihailović and the Yugoslav government.'[156] In February 1943, one of the Foreign Office arguments against the Bailey plan for moving the Partisans into Croatia and drawing a line between them and Mihailović was that it would mean the establishment of a Communist Croatia which might influence Hungary and Austria and lead to a Communist movement in East-Central Europe.[157] The decision to contact the Partisans was regarded as preferable, since there was thought to be a hope of bringing them, if not under Mihailović's command, at least under British influence and control.

As for the Foreign Office's rearguard action on Mihailović's behalf, the subsequent justification for this was given in a top secret paper of 7 June 1944, presented to the War Cabinet:

> the Russians are, generally speaking, out for a predominant position in S.E. Europe and are using Communist-led movements in Yugoslavia, Albania and Greece as a means to an end.... If anyone is to blame for the present situation in which the Communist-led movements are the most powerful elements in Yugoslavia and Greece, it is we ourselves. The Russians have merely sat back and watched us doing their work for them. And it is only when we have shown signs of putting a brake on their movements (such as our continued recognition of King Peter and Mihailović, and more recently the strong line taken against E.A.M....) that they have come into the open and shown where their interests lay.... [158]

Looking back after thirty years, the long-term aim of the Foreign Office seems reasonable enough. But whether it was sensible to persist so long in trying to use Mihailović, or King Peter, for this purpose is quite another matter.

NOTES

1. Captain (later Colonel) D. T. Hudson was the first British officer to enter Yugoslavia (20 September 1941) after the Axis occupation and was in contact both with Tito and with Mihailović; Colonel S. W. Bailey was Senior Liaison Officer with Mihailović from 25 December 1942 onwards; Brigadier C. D. Armstrong was Head of the British Mission to Mihailović from 24 September 1943 onwards.

2. Brigadier Fitzroy Maclean (Sir Fitzroy Maclean Bart.), Head of the British Mission to Tito from September 1943 onwards.

3. Colonel F. W. D. Deakin, the first British officer attached to Tito's headquarters, from 28 May 1943 onwards.

4. Major Randolph Churchill, attached to Brigadier Maclean's Mission from January 1944 onwards.

5. Political Warfare Executive, responsible for propaganda to enemy and enemy-occupied countries. It was subordinated for policy purposes to the Foreign Office and administratively to the Minister of Information.

6. Sir Robert Bruce-Lockhart, K.C.M.G.

7. FO 371/37584.

8. Head of the United Kingdom Commercial Corporation 1940; senior posts in S.O.E. London and Cairo 1941 onwards.

9. FO 371/30220.

10. Lord Selborne, Minister of Economic Warfare in succession to Hugh Dalton, 1941 onwards.

11. Minute from Lord Selborne to Prime Minister F/1627/34 of 11 May 1944. FO 371/44290.

12. Admiral Lord Louis Mountbatten of Burma, K.G., P.C., G.C.B., O.M., G.C.S.I., G.C.I.E., G.C.V.O., D.S.O.

13. FO 371/37585.

14. At a Chiefs of Staff meeting on 17.6.43, Lord Louis Mountbatten presented a memorandum:

...It seems probable...that Mihailović's power is largely the result of the support we have given him; and it is not likely that the prestige of any War Minister, whom H.M.G. have to invite to state categorically that he is against the Axis, can stand very high with his own countrymen, many of whom are actively fighting the Axis. As it appears that Mihailović has actually been in contact with the Italians and is known to be fighting the Partisans, who are being equipped by the Russians [NB: there is no known evidence of this at the period in question. E.B.] we are risking bringing about a situation where we shall have provoked a minor civil war, in which we and the Russians will be backing opposing forces. The military disadvantages of the Foreign Office policy to make the avoidance of 'political issues' with the Yugoslav Government the paramount consideration is obvious. It is proposed that this should be brought to their attention. (FO 371/37609.)

15. General Milan Nedić, the Pétain-type collaborationist head of the puppet government of Serbia under German control.

16. FO 371/37578.

17. Ibid.

18. FO 371/37608.

19. Minute by E. M. Rose of 8.2.43. FO 371/37608.

20. FO 371/37608.

21. Sir Orme Sargent was Deputy Under Secretary in the Foreign Office in charge of Balkan affairs.

22. FO 371/37607.

23. Eden minute of 27.2.43. FO 371/37580.

24. FO 371/37611.

25. *Ibid.*

26. Major Desmond Morton was a member of Churchill's staff at No. 10 Downing Street. FO 371/37609. See also F. W. D. Deakin, *The Embattled Mountain* (London, 1971) p. 223.

27. John Colville, Assistant Private Secretary to Churchill, 1940-1,

1943–5, in *Action This Day: Working with Churchill*, ed. H. Wheeler-Bennet (London, 1968) p. 77.

28. Letter from Cairo, from Sir Ralph Stevenson, Ambassador to the Royal Yugoslav Government from August 1943, to Sargent of 14.10.43. FO 371/37613.

29. Prime Minister's Personal Minute to Foreign Secretary of 28.7.43. FO 371/37610.

30. FO 371/37625.

31. *Ibid.*

32. Letter from Glenconner to Pierson Dixon of the Southern Department of the Foreign Office, of 3.7.42. FO 371/32467.

33. Letter from Douglas Howard, Head of the Southern Department, to Elisabeth Barker, Balkan Region P.W.E., of 2.3.43. FO 371/37580.

34. Letter from Sir Charles Hambro, Head of S.O.E. in London, to Sargent, of 20.1.43. FO 371/37607.

35. FO 371/37607.

36. Letter from Barker to Howard of 4.3.43. FO 371/37581.

37. H. D. Harrison, Reuter's correspondent in Belgrade before (and after) the Second World War.

38. Sir George Rendel, K.C.M.G., was Minister, then Ambassador, to the exiled Royal Yugoslav Government, 1941–3.

39. Letter from Rendel to Dixon of 4.11.42. FO 371/33472.

40. Letter from Rendel to Howard of 12.4.43. FO 371/37583.

41. Eden memorandum to the War Cabinet of 31.10.41. FO 371/30220.

42. FO 371/30220.

43. Gladwyn Jebb (later Lord Gladwyn), at that time detached from the Foreign Office for work with S.O.E., wrote a letter to Howard on 2.12.41:

... With regard to Simović's opinion that the kind of sabotage performed by the Communists only injures the Serbs without hurting the Germans, we can only say that from our point of view we do not agree; more especially as such sabotage is directed against the Belgrade–Niš railway and the industrial area of the Kragujevac–Kraljevo–Kruševac industrial triangle... Reprisals are a double-edged weapon in the hands of the German authorities, since the more savage the measures they adopt, the more do they rouse the people and make them ready to accept any sacrifice... We do not believe that sabotage handicaps Col Mihailović in any way. At the same time he is the leader on the spot who is in the best position to judge... (FO 371/30221.)

See also a letter from George Mallaby, War Office, to Howard of November 1941: 'I note what you say about General Simović's objection to acts of sabotage, but I wonder what the insurgents, whether they be Communists or followers of Mihailović, would find to do if they gave up sabotage. A revolt of this kind must be carried on largely by sabotage...' FO 371/30221. It is of interest that a year later, in November 1942, a S.O.E. 'Appreciation on Yugoslavia', sent to the Southern Department by Peter Boughey of S.O.E. London, contained the passage: '...so far no telegrams received from either of our liaison officers reporting any sabotage undertaken by General Mihailović, nor have we received any reports of fighting against Axis troops.' FO 371/33472.

44. FO 371/30220.
45. *Ibid.*
46. *Ibid.*
47. *Ibid.*
48. *Ibid.*
49. *Ibid.*
50. *Ibid.*
51. See Foreign Office telegram to Cairo of 19.11.41. FO 371/30221.
52. Hugh Dalton was then Minister of Economic Warfare. FO 371/30221.
53. Minute by Dixon. FO 371/30221.
54. War Cabinet conclusions, 27.11.43. FO 371/30221.
55. FO 371/30221.
56. *Ibid.*
57. *Ibid.*
58. Maclagan Report. FO 371/37586.
59. FO 371/30220.
60. Kuibyshev telegram to Foreign Office, No. 132 of 19.11.41. FO 371/30221.
61. *Ibid.*
62. FO 371/33490.
63. Coverley Price minute of 6.8.42. FO 371/33468.
64. Howard minute of 6.8.42. FO 371/33468.
65. Ralph Murray was at that time Head of Balkan Region, P.W.E.
66. Letter from Murray to Howard of 19.8.42. FO 371/33469.
67. Letter from Dixon to Murray of 23.9.42. FO 371/33470.
68. Murray memorandum of 14.10.42, FO 371/33471. The Yugoslav Military Bulletins, broadcast weekly, were prepared by a group of young Yugoslav officers, notably Major Ž. Knežević, and were based partly on messages from Mihailović. They were fanatically pro-Mihailović and contained detailed denunciations of his various enemies, including the Partisans (though the B.B.C. did not know this at the time).
69. Letter from Colonel J. S. A. Pearson, S.O.E. London, to Howard of 20.8.42. FO 371/33469.
70. FO 371/33470.
71. Letter from Dixon to Pearson of 9.10.42. FO 371/33470.
72. Telegram from Bailey quoted in letter from Peter Boughey, S.O.E. London, to E. M. Rose, Southern Department, of 9.1.43. FO 371/37578.
73. Telegram from Hudson of 15.11.42 in reply to question from S.O.E. London about reports of Mihailović's collaboration with the Italians. Hudson replied:
... Mihailović has ... agreed to adopt the policy of collaboration with the Italians pursued by the Montenegrin Četniks ... Mihailović remains opposed to undertaking sabotage against the Italians. He insists that they will collapse shortly, when he expects to secure their arms and equipment, with which he plans to defend Montenegro against the Germans ... In

Serbia, Mihailović's Četniks have considerable freedom of movement. They are however little more than symbols of resistance...When I press for continuous large-scale sabotage, the General and his entourage reply that half a million Serbs have already been killed...When the General is satisfied that victory is certain, blood will not be spared, but until then I consider him perfectly capable of coming to any understanding with either Italians or Germans...I do not know whether Mihailović has an agreement with the Axis involving his inactivity in Serbia and their anti-communist drive in North-west Bosnia...(FO 371/33473.)

74. Letter from Dixon to Pearson of 9.10.42:

...We still feel that we are bound to continue our support of Mihailović because of his potential value, both military and political, at a later stage of the war. This support must, we feel, be given independently of whether or not he continues to refuse to take a more active part in resisting and attacking Axis forces in Yugoslavia....We propose...to review the situation again when our emissary (Colonel Bailey) has reached Mihailović's headquarters and has been able to report on the general position as he sees it...(FO 371/33470.)

75. Dixon minute of 26.10.42. FO 371/33471.

76. Howard minute of 25.11.42. FO 371/33472.

77. Sargent minute of December 1942, quoted in long minute by Howard of 23.4.43. FO 371/37584.

78. Eden minute to the Prime Minister (PM/42/308) of 17.12.42. FO 371/33474.

79. Draft minute from Eden to Prime Minister of 1.1.43. FO 371/37578.

80. Eden minute of 3.1.43 on the above draft:

This seems to me unsatisfactory. The position goes from bad to worse... We are to go back on the decision we had previously taken (because, it seems, S.O.E. and Commander-in-Chief Middle East don't agree, tho' P.M. does) and give full backing to Mihailović tho' he is not fighting our enemies and is being publicly denounced by our Soviet ally. I see no sense in such a policy and every likelihood that we and the Russians will come to an open clash...(FO 371/37578.)

81. Sir Alexander Cadogan, permanent under-secretary at the Foreign Office, minuted on 4.1.43 (after pointing out that Bailey had just arrived in Yugoslavia): ...We have of course hitherto also been influenced by the long-term consideration that it may be wise to support Mihailović in order to prevent the break-up of Yugoslavia after the war into Soviet Republics under Russian domination. And, I suppose, we should have to inform King Peter if we withdrew support from Mihailović.' Eden replied: 'Let us then await Colonel Bailey's report.' FO 371/37578.

82. Howard minute of 23.4.43. FO 371/37584.

83. *Ibid.*

84. Chiefs of Staff meeting of 11.2.43 (COS(43)44). FO 371/37579.

85. Howard minute of 23.4.43. FO 371/37584.

86. The Chiefs of Staff considered the Yugoslav question on 4.3.43, and on 7.3.43 a letter was sent from the War Cabinet office to Sargent, reporting their decision against the diversion of any additional Liberators to Yugo-

slavia, and adding: 'They do not feel qualified to express a strong view, one way or the other, on the intricate political issues involved. In principle, however, they are inclined to the view that it would be a mistake to adopt a policy of supporting both sides, i.e. Mihailović and the Partisans, particularly in view of the fact that the number of aircraft which can be made available is scarcely sufficient to give effective support to either.' On this Howard minuted: 'Not a very helpful suggestion.' FO 371/37581.

87. Memorandum enclosed in letter from Hambro to Sargent of 11.3.43. FO 371/37581.

88. Letter from Pearson to Howard of 13.3.43, commenting on a letter from E. Barker (P.W.E.) to Howard of 9.3.43 arguing against S.O.E. demands for a ban on mention of the Partisans by the B.B.C. FO 371/37581.

89. Selborne letter to Sargent of 9.4.43. FO 370/37583.

90. Pearson letter to Howard of 12.4.43. FO 371/37584.

91. Telegram from Foreign Office to Minister of State Cairo of 8.4.43. FO 371/37583.

92. See Howard minute of 23.4.43. FO 371/37584. The Chiefs of Staff directive to S.O.E. on this issue was also discussed in an exchange of letters between Selborne and Sargent in early April. FO 371/37583.

93. Howard minute of 23.4.43. FO 371/37584.

94. This interpretation of events obviously does not take account of efforts made within S.O.E. Cairo in the early months of 1943 in favour of a policy of contacting and aiding the Partisans.

95. Selborne letter to Brendan Bracken, Minister of Information, of 22.7.43, and Bracken letter to Selborne of 31.7.43; also Howard minute of 1.8.43. FO 371/37589.

96. Howard minute of 15.6.43:

S.O.E. have excelled themselves in their handling of this question. First Lord Glenconner goes and sends Bailey a telegram off his own bat (proposing the Ibar dividing line between Mihailović and Tito) and completely at variance with our own policy, and with the telegram sent to Mihailović the week before. Secondly, Bailey caps this effort by repeating the whole telegram verbatim to Mihailović, when it was clear to all but the totally blind that only one portion was intended for his sight. No wonder then that Mihailović has replied in no unclear terms that we can do what we like with these demands and orders, but that he intends to ignore their existence. We have suggested to the Chiefs of Staff that the disastrous telegram should be rescinded. Unless we do that we shall have ruined our chances of coming to any agreement with Mihailović. (FO 371/37588.)

97. Howard minute of 30.7.43:

Our idea all along has been that we should only supply both sides with material support on condition that assurances were given by both sides that no operations would be taken against the other . . . I suspected all along that S.O.E. had ignored this stipulation so far as the Partisans were concerned and that they had started supplying the Partisans without obtaining the assurances . . . S.O.E. [has now been forced] into the open and our suspicions are justified . . . (FO 371/37610.)

98. Rose minute of 29.7.43. FO 371/37610.

99. Prime Minister's Personal Minute to Foreign Secretary of 28.7.43. FO 371/37610.

100. Sargent minute of 30.7.43; Eden letter to Selborne of 2.8.43; Prime Minister's letter to General Wilson of 3.8.43; Eden minute of 4.8.43; Selborne letter to Eden of 5.8.43; Eden minute of 6.8.43; Eden letter to General Wilson of 9.8.43. FO 371/37610.

101. FO 371/37615.

102. Minute by V. Cavendish Bentinck (Foreign Office) on Chiefs of Staff meeting of 16.11.43:

> The Chiefs of Staff...expressed a desire to hear the Foreign Office comment on Brigadier Maclean's report...It seemed to them at first sight that Brigadier Maclean's recommendations should be carried out. The view was expressed that it was time we ceased to consider the feelings of the Yugoslav Government, if consideration of them in any way interfered with our support for the Partisans, who are doing something against our enemy, unlike General Mihailović...The Chief of Air Staff enquired whether Brigadier Maclean was a realistic observer, or, like many people who go on such missions, a fanatic. I [Cavendish Bentinck] replied that Brigadier Maclean was a former member of this [Foreign] Office, shrewd, hard-headed and rather cynical. The C.I.G.S. said that he regarded Brigadier Maclean as a highly reliable and able officer. All three Chiefs of Staff praised Brigadier Maclean's report...they intended to make recommendations to the Cabinet on Brigadier Maclean's report.

For War Cabinet reactions, see letter from Herbert Morrison to Eden of 6.12.43: 'I have read with very great interest the able report by Brigadier Maclean...I wonder whether it would not be a good plan for the Cabinet to discuss some of the broad questions of policy, present and future, which emerge from the report...' FO 371/37615.

103. Paper presented by M.O.4, G.H.Q.M.E.F., of 19.10.43, transmitted to Foreign Office on 6.11.43. FO 371/37615.

104. Djurić was Mihailović's commander in the Priština area. In October the British had asked Mihailović to remove him because of his inactivity and obstructiveness. However, on 11.11.43 a telegram was sent to Cairo by the British Liaison Officer attached to him, reporting that Djurić said that he had received from Mihailović general mobilization orders for action against the Partisans. A subsequent signal gave a translation of the Serbian text of this reported order:

> ...I order that throughout the whole country, in all our provinces, all Serbs gather together in the common battle against our most dangerous enemy in whose ranks are to be found Ustaši and all the rest of the rabble in the country...Undertake in all provinces the most energetic blows wherever they may be found, for they are the greatest evil in our midst...
> Attack them with parties of three on the roads and everywhere possible in the rear, just as they have attacked us in the rear when we were attacking the Ustaši and the Germans...therefore, when the Communists are fighting the Occupiers, you attack from the rear. It was decided at the Moscow conference [the conference of the Soviet, American and Brittish

Foreign Ministers of late October 1943] that Yugoslavia is to be restored, but on democratic lines. That is in our favour and against the Communists. Act on this order at once...Against all Commandants who fail to carry out this order, steps will be taken as a traitor...(FO 371/37616.) 105. FO 371/37616.

106. See telegrams sent by Pearson to Howard on 12.8.43 and 14.8.43. FO 371/37611.

107. Rose letter to Webb (S.O.E., of 7.10.43, prompted by a telegram from Maclean of 20.9.43, reporting that Tito had said to him that 'it was well-known that Mihailović had long been cooperating with the Germans. Of this he had ample documentary proof, which he had communicated to Major Deakin. He did not know why we ignored it...' FO 371/37612. In this connection, see Howard minute of 17.11.43: '...I hesitate to accept the repeated accusations that Mihailović and the Četniks are in close collaboration with the Germans...Evidence produced by the Partisans must to some extent be discounted.' FO 371/37615.

108. Force 133's 'Appreciation regarding the Military situation in Serbia so as to determine what in the future should be our Military Policy', of 19.11.43; the concluding recommendations were: '1. To discontinue support of Mihailović. 2. To evacuate British Mission with Mihailović by making the necessary arrangements with Tito. 3. To send B.L.Os to the Partisans in Serbia to arrange reception of requisite supplies.' FO 371/37618.

109. Joint Intelligence Sub-Committee report on the situation in Yugoslavia of 25.11.43: '...On military grounds we conclude that there is every reason to discontinue sending supplies to Mihailović, while he is encouraging, or, at best, failing to prevent, the collaboration of some of his forces with the enemy. If supplies were continued, not only is it unlikely that they would be used against the enemy, but they would probably be used against the Partisans with a consequent reduction in the offensive effort against the Germans in Yugoslavia...' FO 371/37617.

110. Telegram from Stevenson, Cairo, to Foreign Office, No. 103 of 20.11.43. FO 371/37616.

111. Telegram from Stevenson, Cairo, to Foreign Office, No. 171 of 11.12.43. FO 371/37618. Eden had already given a milder warning to King Peter on 7.11.43: see telegram from Cairo to Foreign Office of 8.11.43. FO 371/37591.

112. FO 371/37591.

113. Minute by J. Nichols of 14.12.43 and Foreign Office telegram to Stevenson, Cairo, No. 126 of 16.12.43: 'I am seeking Cabinet approval of general line advocated...' FO 371/37618.

114. Vladimir Dedijer, *Tito Speaks* (London, 1953) p. 207; see also Milovan Djilas, *Conversations with Stalin* (London, 1962) p. 14.

115. Monitoring report of Free Yugoslavia Radio of 4.12.43. FO 371/37663.

116. Telegram from Foreign Office to Washington, No. 86514 of 15.12.43. FO 371/37663.

117. FO 371/37636; *Hansard*, 14.12.44.

118. Telegram from Moscow to Foreign Office, No. 1532 of 14.12.43. FO 371/37663.
119. Telegram from Stevenson, Cairo, to Foreign Office, No. 188 of 17.12.43. FO 371/37619.
120. Telegrams from Stevenson, Cairo, to Foreign Office, No. 192 of 18.12.43, FO 371/37619; No. 196 of 20.12.42 and No. 215 of 23.12.43, FO 371/37663.
121. Letter from E. Barker to Rose of 18.12.43. FO 371/37663.
122. Telegram from Stevenson, Cairo, to Foreign Office, No. 193 of 20.12.43. FO 371/37619.
123. Telegram from Stevenson, Cairo, to Foreign Office, No. 198 of 20.12.43. FO 371/37619.
124. Telegram from Foreign Office to Stevenson, Cairo, No. 134 of 20.12.43. On 21.12.43 Sargent minuted:

I think we ought to persevere with our idea that the King should join Tito in Yugoslavia and set up his government there, thus automatically liquidating both Mihailović and the Cairo government...I am inclined to think that...especially if it were reinforced by the Russians and the Americans, Tito would think twice before rejecting it out of hand... Having said this, I must confess that the sudden appearance of all these political declarations by Tito...is rather suspicious. Has it been done, I wonder, under Russian advice and influence? (FO 371/37619.)

125. Telegrams from Foreign Office to Stevenson, Cairo, Nos. 135 and 136 of 21.12.43. FO 371/37619.
126. Telegram from Foreign Secretary to Prime Minister, GRAND No. 723 of 22.12.43:

We were considering plan for elimination of Mihailović...when Free Yugoslavia radio station broadcast statement by Yugoslav Anti-Fascist Council of National Liberation demanding recognition abroad for Tito's committee and formal withdrawal of rights from Yugoslav Government ...All this makes it far more difficult for King Peter to dismiss Mihailović unless he can get some *quid pro quo* from Tito in return. The moment seems to have come therefore when we ought to make ourselves a direct proposal to Tito in order to bring matters to a head, and my telegram No. 134 [see footnote 124 above] shows the form that this should take... (FO 371/37618.)

127. See for instance telegram from Foreign Office to Stevenson, Cairo, No. 153 of 25.12.43, FO 371/37619; Sargent minute of 31.12.43, FO 371/37620; Foreign Secretary to Prime Minister, GRAND No. 1217 of 7.1.44, FO 371/44243; telegrams from Stevenson, Cairo, to Foreign Office, No. 212 of 23.12.43 and No. 222 of 26.12.43, FO 371/37619.
128. See FROZEN No. 807 of 23.12.43: 'Colonel Warden to Foreign Secretary. I quite agree with all you are doing...' FO 371/37619.
129. Telegrams from Prime Minister to Foreign Secretary, FROZEN No. 976 of 29.12.43, No. 996 of 30.12.43, No. 1058 of 2.1.44, No. 1091 of 4.1.44. FO 371/44243.
130. Prime Minister to Foreign Secretary, FROZEN No. 1112 of 5.1.44, FO 371/44243; Nos. 1184 and 1187 of 9.1.44, FO 371/44244.
131. Prime Minister to Foreign Secretary, FROZEN No. 1057 of 2.1.44;

minute by Armine Dew (Southern Department) of 4.1.44; Foreign Secretary to Prime Minister, GRAND No. 1149 or 4.1.44, FO 371/44243.

132. Foreign Secretary to Prime Minister, GRAND No. 1149 of 4.1.44. FO 371/44243.

133. Foreign Secretary to Prime Minister, GRAND No. 1303 of 11.1.44, FO 371/44244; memorandum by Foreign Secretary for War Cabinet WO(41)19, *ibid.*

134. Prime Minister to Foreign Secretary, FROZEN No. 1187 of 9.1.44, FO 371/44244; minute by Dew of 10.1.44, *ibid.*

135. Howard minutes of 18.1.44 and 19.1.44. FO 371/44245.

136. Eden minute to Prime Minister of 19.1.44; minute from Prime Minister to Foreign Secretary of 19.1.44. FO 371/44245.

137. Telegram from Foreign Office to Stevenson, Cairo, of 19.1.44. FO 371/44245.

138. Eden minute of 22.1.44 on telegram from Stevenson, Cairo, to Foreign Office, No. 2 Saving of 5.1.44; Eden minute to Dixon of 23.1.44. FO 371/44244.

139. Telegram from Foreign Office to Stevenson, Cairo, No. 93 of 5.2.44. FO 44247.

140. Telegram from Stevenson, Cairo, to Foreign Office, No. 129 of 9.2.44. FO 371/44247.

141. Minute by the Prime Minister of 11.2.44; minutes by Howard and Sargent of 11.2.44; minute by Cadogan of 12.2.44; minute by Eden of (?) 12.2.44. FO 371/44247.

142. Telegrams from Stevenson, Cairo, to Foreign Office, Nos. 151 and 152 of 14.2.44. FO 371/44247.

143. Prime Minister's Personal Minute, M 122/4 of 16.2.44 to Foreign Secretary. FO 371/44247.

144. Minute from Foreign Secretary to Prime Minister (PM/44/78) of 16.2.44. FO 371/44247.

145. Telegram from Foreign Office to Stevenson, Cairo, No. 117 of 17.2.44; COSMED 37 of 17.2.44 for General Wilson from Chiefs of Staff. FO 371/44247.

146. Minute from Foreign Secretary to Prime Minister (PM/44/89) of 20.2.44. FO 371/44247.

147. Sargent minute of 16.2.44. FO 371/44247.

148. Rendel's valedictory despatch of 4.8.43. FO 371/37611.

149. For instance, minute by Rose of 1.11.43: '...what the Purić Government is prepared to do doesn't matter a rap. It can return to the oblivion whence it came, without anyone being a whit the worse off.' FO 371/37613. Telegram from Foreign Office to Stevenson, Cairo, of 3.11.43: '...The present government has no importance...The King must of necessity be ready to sacrifice the present government...' FO 371/37613. Minute by J. Nichols of 10.11.43: '...The King is the lynch pin of our policy; we don't care tuppence about M. Purić.' FO 371/37591.

150. Dixon minute of 25.6.41. FO 371/30265.

151. Letter from Sargent to Sir A. Hardinge, Buckingham Palace, of 26.2.43. FO 371/37624.

152. Dunlop Mackenzie's confidential report of 25.8.44, sent to Eden by Stevenson on 28.8.44. FO 371/44306.
  153. Rendel's valedictory despatch of 4.8.43. FO 371/37611.
  154. Dixon minute of 8.1.42. FO 371/33133.
  155. Eden minute to Prime Minister (PM/42/308) of 17.12.42. FO 371/33474.
  156. Howard minute of 1.1.43. FO 371/33154.
  157. Letter from Rendel to Sargent of 3.2.43, Sargent letter to C.D. of 23.2.43. FO 371/37579.
  158. Top Secret Foreign Office paper on 'Soviet Policy in the Balkans', WP(44)304 of 7.6.44. FO 371/43646.

3 British Policy Towards General Draža Mihailović

S. W. BAILEY

Much has been published about the activities of the Partisans in Yugoslavia between June 1941 and the beginning of 1945; but very little has been written – at least on this side of the Atlantic – about those of General Dragoljub (Draža) Mihailović. If British policy towards Yugoslavia – tantamount to policy towards Mihailović – is to be understood, it is essential for the reader to have some knowledge of the pre-war history of the Yugoslav peoples and of the events which followed the German attack on Yugoslavia on 6 April 1941.[1]

For three months after Germany's successful invasion of Yugoslavia (whose capitulation occurred on 17 April) and the dissolution of the state, little direct, reliable, detailed information reached the West about conditions inside former Yugoslav territories. However it soon became clear from reports in the Axis and neutral press that resistance to the occupying forces was being put up by numerous groups of armed men operating in practically every mountainous area of the country. But it was equally apparent that these groups were isolated and acting independently of one another, and that their efforts were quite unco-ordinated.[2]

These press reports were subsequently borne out by more up-to-date and direct evidence smuggled out of the country in various ways, and by the personal submissions of Yugoslavs who had succeeded in escaping from the country, often in suspicious circumstances. The doubtful value of such testimony notwithstanding, it was obvious that the resistance reported in the Axis and neutral press was on a more considerable scale than had been suspected.

In the middle of August 1941, the Naval monitoring station

at Portishead began to pick up weak, intermittent signals from an unidentified wireless transmitter which purported to be working inside Yugoslavia. The contact was carefully nursed, and by the end of the month it had been established beyond doubt that the station was being operated by units of the Royal Yugoslav Army which were still offering vigorous and well-organised military resistance to the enemy in the hills of western Serbia. The headquarters of these forces were on Ravna Gora, some twenty miles due north of Čačak, and they were under the command of a Colonel Draža Mihailović, the senior officer present.

The establishment of this W/T link was followed at the end of August by the arrival in Istanbul of a Dr Miloš Sekulić, who said he was an emissary of the Serb Agrarian (Peasant) Party. From Istanbul, Sekulić went to London where he reported both to the Yugoslav and to the British Government, claiming to have had personal contact with Mihailović who had asked him to establish links with the outside world on his behalf.

Reports about resistance in other parts of Yugoslavia continued to come in from many sources. The British military authorities in Cairo therefore decided to send an exploratory mission into the country. Captain (later Colonel) D. T. Hudson, probably the best qualified officer available in the Middle East with the necessary knowledge of the country and language, was selected as the British member of the mission.

There could however be no question, in the light of assurances given to the Royal Yugoslav Government-in-exile in London, of placing Yugoslav Army units under the direct orders of British officers. Satisfactory contact between the Yugoslav Government and its forces in the homeland would have to be maintained through Yugoslav officers. This arrangement proved an embarrassment throughout our period of co-operation with Mihailović.[3] Consequently two Yugoslav officers (Majors Ostojić and Lalatović) were posted to the party. The fact that these two men, who became Mihailović's principal lieutenants on the military side, were *Air Force officers* with little understanding of guerrilla warfare or for land fighting generally, had, in my view, the gravest repercussions on Anglo-Yugoslav relations between 1941 and 1944.

Although the British authorities had no control over the

instructions given by the Yugoslav Government to the Yugoslav members of the mission, they did provide a clear and un-ambiguous British brief. This laid down that in addition to the collection of technical military intelligence about the disposition, strength and armament of Axis forces and related matters, the party's task was to make contact with, investigate and report back on all elements offering resistance to the enemy, regardless of nationality, religion or political belief. No copy of this brief has survived in British hands as the relevant documents were destroyed at the time of the Axis threat to Cairo in July 1942; but the text may well be in the hands of the present Yugoslav Government since, in accordance with the general instructions to make as many contacts as possible, the wireless operator of the party, with one W/T set, was left behind with the Montenegrin 'patriots', who were merged with Tito's National Army of Liberation.

Hudson himself, accompanied by Ostojić and escorted by 'patriots' (who were actually Partisans), made his way to Serbia where he finally found Mihailović on Ravna Gora towards the end of October. He confirmed in his earliest reports that the forces under Mihailović's command were numerous, and that they were causing considerable trouble to the Axis. He asked for the urgent despatch of money, small arms, explosives and clothes, so that resistance could be expanded into a general revolt. For operational reasons – chiefly lack of aircraft with suitable range and lift (which were in the first place required for vital anti-submarine warfare) – we found ourselves unable to give Mihailović substantial military aid. Study of this problem produced the first expression of British *operational* policy towards Mihailović's movement. This was to the effect that, while it was desirable to keep resistance alive, it should not be encouraged to spread to such an extent as to provoke ruthless counter-measures by the Germans.

However the Germans themselves decided to nip the revolt in the bud. During October and November 1941 they carried out two large-scale drives against not only Mihailović's forces, but also those of Tito, who after the German attack on Russia on 22 June had likewise taken to the hills to build up, on the foundation provided by the pre-war clandestine organisation of the Yugoslav Communist Party, a second resistance movement.

Most unfortunately the appearance on the battlefield of this rival movement led to armed clashes between the two resistance movements even before the onset of the German offensive. In these clashes were sown the seeds of mutual aversion and intolerance which, fed by the atavistic traditions of the blood feud common to all the Balkan peoples, soon came to yield a bloody harvest of civil war.

Despite this, during October and November 1941 at least two meetings took place between Mihailović and Tito in western Šumadija. At these meetings genuine efforts seem to have been made by both sides to reach an agreement which, if it would not have unified their efforts under a single – or even a joint – command, would at least have ensured adequate co-operation in joint actions against the occupying forces. Captain Hudson was in an adjacent room on the occasion of one of these meetings although he took no active part in the negotiations, and later he spent a short time with the Partisans forces of which he formed a favourable opinion.

Despite these attempts to evolve a common *modus operandi et vivendi*, the conflict between the two groups, exacerbated by political complications, assumed serious proportions towards the middle of November. On the 13th of that month the Yugoslav Prime Minister informed Anthony Eden that he had told the Soviet Government, with which his country had concluded a pact of friendship and non-aggression on 5 April 1941, that the Yugoslav Government considered Mihailović to be the national leader in Yugoslavia, and would therefore be grateful if Moscow would urge Tito not only not to attack Mihailović's forces, but also to collaborate with him in fighting the Germans.[4]

His Majesty's Government agreed with this action, and encouraged by the hope expressed on 22 October by Ivan Maisky, the Soviet Ambassador in London, that all the insurgents in Yugoslavia would be helped, Eden instructed the British Ambassador in Moscow to support it. At the same time, the British Government requested the Yugoslav Government to instruct Mihailović to reciprocate by refraining from retaliating if attacked by the Partisan forces, and by renewing his attempts to come to an understanding with them. It was made abundantly clear that British policy was to promote the utmost solidarity between all Yugoslav resistance elements.[5]

The outcome of this diplomatic activity was that Mihailović reported on 22 November that he had reached an agreement with Tito. Despite a move by the Foreign Office to step up the revolt by increasing supplies and intensifying propaganda to both sides, military considerations prevailed, and the policy of limiting aid to the minimum required simply to keep resistance alive was reaffirmed. At the same time it was suggested to Maisky that his government should send a message of congratulation to Tito on the agreement reached with Mihailović, urging that the united front thus created be kept up.[6]

While these exchanges were going on at diplomatic level, the German drives had resulted in the expulsion of Tito's forces from western Serbia, whence they made their way to north-west Bosnia, and in the temporary disruption of Mihailović's movement, most of the members of which, obeying his explicit orders, returned to their normal calling or otherwise went to earth behind the advancing German forces. Mihailović himself, with a small group of staff officers and political advisers and a substantial bodyguard and support group, also quit Serbia for Montenegro.

One of the ways in which the followers of Mihailović concealed their true nature was by enlisting in the Serb Quisling forces of General Nedić, Prime Minister in the puppet government in Belgrade, and in those of Dimitrije Ljotić, a notorious near-Fascist. Mihailović maintained that this ruse was legitimate, since such followers were pledged to come over to him when so ordered with at least their arms and equipment, and if possible with their comrades as well. But to other observers the practice looked less justified, and it was by this action that Mihailović first laid himself open to the charge of collaboration with the enemy which in the end brought him to grief.

These widely differing reactions to the German offensive crystallised for the first time the irreconcilable divergence of the policies which must already have been decided upon by Mihailović and his supporters and the Partisan staffs, respectively. Whereas Tito stood for continual harassment of, and constant active resistance to, the occupying forces at no matter what cost either to his own forces or to the civilian population, Mihailović's policy was one of passive resistance, comparatively speaking. By this he hoped not only to shield the peasantry from extensive enemy reprisals, but also to gain time and relative peace in which to complete the progressive organisation of a country-wide regular army in the homeland, to be used only when it had become certain that the Germans could no longer hold the Balkans, first to expedite the expulsion of the occupying forces, in concert with Allied operations from outside; and later to secure law and order pending the return of the King and the government-in-exile.

This author believes there is an historical explanation of these diametrically opposed attitudes. Serbian guerrilla tactics, as adopted by the remnants of the Yugoslav Army, were largely based on the 'četnik' tradition which had gradually grown up during the 550 years of Turkish occupation, on the same lines as the Bulgarian 'komitaji'. But in the case of Serbia the tradition degenerated into a kind of sport or game, especially in the late eighteenth and early nineteenth centuries. There was a close season during which Turkish troops and Serbian četniks fraternised in the village *kafanas*. But as soon as the forests put on their foliage and the snow cover melted away (traditionally on St George's Day), the guerrillas took to the hills and woods again and a bloodthirsty struggle went on until *Mitrovdan* (31 October O.S., 13 November N.S.), by which time the fall of the leaves and the freshly fallen snow had usually increased the risk of detection. Operations were then suspended until the following spring. Such habits could hardly fail to corrupt, and that corruption was transmitted to the great majority of Mihailović's forces. Many of the leaders of the Partisan forces, however, were fresh from the Spanish Civil War where they had won priceless experience which their ideology enabled them to put to most effective use by continual harassment of the enemy in Yugoslavia. There cannot be the slightest doubt that the Partisan policy paid off much the better in the conditions prevailing in Yugoslavia at the time.

In the meantime, British knowledge of the true state of affairs inside Yugoslavia had relapsed into uncertainty.[7] Hudson, still anxious to respect his brief to the letter, went off to visit Tito again in the hope that it might still prove possible to engineer some sort of agreement between him and Mihailović, but he found himself cut off from both sides by the German offensive. When he at last succeeded in rejoining Mihailović he found that he had forfeited the latter's trust because of his brief stay with the Partisans. Mihailović held Hudson responsible for the cessation of supply drops, although it was still essentially lack of suitable aircraft that had led to the suspension. For some five months Hudson remained a virtual outcast, deprived of contact, either with the outside world or with Mihailović. At this stage of the war the development of the highly specialised W/T equipment needed for clandestine and irregular operation had barely got beyond the experimental stage. Moreover, Hudson lacked a safe cipher during this period. At the same time, the reliability of the reports coming out not merely from Serbia, but also from other parts of the country, especially Croatia and Slovenia, were equally uncertain – an uncertainty which was if anything heightened by the circumstance that they provided quite a different picture from that presented by Mihailović in telegrams sent direct to his government in London, which for most people constituted the only regular source of information from within the country at that time.

It was therefore decided to make other attempts to penetrate the country and in the first instance to strengthen our contacts with Mihailović. One of the first fruits of this decision took the shape of the despatch of the ill-fated Atherton mission.[8] Failure to maintain continuity of supply operations to Mihailović and the consequent loss of contact with him still further intensified our ignorance of what was going on in Yugoslavia. In March 1942 therefore the British Government turned to Maisky for help in restoring contact; but the Ambassador reported in due course that his government had no communication whatsoever with Yugoslavia.

By the time that the Russian reply came in, communications had been re-established between Cairo and Mihailović. In January the latter had been promoted to the rank of General and appointed Minister of War in the cabinet of Slobodan Jovanović, who had succeeded General Simović as Yugoslav Prime Minister on 12 January 1942. Almost the first message received from Mihailović revealed that serious trouble had again broken out between his forces and the Partisans. In his message, Mihailović complained that 'Communists' were constantly disturbing his work, and went on to allege that they were receiving support from the occupying forces, who were naturally interested in keeping both sides busy fighting one another.

The British Government, much perturbed by this news, returned to the charge with the Soviet Government. The suggestion was made through Maisky that a word of authority broadcast from Moscow might induce the 'Communists' to desist from interfering with Mihailović's work. This approach was in vain. That this disinclination to help reflected a change in Soviet policy was made clearer by a conversation between the Soviet Ambassador to the Yugoslav Government and his British counterpart, in which the latter was told that the Soviet Union intended to steer clear of Yugoslav quarrels, and that in its view the importance of Mihailović's activities had been greatly exaggerated. Other information reaching the British Government confirmed its fears that the Soviet Government no longer intended to assist in the formation of a united front in Yugoslavia bringing all resistance movements together and that it was probably in direct touch with the Partisans.

Nevertheless the British Government continued to pursue its declared policy of supporting organised resistance in Yugoslavia. This it still considered to be headed by Mihailović. It also believed that such resistance was being weakened by the Communists. Further approaches to Moscow designed to secure Partisan co-operation with Mihailović were therefore contemplated; but before they could be made the Foreign Office was informed that the Russians had reason to believe that Mihailović was in touch with Nedić and therefore not to be trusted.[9] This allegation was challenged in vain, and a little later the Foreign Office was told of the contents of a note handed to the Yugoslav Ambassador in Kuibyshev in which Mihailović's local commanders were accused of joining the Italians in attacks on the Partisans in south-west Yugoslavia.

This confirmed British doubts about Mihailović's effectiveness and reliability as an ally. Hudson was instructed to remind him that continued aid was dependent on his reaching an agreement with the Partisans; and an investigation was begun into the possibilities of establishing direct contact with the latter. Simultaneously the Russians were told that the British Government was convinced that the accusations against Mihailović were instruments of Communist propaganda, wielded by the Partisans and taken up by Russian English-language publications circulating in the British Isles as well as by the official press in Russia. Exception was also taken to the material broadcast by the 'Free Yugoslavia' radio station, known to be situated near Kuibyshev. There was no reaction by the Russians to this *démarche*. None the less, the British Government's faith in Mihailović had been shaken. A further observer, Captain Charles Robertson (a ship's W/T operator of Yugoslav nationality), was therefore dropped to Mihailović's headquarters in September 1942.

As a last step in this campaign to incite Mihailović to take positive action, the Commander-in-Chief Middle East sent him, through Hudson, in September 1942 a telegram in which he urged him to do everything in his power to attack Axis lines of communication, explaining that constant sabotage attacks on these lines would appreciably impair the enemy war effort in the Balkans. In November this message was backed up by another telegram from the Yugoslav Prime Minister. Neither produced any visible effect.

At about the same time as Robertson was infiltrated, a full-scale signals unit was dropped to Hudson. This at last gave adequate daily two-way communication between Cairo and the field. As a result by the end of the year the British Government had a much clearer and more accurate picture not only of conditions there and elsewhere, but also of Mihailović's practices and intentions. This information confirmed that Mihailović's policy remained one of abstention from serious action against the occupying forces largely because he feared that consequent reprisals on the civilian population would cost him the support of the peasantry, but also to secure favourable conditions for the consolidation of his political position in the areas under his control, and time in which to extend such control to the entire country.

Moreover both British liaison officers confirmed that certain of Mihailović's Montenegrin commanders had reached accommodations with the Italians under which, in return for food, arms and clothing, they undertook to maintain reasonable law and order in the area. At the time Hudson reported these facts (October to December 1942) conditions in Montenegro were relatively calm. Certain members of S.O.E. in the Middle East decided that they were prepared to turn a blind eye to such accommodations providing that they were arrived at in good faith, i.e., constituted true exploitation of the enemy with the object of securing to Mihailović arms and supplies which would be turned against the Italians on orders from the Supreme Allied Command outside the country; an additional reason was the fact that the volume of material support which the British found it possible to send direct to Mihailović was still very small. Instructions in this sense were therefore sent to Major Hudson, who was however warned to watch developments most carefully.

Meanwhile, other British departments, notably the Political Intelligence Department of the Foreign Office, the Ministry of Information, and the Intelligence Services of the Army, Navy and Air Force, had been steadily accumulating information about conditions inside Yugoslavia from many and varied open sources; covert information was also arriving in increasing volume. The net burden of all this was that while in Serbia proper and other areas of southern and eastern Yugoslavia small-scale sabotage and minor skirmishes were taking place which – although of no great military value – could justifiably be ascribed to Mihailović's forces, more significant operations were being carried out in the north and west of the country (especially in Croatia and Slovenia) which were certainly not the work of Mihailović's Četniks, though it was still uncertain to whom they should rightly be credited. The vital fact was that these activities seemed to be making a greater contribution to the Allied war effort than were those of Mihailović's followers; indeed they bore some resemblance to the work of the Republican irregulars during the Spanish Civil War.

As these conflicting facts became better appreciated, the question of the possible revision of Britain's declared policy towards resistance in Yugoslavia became immediate. After full consultation with all the departments concerned, the Foreign Office reached the conclusion that it could not recommend to the Cabinet any radical change in the position.[10]

It was however realised that other resistance movements were emerging in parts of the country where Mihailović exercised no real control, and the preparation of plans for contacting them was speeded up, always with the ultimate objective of unifying all such elements in a single movement, under Mihailović's leadership. At no time was any suggestion made to any side that it should eliminate its rivals. On the contrary, it was constantly emphasised that British arms would be supplied on the sole understanding that they would not be used against other Yugoslavs engaged in fighting the Axis forces, except in legitimate self-defence. This issue was raised by the public prosecutor at Mihailović's trial in Belgrade, and caused the British Government acute embarrassment.

Furthermore, it was now clear that Mihailović intended to go on playing his waiting game. Accordingly, at the end of October 1942, the B.B.C. (which had up till then given most of the credit for resistance operations in Yugoslavia to Mihailović's forces) was authorised to mention Partisan activities alongside those of Mihailović in the hope that this would spur the latter to action. Not unexpectedly, this gave offence both to the Yugoslav Government in London and to Mihailović in the field, but, in the light of reports received from Hudson, it was decided to ignore their protests and to persevere with the new propaganda line.

Another reason for postponing any drastic change of policy at that stage was that during the summer of 1942 it had been decided to send a more senior British officer into Yugoslavia to relieve Hudson, who, it was felt, more than deserved such a change. Operational difficulties delayed the departure of this observer for some months, but finally, on Christmas Day 1942, I was dropped by parachute to Mihailović's headquarters, landing at a point on the mountain of Sinjajevina, some ten miles due north of Kolašin in Montenegro. I carried with me letters of introduction from the Foreign Secretary and the Commander-in-Chief Middle East. These impressed upon Mihailović the necessity for him to make the utmost and most immediate contribution to the war effort. It had proved impossible to secure a similar letter of introduction from either King Peter II or the Yugoslav Government; but I did take in unofficial letters from some of Mihailović's personal friends and brother officers, then in Cairo.

I found Mihailović cosily installed in headquarters situated on a little knoll above the village of Gornje Lipovo, some twelve kilometres north east of Kolašin, in Montenegro, and immediately under Sinjajevina, where I had landed. When I first visited him on Boxing Day 1942 to present my credentials, so to speak, I found him flanked by his staff in a smallish room filled with lesser officerdom, bodyguards, batmen and other hangers-on. This was to prove one of the banes of my association with the general. It was virtually never possible to deal with him alone. On the few occasions when I insisted, Lalatović was always present; but this I countered by taking Hudson with me.

I found Mihailović to be a medium-sized man, with a fundamentally melancholy cast of countenance. Strangely for a career officer, one would have said he was introverted rather than extroverted. His slight build and somewhat retiring nature made him only too suitable material to be caught up in the whirlwind of the world, to repeat the dramatic phrase he used in his final speech at his trial. At our first meeting he was in good spirits, as well he might have been, for perhaps naively, he saw in my arrival the answer to all his problems – supply, propaganda and political.

The person who made the greatest impression on me at this first meeting was Lalatović (Ostojić was in the field in another part of Montenegro), who had grown a luxurious auburn beard and bore an uncanny resemblance to the males of the Romanov family; indeed he looked like a cross between the last of the Tsars and our own King George V. The striking impression was strictly confined to his physical appearance. Everyone present wore beards and hair longer than that of young people today. This was bound up with ecclesiastical tradition. It was customary in the Orthodox Churches for the males of a bereaved family not to shave or have their hair cut for forty days after the death – i.e., until after the final requiem mass. Mihailović and his men had decided to go one better than this. Considering that the entire country was in mourning after its shameful defeat at the hands of the Axis powers, they had taken an oath – whether on Mihailović's orders or not I do not know – not to shave or cut their hair until the country had been liberated. Most of those present had also abandoned formal uniform for the homespun peasant jacket and breeches, and boots for the traditional Serbian bast slippers – *opanci*. However they kept their cap badges and shoulder indications of rank, all but Mihailović himself, who like certain better known contemporary leaders took precedence by anonymity.

The members of the British mission already at Mihailović's headquarters had become infected by these unorthodox practices. There were some fine facial adornments and some rather irregular kit. I made myself unpopular at the outset by insisting on strict observance of King's Regulations in this respect. I realised at once that if the British mission, which was now of some strength, was to achieve anything at all, it must maintain its identity as a *British* formation.

Near at hand were Mihailović's W/T and general administrative units. It was thence that he maintained contact with his local commanders in all parts of the country, issuing his orders to them and receiving their intelligence reports. Having been Yugoslav Director of Military Intelligence for a spell shortly before the war, Mihailović set a good deal of store by these activities, which so far as one could judge from a static observation post, were efficiently run. A paraphrase (2 February 1943) made for the Foreign Office of some of my early telegrams stated: 'In general, Colonel Bailey confirms the existence of General Mihailović's network of organisations in Serbia, Montenegro and Hercegovina... At his headquarters Mihailović has only a skeleton staff and a personal bodyguard who accompanied him from Ravna Gora last year... This staff is entirely absorbed in details of planning and communication and the bodyguard with guard duties. General Mihailović does not dispose of any fighting units in this area and is really the guest of Pavle Djurišić, on whose loyalty his safety depends. General Mihailović's intelligence services appear to be weak... [his] internal security is far from good... communication (with) sub-missions very slow; W/T communication sporadic.'[11] As to the internal W/T communication system, it was not at that time realised that the Germans had already cracked the general's somewhat low-grade military ciphers, and were thus able to follow his aerial communication with his subordinates; but as this largely consisted of such routine matters as promotions and postings, the enemy may well have got bored with decoding everything. This obsession with military administration was perhaps Mihailović's greatest mistake on the practical front. The administrative procedure itself was based on the pre-1914 Serbian model and was hardly conducive to efficiency. The net result was a great expenditure of time and energy, both at the centre and at the periphery, which could have been put to far better use against the Germans and Italians. On 15 February 1943 I telegraphed

... Mihailović's units from Kalinovik are undoubtedly active in central Bosnia, ostensibly against the Ustaši but to some extent against Croat peasants and possibly against the Partisans. I do not believe however that he is in conflict with Croat Peasant Party bands.

Recent arrangements made between the Četniks and the Italians to transport Četniks from both Nikšić and Kolašin in Bosnia to fight the Partisans were cancelled at the last moment, probably at German instance. It is probable that the Germans do not desire a concentration at Bosnia in view of their apparent intention to clear up the whole area as far as Split.

As a result of Russian military successes and to some extent of the arguments I have put forward, Mihailović is changing his policy towards the Partisans. He states, and I am inclined to believe him, that he has instructed his commanders to filter into and occupy the (Partisan) 'Independent Republic' should the Germans expel the Partisans. It is however doubtful whether he could adequately enforce these orders.[12]

Theoretically, Mihailović, as Commander-in-Chief and Minister of War (I am speaking of the time after my arrival in the country), had power of life and death over his local commanders and their troops. But the power was one thing, the possibility of exercising it quite another, largely because of the tenuous nature of communications, particularly by courier; while the long distances usually involved made the use of melodramatic measures, such as the despatch of extermination parties to liquidate turbulent lieutenants, a problematical solution to say the least. Perhaps the best way of describing the true situation is to liken the position of anyone incurring Mihailović's disfavour to that of a member of the British House of Commons from whom the Whip has been withdrawn. Their isolation would then have made them very vulnerable to the settlement of private accounts. None the less, several are known to have gone over to the Partisans.

One of the first matters I had been instructed to look into was the question of the nature of Mihailović's relations with the Germans, with the Italians and with the Partisans. Within a month of arrival I reported that the feud between the Partisans and the Yugoslav Army had already grown so deep and bitter on the latter's side that there was no hope of bringing them together on *the same* territory. I also confirmed that there was a working agreement between certain of Mihailović's local (Montenegrin) commanders, as already reported by Hudson, but that I had no evidence of direct collaboration between Mihailović himself and the Germans or Italians. I also emphasised the static nature of Mihailović's policy and organisation. I wrote,

> The time has come to treat Mihailović firmly. He must be made to realise that we can make or break him. In return for former we demand frank and sincere co-operation. The blind unquestioning support given him in the past has convinced him that...this Mission is here merely to transmit his demands to the British authorities and see that they are met as quickly and smoothly as possible – hence his anger when we questioned his facts...If our work is to prosper...he must now be...made to realise we will no longer tolerate deceit ...[13]

In an attempt to dispose of the disadvantages which this state of affairs was inflicting upon the common war effort, Hudson and I submitted a joint plan to Cairo for discussion with London. The essence of this plan was to deny to the Axis Powers the benefits they were deriving from the fighting between Mihailović's forces and those of Tito, by delimiting two operational areas, one of which would be allotted to Mihailović and the other to the Partisans. The line of demarcation would run roughly from the Yugoslav–Bulgarian frontier on the Danube in the north-east, to the Montenegrin–Albanian frontier in the south-west. Each movement would enjoy full British support in its own area in return for an understanding to eschew all contact with the occupying forces and to abstain from all conflict with, or attempts to penetrate the territory of, the other. Political expediency made it impossible to give a trial to this plan, which was recognised by its authors to be something of a counsel of despair.

Towards the end of February 1943 I further suggested that a determined effort be made to bring Mihailović either to dismiss the Montenegrin commanders who were in direct and friendly contact with the Italians (Djukanović, Stanišić and Ljašić) or to order them to quit the sanctuary of the Italian garrison towns forthwith, and take to the hills. The officers concerned were shortly to visit Mihailović's headquarters and I sought, and received, authorisation to speak to them and Mihailović on these lines. The meeting proved abortive. Mihailović persisted in his contention that his tactics constituted justifiable exploitation of the enemy and penetration of his organisations, while the subordinate commanders proved bigoted and too stupid to be susceptible to persuasion, reason or threat.

As regards the position of Major Pavle Djurišić, Mihailović's commander in Eastern Bosnia and the Sandzak who had his base headquarters in Kolašin, the British Liaison Officers, after visiting that town in the middle of February 1943, came to the reasoned conclusion that although his troops were recognised by the Italians under the name of the Limsko-Sandzački Četnik Detachments, Djurišić should be allowed to maintain his connection with the enemy. They were convinced that ultimately the arms, equipment and clothing which he was receiving from the Italians would be used to good effect against them; while the need to feed his troops would further increase the Italians' difficulties with the civilian population if they tried to requisition the victuals on the spot, or alternatively, compelled them to bring food into Montenegro from other Italian-held territories, or even from Italy itself. Moreover, the fact that Djurišić's troops were policing this part of Montenegro promised to facilitate the reception of supplies from Egypt, not only by air but also by sea; it being hoped that, after getting sufficient arms from the Italians, Djurišić would be able to secure a channel to the coast and cover the landing of supplies. In the outcome, all this material went to the Partisans, who were at the gates of Berane in much greater numbers than Mihailović's forces immediately after the Italian capitulation.

It was at this time that a number of messages from other resistance leaders, including General Napoleon Zervas in Greece, were passed to me by Cairo for transmission to Mihailović. The one from Zervas had been sent out by the Senior

British Liaison Officer with the Greek National Army of Liberation. The messages were of an exhortative and complimentary nature and harmless in content. Zervas's message was directed against no other resistance group, and certainly merited neither the importance nor the sinister motives read into it by the prosecution at Mihailović's trial.

Meanwhile, I found myself in difficulties with Mihailović, who had, not unreasonably, taken my arrival as an indication not only that material support would in future reach him on a greatly increased scale, but also that what he regarded as the monstrous publicity being given by the B.B.C. to Partisan activities would cease. Regrettably the continued necessity for allocating long-range aircraft in the Mediterranean theatre to anti-submarine warfare and to the support of land operations in Libya made an increase in air sorties to Yugoslavia or other parts of the Balkans impossible. In fact during the ten weeks following my arrival at Mihailović's headquarters we received only two sorties. The few tons of supplies dropped included thirty million Italian occupation lire, overprinted in bright red 'Ethiopia', and several hundred boxes of tropical anti-snake-bite serum. Mihailović's rage was matched only by my own when I got instructions from Cairo to the effect that I was to count the lire myself, then have them checked independently by Hudson and the other officer on the mission, before formally acknowledging receipt. This was but one of many foolish demands from Cairo to which I turned a deaf ear.

Mihailović's disappointment over the lack of adequate support, the realisation that the truth about his relative inactivity and his Montenegrin commanders' fraternisation with the Italians was coming to be known to the outside world, and the continued references to the Partisans by the B.B.C. all combined to provoke him into a public outburst on 28 February 1943. The occasion was the christening of the youngest child of the mayor of Gorne Lipovo where his headquarters still were; and it is only fair to admit that by the time Mihailović lost control of himself a good deal of plum brandy had been consumed by all present except the baby. In this speech he bitterly criticised Allied policy towards his country and his movement, making it absolutely plain that he considered it imperative for military reasons to concentrate first on liquidating his internal

enemies, whom he named as the Partisans, the Croats, the
Moslems and the Ustaši – in that order – before turning his
attention to the Axis forces. He added that nothing the Allies
could do or threaten would turn him from his objective of
exterminating the Partisans, or change his attitude towards the
Italians (whom he called 'his sole source of supply'), and that
he needed no further contact with the Western democracies.

When I reported this tirade to Cairo and London, the British
Government decided that it could not be overlooked. On 29
March – some four weeks later – Churchill himself addressed a
note to the Yugoslav Prime Minister, drawing attention to
Mihailović's statements and saying that it was not believed that
they reflected the views of the exiled Yugoslav Government.
But Churchill pointed out that as Mihailović was Yugoslav
Minister of War, the British Government believed that he
should be fully and properly informed of the views of his own
government, and that he should be instructed to take a line
more in accord with the common approach followed by the
Yugoslav and British governments. Churchill ended by saying
that unless Mihailović was prepared to change his policy towards both the Italians and his compatriots who were actively
resisting the enemy, the British Government might feel obliged
to revise its policy of favouring him to the exclusion of other
resistance leaders in Yugoslavia.

The Yugoslav Government agreed to send a signal to
Mihailović in this sense and in due course a somewhat un-
convincing reply was received from him in which he once again
stressed the necessity of removing all those standing in the way
of his engaging the Germans and Italians whom he had always
regarded as his principal enemies.

This first indication that the British Government was not
prepared to tolerate indefinitely Mihailović's policy of inactivity, procrastination and internal account-settling was
partly the result of the rapid growth of evidence that the Partisan forces were a serious thorn in the side both of the Germans
and of the Italians.

About this time, the British mission at Mihailović's headquarters began to report rumours of heavy fighting on the borders of Bosnia–Hercegovina, and by early March heavy and
continuous gunfire was audible from the north-west. Mihailo-

vić's local forces were obviously also on the move though every effort was made to conceal this from the British. It later became clear that this fighting involved considerable Partisan forces, but the British Liaison Officers were unable to determine exactly what part Mihailović's forces (hereinafter referred to as the 'Četniks') had played in the action.

In the meantime, I had reported that in the middle of March, Mihailović, with whom I had had no contact since the embarrassing meeting at the christening on 28 February, had left his headquarters secretly for an unknown destination. The ostensible reason given by his staff for this departure was that he had gone to Hercegovina to confer with certain of his commanders from Dalmatia. On 16 March 1943 I telegraphed: 'Mihailović left headquarters somewhat mysteriously at 16 hours today...He may be assuming personal command of operations against Partisans or visiting Kalinovik. There have been attempts recently by Germans, Italians and Ljotić to arrange a meeting with General Mihailović. Despite protests to the contrary, I do not consider impossible that he has gone to some such meeting...He may have gone ahead select summer headquarters...'[14] I added in a telegram of 23 March 1943: 'Confirm present fighting in Bosnia and Hercegovina is going against Četniks. It is not impossible that General Mihailović and Company will flee without worrying unduly about fate of this mission as they did Major Hudson last year!'[15] However after consulting Hudson I gave it as my view that Mihailović had in fact gone to assume command over those of his forces engaged in preventing the Partisans, who it was now established were being driven south from Bosnia–Hercegovina by the Germans and Croats, from entering Montenegro.

I was still without news of Mihailović at the beginning of April and therefore asked that the British Government should prevail upon the Yugoslav Government to instruct him to return to his headquarters forthwith, as there were many outstanding questions of prime importance to Allied plans to be discussed with him. Such an instruction was issued and promptly obeyed, though it seems that this was due not so much to the order itself as to the fact that the resistance of his forces to the influx of the Partisans had for the moment collapsed. On 15 April, to get out of the Partisans' way, Mihailović struck camp and moved, first to a point above Berane, still in Montenegro, and then to Serbia which he reached on 30 May 1943.

Meanwhile Mihailović's reply to the message from the Yugoslav Prime Minister had been under consideration by the British Government. On 7 May the Foreign Secretary asked Jovanović to convey a further message to Mihailović. This was in effect a directive. It opened by saying that while His Majesty's Government hoped soon to be in a position to send Mihailović material support on an increased scale, it must be satisfied before the necessary action to this end was set in motion, that there was complete agreement on certain points. These were: (a) The primary object of Mihailović's movement, from which he must not allow himself to be deflected by internal differences, must be resistance to the occupying forces. (b) There must be the closest and most constant collaboration between him and the Commander-in-Chief Middle East. (c) All collaboration with the Italians and Nedić must cease, except in specific cases with the explicit prior approval of the Yugoslav and British governments. (d) Special efforts must be made to co-operate with the guerrillas active in Croatia and Slovenia. (e) Every effort must be made to reach a peaceful settlement with the Partisans, and in no event should operations be conducted against them except in self-defence. In a private letter of the same date, Eden made it clear to the Yugoslav Prime Minister that if Mihailović refused to agree to these terms the British Government might come to feel that it was no longer justified from the military point of view in giving him the support it was anxious to extend. The directive was despatched to Mihailović on 10 May 1943.

Before Mihailović could frame his reply to this quasi-ultimatum, the situation was complicated by the despatch by General Headquarters Middle East, of a telegram on 26 May instructing me to ask Mihailović (i) to break off all collaboration with the Axis forces, and (ii) to withdraw across the river Ibar into Eastern Serbia, on the grounds that the war in the Mediterranean theatre had reached the stage at which Allied offensives might be considered imminent, and this in turn made it imperative that Mihailović honour his pledge to co-operate unreservedly with the British High Command in that area. The latter, arguing that as Commander-in-Chief of the Yugoslav Army he could not accept limitation of his territorial command on unilateral order from Allied Headquarters in Egypt, took strong exception to these instructions. The message was eventually cancelled, and Mihailović informed that as soon as he had accepted the British directive, it would be desirable that there should be an exchange of views on operational possibilities between him and the Commander-in-Chief Middle East.

While this triangular exchange of communications between Mihailović, the British Government in London and the General Headquarters Middle East was going on, considerable progress had been made in implementing the decision taken in 1942 to secure direct information about the Partisans' activities, regardless of the Soviet Union's disinclination to co-operate. Exploratory mixed parties of British and Yugoslav personnel similar to those sent to Mihailović in 1941 and 1942 had been dropped into Montenegro, Bosnia and Slovenia. The most important of these was that which came to be led by Captain (later Colonel) F. W. D. Deakin, which reached Tito's headquarters on the borders of Montenegro and Hercegovina on the night of 27/28 May 1943.[16]

In briefing these missions the greatest care had been taken to ensure that they should in no way suggest to their hosts that the British Government had decided to transfer its support from Mihailović to Tito. The British officers concerned were instructed to make it clear beyond possibility of misunderstanding that British policy was to support all those in Yugoslavia regardless of their political orientation who were prepared to take up arms against the Axis powers, and that the supply of war materials to such resistance elements would be dependent on their abstaining from attacking other Yugoslav guerrillas except in self-defence.

The introduction of these missions resulted in a vast increase in information not only about the activities of the Partisans, but also indirectly about those of Mihailović's Četniks and commanders in Dalmatia, Slovenia, Croatia and Western Bosnia. For the first time the British Government had direct evidence of an overall picture of the conditions prevailing over the greater part of Yugoslavia, against which it could review its policy.

These additional sources of knowledge confirmed earlier evidence that Mihailović's commanders, not merely those in Montenegro but also those in all the areas newly opened up, were much more deeply involved with the enemy than many people had suspected. This was particularly true of the remoter areas of Northern Dalmatia and Western Bosnia, from which, because of their inaccessibility, information had previously been scanty in the extreme.

This irrefutable evidence of the reality and value of Partisan activities against the Axis forces led the British Government to the conclusion that it could no longer persevere with its policy of exclusive support for Mihailović. The policy was therefore modified to allow the despatch of war supplies to Tito's forces, on the usual conditions concerning their use.

To revert to developments in South Serbia and Macedonia where Mihailović was certainly in control, I had succeeded (before relations with him had become strained) in securing his agreement to the introduction of British sub-missions at a number of points, selected in the first place for their proximity to the vital military and economic objectives which it was desired to attack. In April and early May 1943, sub-missions had been established in north-east Serbia (Homolje) near the Danube and the copper mines at Bor, on the Kopaonik range near Raška, and in the hills south of Priština, on Kosovo, from both of which points it was hoped to deal with the Trepča lead-zinc mine and metallurgical plant at Kosovska Mitrovica, the Allatine chrome mines under Šar Planina, and the Skopje–Niš and Skopje–Kraljevo railway lines. Later in the summer other missions were dropped, some independent, some subordinated to other sub-missions. In the same way that the introduction of the missions to the Partisans revealed the serious gaps in our knowledge of conditions in western Yugoslavia, so the arrival of these sub-missions shed a penetrating if unhappy light on a wide area of Mihailović's territory. Initial contacts were excellent and at first held every promise of stimulating the Četniks into profitable anti-Axis activity. The instructions given to all sub-missions were to collect intelligence about Axis military dispositions and to encourage and organise resistance and sabotage by the guerrillas, especially against the targets mentioned above. They were told to avoid politics at all costs, and explicitly that in the event of an outbreak of fighting between the units to which they were attached and other resistance elements, they were to take no part, but on the contrary to do everything they could to limit such wasteful internecine warfare and promote friendly relations between all resistance groups. The instructions were none the less proper for being virtually impossible to obey. But the sub-missions had not long been established before their reports began to confirm the now well-documented suspicions that a policy of procrastination and downright inactivity was common to all Mihailović's forces.

The next development occurred in the latter half of August, when a reply was at last received in London to the British directive of late May. Mihailović seemed to accept the conditions imposed upon him; none the less his operational behaviour remained one of inaction. Although in certain areas (e.g. between Užice and Ivanjica) the Četniks engaged, largely on the initiative and personal responsibility of local commanders, in operations against the Germans; in others the work of the British sub-missions was nullified by the impossibility of getting Mihailović to give the necessary orders authorising local operations to be undertaken.

The usual course of events in such cases was somewhat as follows. The British Liaison Officer with a local commander would suggest certain action. The local commander would agree, subject to Mihailović's approval. I would be asked to secure this and would be assured by Mihailović that the necessary authority had been given. But when the British Liaison Officer returned to the charge, he would be met either with a flat denial that the instructions had arrived, or with evasion. The end result in either case was that the planned operation had to be abandoned.

The persistence of this irritating and unsatisfactory state of affairs prompted me in August 1943 to deliver on my own initiative and without reference to Cairo, an ultimatum to Mihailović. This again produced a reply which, although on the surface conciliatory and promising an improvement of relations, never yielded any concrete result.

Meanwhile, the encouraging progress of military operations in the Mediterranean theatre had greatly increased the importance of Yugoslav resistance. It was therefore decided in July 1943 to send in full-dress military and political missions, both to Mihailović and to Tito. Brigadier C. D. Armstrong, a regular officer with twenty-five years' service behind him, who had acquired considerable battle experience at Dunkirk and in

North Africa, was appointed to the command of the mission to Mihailović. I remained with him as political adviser. Brigadier Fitzroy Maclean was appointed to the corresponding post with the Partisan forces.[17]

Brigadier Armstrong reached Mihailović's headquarters by parachute on 25 September 1943. He carried a letter of introduction from General Sir Henry Maitland Wilson, Commander-in-Chief Middle East, as well as a telegraphic message from King Peter II to Mihailović. It was intended to send in the signed original of the King's message later, but it proved impossible to secure this, and Armstrong was thereby deprived of the backing which production of the authentic message might well have given him.

Mihailović replied to General Wilson in what may be called his customary evasive–co-operative style; and for some six weeks after Armstrong's arrival a campaign of anti-German operations which had been launched with considerable success in the Sandzak and Eastern Bosnia after the Italians capitulated on 8 September, was continued with further local success. Brigadier Armstrong and the specialist staff officers who had come in with him played an important part in the planning and execution of these operations, which led to the capture of several towns, including Višegrad. Most regrettably, it proved impossible to restrain the Partisans from Western Bosnia and Hercegovina from irrupting into the territories won from the Italians and Germans by the Četniks (chiefly in the valley of the Lim), although at Armstrong's insistence – based on his standing instructions from the Commander-in-Chief Middle East – Mihailović withdrew his forces before the Partisan advance in order to avoid conflict with them. This experience had the most unhappy effect on Mihailović; he at once relapsed into stubborn obstructionism and inactivity.

Simultaneously, reports from Maclean and other British officers with the Partisans had demonstrated effectively that in all parts of the country except Serbia, Eastern Bosnia, the Sandzak and South Serbia, Tito's forces presented a military instrument considerably more efficient than that wielded by Mihailović. Moreover, evidence of the undeniable collaboration with the Italians of many local Četnik commanders who claimed to be members of the Četnik movement, and who were recognised as such by Mihailović himself, continued to accumulate. Lastly, there was a serious recrudescence of the difficulties experienced earlier by the British officers at Mihailović's headquarters in securing the issuance to local commanders of orders authorising operations against the Germans.

Towards the end of November 1943 therefore the British Government was constrained once more to review its policy to Yugoslavia in general and *vis-à-vis* Mihailović in particular. The situation with which it was faced can be summed up as follows: while the Četniks still provided the only effective resistance movement in Serbia proper, Mihailović himself was still bent on pursuing his dual policy of eliminating internal enemies before attacking the Germans, and of conserving Serb blood, regardless of all other considerations. He seemed to be so obsessed by what he regarded as the Communist threat to his country and people that he could unashamedly argue that the protection given by the quisling Serb Government in Belgrade, and even perhaps that given by the Germans themselves, was preferable to a composition with the Partisans. So long as he persisted in this attitude (and everything went to show that he was becoming more and more stubborn) not only was his movement of no military value to the Allies, but also he himself was a standing obstacle in the way of the unification of the Yugoslav resistance movement.

On the other hand, reports from the other side suggested that while the Partisans' view of Mihailović himself was utterly uncompromising, there was nothing to show that they would refuse to treat with other leaders representing forces under Mihailović's nominal command. To complete the picture, the British Government had the general's reply to a final appeal made to him, with the support of Božidar Purić, who had formed a new Yugoslav Government in July 1943, to rid himself of the collaborationist commanders in Dalmatia and Montenegro. This reply allowed of no doubt about the impossibility of reaching an understanding with Mihailović on any terms but his own.

With all this in mind, as well as the views of the British officers in Serbia that not all of Mihailović's followers shared his extreme position regarding non-co-operation with the Partisans, the British were reluctantly led to the conclusion that in the general interest of Yugoslav resistance and the unification of its main components, the possibility of replacing Mihailović by a man of more reasonable views must be looked into. This conclusion was reinforced by answers received from Mihailović to a number of letters addressed to him by Armstrong in the field as a final, direct and personal attempt to persuade him to abandon the civil war, and to concentrate his efforts against the Axis powers.

Approaches to this end were therefore made both to the Yugoslav Government and to the British mission at Mihailović's headquarters. Military considerations alone made it imperative that the utmost assistance to the Allied armies fighting to drive the Germans from central and northern Italy should be forth-coming from the properly organised and co-ordinated operations of a unified Yugoslav resistance movement.

If further justification were required for a complete reversal of policy, it was provided by Mihailović himself by his ultimate failure to respond to an appeal from General Wilson in December 1943. General Wilson called on Mihailović to attack before 29 December two vital railway bridges, one over the Morava and the other over the Ibar. Both lay well within the area in Serbia over which he claimed to have absolute control. Cutting off the enemy lines of communication concerned was required to disrupt the German organisation in Macedonia and Greece so that guerrilla activity there could be increased to the point at which it would compel the German command in the Balkans to consider seriously the question of withdrawal of their occupation forces in the Balkans.

Mihailović's first reactions appeared to be satisfactory. He gave the usual assurance that authority to carry out the operations would be sent to the local commanders concerned and even went so far as to discuss with Brigadier Armstrong operational plans, including the dropping of necessary supplies. This good start was not kept up. The old bogey of procrastination soon raised its head again, and although an extension of time was granted, it became clear by the middle of January 1944 that the operations would never be carried out, despite such preparations as the mobilisation of Četniks on a considerable scale.

At the same time, during the negotiations for the execution of the operations requested by General Wilson, Mihailović at last told Armstrong of his wish to put an end to the civil war. He solicited the assistance of the British Government not only in arranging a meeting between representatives of Tito and of himself, but also in guaranteeing the implementation of any agreement reached. This offer was transmitted to London, but the British Government declined to act as intermediary in this belated proposal, which savoured too much of a death-bed repentance, and Mihailović was so informed. The Foreign Office, in agreement with the Middle East Defence Committee and the Supreme Allied Commander Mediterranean, then recommended to the War Cabinet that all supplies to Mihailović be cut off on the grounds that not only had he signally failed to attack the Germans, but also that he had given his blessing, tacitly if not explicitly, to collaboration with the enemy on the part of some of his commanders.

This decision was communicated to the British officers with the Četniks in the various parts of the country early in January 1944, though it was not, in view of the delicate situation of the majority of the British missions and sub-missions, simultaneously communicated to the Yugoslav Government which had moved to Cairo when Purić became Prime Minister, nor to Mihailović in the field. Instructions were also sent to certain of the sub-missions authorising them, at their discretion, to go over to the nearest Partisan formation.

From this stage – in effect a vote of no confidence in Mihailović – the logical development was towards a formal withdrawal of support from him. This decision was recorded in a minute addressed to Churchill by Eden as Secretary of State for Foreign Affairs on 17 February 1944 and communicated both to the Yugoslav Government by the British Ambassador and shortly thereafter to Mihailović, by Lieutenent Colonel Howard, senior British officer at Mihailović's headquarters (Brigadier Armstrong having left to direct the proposed demolition of the bridges), acting on instructions from General Sir Bernard Paget, Commander-in-Chief Middle East. To complete the procedure, Churchill included a passage on Yugoslavia in a statement on foreign policy made in the House of Commons on 23 February 1944.[18]

In his message, General Paget asked for Mihailović's full cooperation in evacuating all British personnel attached to Četnik forces – who had in the meantime been concentrated at his headquarters – together with a number of Allied escaped prisoners-of-war who had been given shelter and guaranteed safety by the Četniks. Mihailović accepted this obligation unreservedly and he and his staff gave full and loyal co-operation in preparations for and carrying out of the necessary operations. All Allied personnel were thus successfully brought out by air from a landing strip in Central Serbia secured by Mihailović's troops on 29, 30 and 31 May 1944.

I myself had already left Yugoslavia, arriving in London on 3 March 1944. I made a full report there, mainly orally, but His Majesty's Government saw no reason to alter its decision in the light of such additional knowledge as I was able to provide.

The governments of the United States of America and the Soviet Union were kept fully informed at all stages of the consultations which led up to the final rupture of relations, and the former was persuaded of the desirability of withdrawing the sole remaining American liaison officer with the Allied missions, Colonel Albert Seitz, though it did later decide to send in an intelligence mission under Lieutenant Colonel R. H. McDowell. No such action was required on the part of the Soviet Union as it had never sent officers to Mihailović, despite an approach made at the time of the despatch of the Russian mission to Tito's headquarters.

The inevitability of the progressive deterioration in relations between the British Government and Mihailović will be abundantly plain from the foregoing narrative. There can be no real quarrel with the final decision to leave Mihailović to his fate. But this account should not be interpreted as condemnation *per se* of the policy which Mihailović felt obliged to adopt, many aspects of which are understandable and must command both sympathy and respect. Rightly or wrongly, he made it clear at an early stage that he would not lay his organisation open to destruction by taking what to him was premature action, but would endeavour to keep it alive until he considered that the moment was ripe for him to strike. There can be little doubt that nothing less than the opening of a third, Balkan front by the Allies would have created the necessary conditions. Mihailović was still obsessed by his memories of the Allied breakthrough on the Salonika front in 1918 in which he had taken part as a junior officer.

Even this policy which would have yielded negligible results militarily at all times before the Grand Finale, might in my view, have been fitted into the overall Allied plan had not Mihailović insisted so fanatically on opposing, by force where necessary, other elements in Yugoslavia who were themselves carrying out operations against what should have been regarded as the sole enemy – the occupying forces. His stubborn adherence to this objective, fired by his strong Slav mysticism and violent anti-Communist feelings, in the face of the lengthy and patient efforts of the British Government – which did not always receive from the Yugoslav government-in-exile all the support which its intentions warranted – to bring him to a more reasonable frame of mind, made Mihailović a stumbling-block in the way of the unification of active resistance to the Axis in Yugoslavia. This, at a time of intense and widespread military operations all along the periphery of Europe, was perforce the sole criterion by which the worth of a resistance group could be measured.

Mihailović himself made it impossible for the British Government to go on regarding him as that central figure of resistance in Yugoslavia, and of the country's future unity, which lay at the roots of the support extended to him from the summer of 1941 onwards. Moreover, he found it impossible to carry out his policies without recourse to certain contacts and accommodations with the occupying forces, if not directly, then through his subordinates, whom he steadfastly refused to dismiss or disown. Once his indulgence in such practices had been demonstrated beyond reasonable doubt, the British Government had no option but to withdraw support and recognition from him. Failure to do so would have put it in an untenable position *vis-à-vis* its Allies.

It must remain a matter for conjecture whether this disaster, for such in fact it was, could have been averted had the Soviet Government shown a more co-operative spirit when in 1942 His Majesty's Government appealed to it for help in resolving the discord between Mihailović and Tito; for at this critical period neither the antagonism between the two movements, nor the duplicity of Mihailović and his commanders in their contacts with the enemy, can with justice be said to have reached the limit beyond which reconciliation with one another and with the Great Allies became impossible.

There are a number of intriguing points which should be investigated sometime, such as the mechanics and security of Mihailović's communications, both internal and external; also the relations, probably clandestine, between Mihailović and his government, of which we have no direct knowledge (there are many mystifying features of the peculiar three-four-way, if not indeed five-way, links between British and Yugoslavs in London, Cairo and the field); the attribution of responsibility for the gradual loss of mutual trust between the parties concerned – the several British missions and sub-missions are by no means guiltless in this regard; and the lack of co-ordination, if not downright rivalry, between London and Cairo at S.O.E. level.

Although there are still many unsolved problems relating to Mihailović, it is still essential to try to identify the causes of the breakdown of British relations with him. On the British side was the inability to supply the Četniks with anything like reasonable, far less adequate, supplies on a scale that might have spurred Mihailović into action; there was also British inability to understand either his general strategy or his strong views about courting enemy reprisals on the civilian population (the problem of reprisals was carefully swept under the carpet - it was never faced squarely at any level in either its moral, its ethnical, its social or its military aspects, for any European resistance movement); and the frequent and embarrassing evidence of a lack of co-ordinated aims and objectives among various British Government departments themselves and between them and other national institutions, such as the B.B.C.

On Mihailović's side, there were certain characteristics which militated against co-operation between him and the Allies: an innate Slav mysticism which, combined with his professional loyalty to his King and country, dictated his overall objective, namely, to hand back the latter to the former, intact both geographically and constitutionally; a cognate Slav fatalism, which made him indifferent to the consequences of his actions; an almost pathological obsession with military administrative procedures; a fanatical hatred, inculcated firmly during his military training, of anything such as Communism, which in his narrow view, was inimical to the interests of the monarchy – essentially Serbian – and to a lesser extent the Church – essentially Orthodox; and finally, his inability to appreciate that the military, political and social set-up in Europe had changed irreversibly since the halcyon days of the First World War, the Salonika Front, and the subsequent restoration of quasi-absolute monarchy in virtually all the countries of south-eastern Europe: in other words, his failure to realise that the clock could not be put back.

In a way there never was a British policy towards Mihailović in the true sense of the term – a definite course of action selected from among alternatives in the light of established facts and designed to achieve desired ends. Nor could there have been a properly conceived policy given the United Kingdom's own desperate position during the first three years of the war, fighting as it was not merely for its own life but for the lives of all the occupied countries of Europe, and determined to fulfil its treaty and moral obligations towards them, while itself deprived of any but the scantiest of military or civilian resources save courage. The situation was also aggravated by the lack of time to prepare a policy worked out on the basis of a thorough appreciation of conditions within Yugoslavia. The United Kingdom can be said to have defined its policy towards that country finally only by its decision to withdraw support from Mihailović and his Četniks in favour of Tito and his National Liberation Army. Naturally, much has been written about the winning side in the struggle for post-war control of Yugoslavia; but there is also something to be said for the losers, and I hope that this paper has been able to make some contribution, however tentative, to the explanation of why they lost.

NOTES

1. There are only a limited number of books in the English language giving information about the history of Yugoslavia in the inter-war years. Among others, the reader may consult the following books: W. Vucinich (ed.), *Contemporary Yugoslavia* (Los Angeles and Berkeley, 1970) Ch. 1, J. B. Hoptner, *Yugoslavia in Crisis 1934–1941* (New York, 1962), G. H. N. Seton-Watson, *Eastern Europe between the Wars, 1918–1941* (London, 1945), P. Auty, *Tito; a Biography* (London, 1970) Parts I–III.

2. The author wishes to make clear that this paper is not as thoroughly

documented in footnotes as he would have liked it to be. The reason is that on two occasions – the first while he was being briefed before going into Yugoslavia at the end of 1942 – the author had entirely unrestricted access to all manner of documents, many of which, for various reasons, are no longer available; he also received, by word of mouth, much secret information which was never committed to paper, and cannot be published. When Mihailović was finally captured in the summer of 1946, the author was First Secretary (Commercial) at the British Embassy in Ankara. When the prosecution at Mihailović's trial in Belgrade associated the author with the charges made against the General, the Turkish authorities intimated that they would rather he be moved elsewhere. He was therefore recalled to London and asked to draft a White Paper refuting the charges levelled in Belgrade against His Majesty's Government. In the event, the White Paper had to be abandoned for a number of delicate diplomatic reasons. Moreover, many of the documents which the author saw and which still exist, are not available to the public or to serious research workers.

3. The arrangement, of which the author was informed during his briefing – he was naturally anxious to know exactly what the position was in this respect – seems never to have been embodied in a formal document.

4. 20 Oct. FO 371/30221.

5. *Ibid.*

6. See pp. 33 above.

7. Some senior military and Foreign Office officials had knowledge, and evidence, of the true resistance situation in many parts of Yugoslavia (Serbia, Montenegro, Bosnia-Hercegovina especially), see pp. 33–5 above. Also see FO 371/37586 *passim.*

8. Colonel Deakin has dealt brilliantly with this in his book, *The Embattled Mountain* (London, 1971) pp. 156 et seq.

9. The Foreign Office had its own independent sources of information about Mihailović's negotiations with Nedić's organisation. See FO 371/37586/37, 39.

10. See Chapter 2.

11. FO 371/37579.

12. FO 371/37580.

13. FO 371/37582.

14. *Ibid.*

15. *Ibid.*

16. A detailed account of this mission is given in Deakin, op. cit.

17. Brigadier Fitzroy Maclean had parachuted to Tito's headquarters on 17 September 1943 to be Commander of the Allied Mission to the Partisan forces, with all British Liaison officers who were with Partisan forces in Yugoslav territory under his control. See below p. 226.

18. *Hansard,* 23 Feb 1944. See also *Hansard,* 4 May 1944.

NOTE ON COLONEL D. T. HUDSON'S ACCOUNT OF HIS MISSION TO
YUGOSLAVIA 1914-4

Colonel D. T. Hudson D.S.O., O.B.E. was unable to attend the conference
which provided the material for this book; but he later (8 July 1974) gave
his own personal account of his mission to Phyllis Auty, one of the editors.
He said that when he was sent by S.O.E. in mid-September 1941, as the
first British officer into Yugoslavia, he was given a roneoed sheet of paper
on which the brief for his mission was described as 'to co-ordinate the forces
of resistance against the enemy'. He later showed this paper first to Tito,
then to Mihailović, both of whom he met within a short time of his arrival
in Yugoslavia. He was landed by a British submarine operating from Malta
on the coast of Montenegro near Petrovac on the night of 17/18 September
and soon met Partisans; among them were Milovan Djilas, Mitar Bakić and
Arso Jovanović. The Partisans in general were pleased to see a British
officer returning to Yugoslavia so soon after the beginning of resistance,
but their leaders were not greatly interested at that time in official con-
tracts with the western allies as they were confident of getting help from
the Soviet Union. 'Remember, the sun will not rise in the west,' was Djilas's
rebuke to over-enthusiastic Partisans. On Tito's instructions, Hudson was
given every assistance in his journey onwards into Serbia to contact Mihailović and the Četniks.

Hudson interpreted his brief to mean that he should travel anywhere
and meet anyone to further his task of co-ordination. He was very disappointed at his reception by Mihailović when he reached Ravna Gora
on 26 October. By this time, Mihailović had made radio contact via Malta
with the British and the Yugoslav government-in-exile, he was certain he
would receive British aid, and was determined not to make agreement with
communist-led Partisans. Mihailović's reception of Hudson was cold and
reserved. He refused to allow Hudson to be present at the meeting with
Tito on 27 October, saying that discussion between the two opposing resistance leaders was a matter of internal politics only. Tito would have agreed
to Hudson attending the talks. In November Hudson left Mihailović's
headquarters to go and see conditions in Partisan-held territory. He met
Tito again and talked with him alone on several occasions. They were
together when the German counter-attack reached Užice, and they escaped
together. By this time relations between Partisans and Četniks had broken
down and possibilities of 'co-ordination' of their activities were very remote.
Yet Hudson refused to stay with the Partisans and made his way back into
Četnik territory to see what he could do to fulfil his mission.

Hudson obtained important information about the activities of both
Četniks and Partisans, but only a very small amount of this could be
relayed back at the time to British authorities (S.O.E. Cairo) because of
his difficulties with radio equipment. Of the two sets with which he had
been provided for his mission, one was battery operated and used to send
back messages immediately after his landing. He sent S.O.E. an account
of his first meetings with Partisan resistance *odreds* in Montenegro and gave

the name of Tito as the leader of the Partisans (October 1941). Hudson's other radio set weighed thirty kilograms and operated only off 220 volt mains. He left it with the Partisans in Montenegro (they too could not use it) in order to be able to move quickly when he first went to join Mihailović; although he recovered it later, it again had to be abandoned and was never used. From the time he joined Mihailović, he was dependent on the latter's radio link, and although Hudson had his own cipher the despatch of his message to Cairo was dependent on Mihailović. When Milhailović himself was in retreat in the winter of 1941–2 radio contact with Cairo was broken. By the time it was resumed in the spring of 1942, Hudson was unable to get out any messages. This was the period when Hudson was posted 'missing presumed dead'.

Sometime in early summer 1942 Mihailović, in response to British enquiries, informed Cairo that Hudson was still alive. Hudson was joined by a new radio operator with equipment and was able to send out his own account of resistance conditions and the co-operation of Četniks with enemy occupying forces as he had seen them in the 1941–2 period. These messages were later (1943) expanded into the series known as the Ploz telegrams. Whilst Hudson had been enduring the rigours and dangers of the winter and spring of 1941–2, British policy had changed to support for Mihailović, who had been appointed Minister of War in the Yugoslav government-in-exile. The idea of co-ordination of resistance activities of Partisans and Četniks which had been the original purpose of the Hudson mission had been abandoned. Though Hudson was aware of the effect of these changes on Mihailović, as well as of the hardened anti-Četnik attitude and increased organisation of the Partisans, he never received any instructions changing his mission until the arrival of Colonel Bailey on 25 December 1942 indicated that policy had changed and he had in effect been superseded. Colonel Hudson eventually left Yugoslavia, in March 1944.

4 The Myth of an Allied Landing in the Balkans during the Second World War (with particular reference to Yugoslavia)

F. W. D. DEAKIN

A. THE POST-WAR CONTROVERSY

In a series of publications, mainly in the United States, which appeared during the Cold War and continue to be written, a strategic theory has been put forward which it is the purpose of this paper to study in light of the British documents now available.

Briefly stated, it is held that, with the opening of the Mediterranean theatre after *Torch* as a major front of operations by Anglo-American forces, the British evolved a coherent Mediterranean strategy in sharp conflict with the American 'grand design' of an exclusive landing in Northern France (*Overlord*); that an integral and central element in British planning was a Balkan landing. Such a concept was consistent with the historical traditions of the British conduct of war on the European continent: the 'eccentric' operations of the Napoleonic Wars; the Dardanelles and Salonika in the First World War; the lessons of the Western Front and the incubus of another frontal assault; and the continuing preservation of exclusive British imperial interests in the Mediterranean. This alleged Balkan operation was deliberately planned and conceived as an alternative to *Overlord*. It had an essentially longer-term political motivation to beat the Russians into central Europe, and to forestall and limit the Soviet drive westwards and the spread of

Communist control: in other words, to enable the reconstruction of the 'Cordon Sanitaire' of the 1920s.

The protagonists of this theory favoured these implications,
and were ideological critics of Roosevelt's opposition to this
British 'design'. Churchill, as its architect, was right in the event,
and Roosevelt wrong.

Two leading exponents of this theory of a Balkan operation
are Hanson Baldwin in his essays, *Great Mistakes of the War*
(1950), the main military expert in American journalism, and
Trumbull Higgins (in *Soft Underbelly* (1968)).

Both writers, in varying degrees, draw on the statements of
American leaders such as General Mark Clark and certain of
the American Chiefs of Staff, and on arguments quoted (often
out of context) from Alanbrooke's diaries, Lord Moran, and the
late Chester Wilmot's *The Struggle for Europe* (1952). Their thesis
'has been so widely held in American official and unofficial
histories of the War that it is virtually accepted as a self-evident
truth'.[1]

The British official historians, John Ehrman and Michael
Howard, have effectively demolished this legend in general
terms.[2] The purpose of this paper is to review their case in
the light of British documents now available in the Public
Record Office, and to attempt to define British attitudes towards
the Balkans as a theatre of war.

It is proposed to take in order (a) the unrealised plans for a
Balkan front put forward by the French to their British allies in
1939 and 1940 (in particular as they have not yet been documented in published terms); (b) the conception of British
'irregular' operations after the collapse of France and in relation to the first 'rebellion' in Yugoslavia and the short-term role
of the Special Operations Executive (S.O.E.) as a substitute for
regular military operations and as representing an experimental and precursory stage for future action; (c) the events of
1943 and the 'real' Anglo-American strategic controversy over
the Balkans.

B. BRITAIN, FRANCE AND AN EASTERN FRONT
(September 1939–June 1940)

After the outbreak of war in September 1939 it was the French who pressed for the early creation of an Allied Eastern Front. Their case was presented by Daladier at a meeting of the Allied Supreme War Council on 22 September.[3] In Anglo-French terms, he considered that there were three immediate problems of key importance: the front in France, collaboration in the manufacture of armaments, and the constitution of an Eastern Front.

As regards the last, Daladier 'thought that it was essential to have an allied force ready to prevent a German advance towards the Mediterranean and the Straits'. Although the original conception of a Polish front had collapsed, a 'dislocation of the Balkan States' must be prevented – in particular Rumanian oil must be denied to the Germans. 'The French government, therefore, thought it most important to establish a force either at Salonika, if this could be done without endangering the neutrality of Italy, or at Constantinople with the agreement of the Turkish government.' Chamberlain expressed his scepticism. 'He wondered how a force, wherever it was established, could prevent a German attack on the Balkans or the dislocation of the Balkan States.'

Daladier then defined more closely his original proposal. 'All he had in mind was to send a token force to strengthen the will of the Balkan States to resist German oppression,' but, at the same time, he underlined the key significance of the danger. 'If Germany were allowed to dominate the Balkans, the consequences could be catastrophic, since she would thus obtain the raw materials which were essential to her for a long war.'

The pressure for opening a south-eastern military front was essentially the work of Generals Gamelin and Weygand. The direct implications of such a move must be the creation of a pro-Allied Balkan *bloc* (both the French and British governments had already made unilateral guarantees to Greece and Rumania at the time of similar assurances to Poland in April 1939), and the French proposed secret talks with the Balkan General Staffs.

The British leaders based their assumptions on the need to

keep Italy neutral at all costs, and were convinced that they, rather than the French, could secure this end. They had conceived, for a time, of a neutralised Balkan *bloc* under Turkish initiative which would dissuade the Germans from military action south of the Danube, and, above all, remove any temptation from Mussolini to penetrate these regions.

As Halifax, the Foreign Secretary, wrote in a memorandum for the Cabinet on 12 September 1939:

> Our intervention in the Balkans in present circumstances, such as an expedition to Salonika which General Weygand seems to have been toying with, would almost certainly involve the violation of Greek, and perhaps Turkish, neutrality ...In a word, we cannot at one and the same time pursue a policy of keeping Italy neutral and the policy of mobilizing the Balkan states against Germany... A neutral and *a fortiori* friendly Italy seems more valuable to us than a Balkans forced by us into belligerency.[4]

French strategic proposals regarding the Balkans were discussed again at Cabinet on 7 December, on the basis of a Chiefs of Staff memorandum, 'Policy in the Balkans and the Middle East'.[5] This stated that 'the French are in favour of a forward policy in the Balkans. They anticipate that events may render the presence of an allied expeditionary force in the Balkans necessary as early as next spring. They therefore advocate immediate negotiations, which are to be completed by the end of this year or the early days of 1940.' They appeared to ignore the political dangers involved and the 'administrative dangers and strategic risks to which an allied force would be exposed if hastily committed in the Balkans'.

There was, however, as the Cabinet recognised, the danger of a German attack in south-east Europe 'on a broad front', and the general British objective had been defined by the Chiefs of Staff as 'to keep the Straits in the hands of the Anglo-French-Turkish coalition (sic) in any event, and, if possible, to deny the enemy access to the Aegean'. It could be argued that a bridgehead should be established and held at Salonika, but 'we had not sufficient forces to hold Salonika against a determined attack. An attempt to do so might result in a disaster.'

The British and French Chiefs of Staff met in Paris on 11

December and agreed to proposals by General Gamelin that the French should make cautious approaches in Athens, Belgrade, and Bucharest, 'provided that this can be done without offending Italian susceptibilities', and that the two staffs should 'study the problem of intervention in the Balkans in the spring of 1940'.[6]

The War Cabinet accepted these proposals on 14 December as the 'dominant consideration which should govern all action by the Allies in the Balkans'.

By the end of the year the general position was modified by signs of Russian 'aggressive imperialist ambitions in the Balkans', and the possibility of joint Russo-German action which in turn might bring in Italy, 'e.g. by an attack in the direction of Salonika from her bases in Albania, in order to obtain what spoils she could'. (Memorandum by the Foreign Secretary, 'Situation in the Balkans', 16 December 1939.)[7]

Throughout the spring of 1940 there were rumours of an impending Italian attack on Yugoslavia, in particular to occupy the Dalmatian ports (in April), and of an Italian invasion of Corfu. The Chiefs of Staff recommended that war should be declared on Italy if she moved against either Greece or Yugoslavia and Halifax accepted, on 29 April, the latter proposal, and the Cabinet agreed, in general terms, to send troops to Crete if Italy invaded Greece. This stand was speedily modified. On 8 June the Chiefs of Staff reported their considered view that 'there can be no question of creating a diversion in the Balkans unless Italy has already intervened against us or attacked one of the Balkan powers'.[8]

In effect, British policy in south-east Europe, and the eastern Mediterranean, was based on two alternative assumptions: the continued Italian neutrality in the conflict with Germany; or an Italian attack on one or more of the Balkan powers, in which case we were committed to assist, by formal obligation, Greece, Rumania, and/or Turkey – and equally in the event of German aggression. But, in such an eventuality, no common strategic plan of Anglo-French military action had been worked out by the critical summer of 1940. Within two days of the drafting of this memorandum of the Chiefs of Staff, Italy declared war on Britain and France.

On the day following this announcement, the British Chiefs

of Staff produced a memorandum on 'Balkan Policy in the New Situation'.[9] Britain was faced not only with Italian hostility but the critical situation in France. 'Moreover, we are advised that, unless Germany is able to improve her economic position in the near future, she will be in danger of collapsing in 1941.' In other words, the resources and raw materials (oil, copper, and chrome especially) of the Balkans must be acquired, and rapidly, by the Germans in the near future. It was recommended that 'we should make a direct and frank approach to Turkey to concert with Greece and Yugoslavia to form a common Balkan front on our side' in consultation with the French 'with the minimum delay.' This recommendation was deferred by the Cabinet 'until the policy of Turkey has been completely revealed', and no immediate action was taken. In less than a week the French had sought and obtained an armistice with Germany.

The subsequent diplomatic moves by Britain, after the fall of France, to maintain an independent and neutral Balkan bloc, are outside the subject of this paper. The shadow of Axis oppression hung over the whole region and the material resources of an isolated Britain could not permit of any supplies of military equipment – the prerequisite of any mutual and concrete obligations – to the now demoralised Balkan powers.

As, for example, a Chiefs of Staff report of 25 November 1940 put it: 'The best way in which this country could assist the Yugoslavs was to carry on the war relentlessly against the Germans and Italians.' Direct armed assistance could only be on a very limited scale.[10]

C. FROM THE FALL OF FRANCE TO THE NORTH AFRICA LANDINGS. THE PREPARATORY ROLE OF S.O.E.

The French surrender ended the argument both for and against a joint Balkan operation. During the remaining months of 1940, the Italian attack on Greece in October, followed by the movement of German troops into Rumania and the pro-Axis 'neutrality' of Bulgaria, completed the control by the enemy of the south-eastern coastal approaches to Continental Europe – with one exception for a brief space: uncommitted Yugoslavia.

Britain was confined to the defence of her islands, her *place d'armes* in Egypt and on the Suez Canal, and her naval bases at Gibraltar and Malta. The concept of the 'long war' had become a grim reality. As Churchill put it: 'The only plan is to persevere,' and to plan, under the shield of naval and air power, for a decisive return to the Continent.

As early as May 1940 the Chiefs of Staff considered the eventual collapse of Germany: 'The German army, paralysed by lack of petrol and by patriot revolts . . ., might be unable to fight; and the British army could then return to the Continent . . . to receive its surrender and restore order.'[11] Armed rebellion would be provoked by skilful subversion (Chiefs of Staff paper, May 1940); from the vital bases in Egypt and Palestine, direct if limited damage could at an early stage be inflicted on the southern fringes of the Axis European fortress. In this strategic task the role of S.O.E. as an ancillary 'Fourth Arm' was recognised as central at its foundation in the summer of 1940. 'Subversion ranked with bombing and blockade as one of the three weapons at Britain's disposal.' The pattern was set, in somewhat euphoric terms, in a paper drafted by the Joint Planning Staff in June 1941. At some stage the subjugated peoples of Europe would rise in revolt. 'Such rebellions can only occur once. They must not happen until the stage is set. . .' An invasion force of ten divisions at most, mainly of armoured troops backed by air and naval superiority, would be dispatched. 'Smaller forces might be sent from the Middle East to the Balkans.'

'We should be able overnight to produce the anarchy of Ireland in 1920 or Palestine in 1936. . . Powerful air forces will be used to interrupt the German communications and harass their troops. If we have access to the country by sea, armoured formations will be landed to strike swiftly and deep into the area.'[12]

The aim, as stated in this paper, was therefore not the promotion of an extensive guerrilla movement as such in occupied Europe but a fixed and single revolt at a chosen moment without rehearsal – a concept to be torn up later in the realities of isolated and spontaneous explosions.

But this first concept of European rebellion was to play its part – and further and changing definitions were forced on

the British planners by events. The project of mid-1941 was
elaborated by Churchill at the Washington Conference in
December to a somewhat sceptical American audience. 'If
the incursion of armed formations is successful, the uprising of
the local population, for whom weapons must be brought, will
supply *the corpus of the liberating offensive.*'[13]

This mass revolt must also be supported by 'underground'
armies – an attractive early theory soon to be abandoned. The
figures, after drastic reduction, of air support needed to provide
such a force of 45,000 men (the nucleus to be drawn from the
'free' Allied contingents in exile) in France, Belgium, and
Holland would require more than 2000 air sorties (the total of
one month's offensive at the time by Bomber Command).[14]
Although the Chiefs of Staff rejected this original plan, the
policy remained as a final objective of S.O.E.

The first explosion had already erupted (as all those which
followed) unheralded and spontaneous. A military *coup d'état*
in Yugoslavia in March 1941 led to an urgent appeal for British
aid. Conventional military support was out of the question. As
the Chiefs of Staff reported on 10 April, 'There was nothing
that we could do at this end as regards army resistance.' But
the challenge raised the prestige of Britain in the future. Arms,
supplies, and equipment must reach the rebel allies somehow.
As Eden was to put it at a Chiefs of Staff meeting (4 November
1941), 'Other enemy-occupied countries would tend to regard
it as a "test case".'[15]

With the collapse of the Yugoslav state, the German and
Italian armies overran the country, and the iron curtain des-
cended.[16] By August the first reports reached London of the
existence of guerrilla bands in the mountains of Serbia. The as
yet untried organisation of S.O.E. was to meet its first test as an
arm of war. The directive by the Prime Minister to Hugh
Dalton in August 1941 was to set the first limited and experimental pattern of its operations:

> The Yugoslavs (i.e. the exiled Royal Yugoslav Government),
> the War Office and we are all agreed that the guerrilla bands
> now active in Yugoslavia should show sufficient active resist-
> ance to cause constant embarrassment to the occupying

forces, and prevent any reduction in their numbers. But they should keep their main organization underground and avoid any attempt at large scale risings or ambitious military operations, which could only result at present in severe repression and the loss of our key men. They should now do all they can to prepare a widespread underground organization ready to strike hard later on, when we give the signal.[17]

From the autumn of 1941 to the end of the following year S.O.E. evolved, with a scant allocation of supplies and aircraft and tenuous sources of vital intelligence, a policy of supporting the only leader of Yugoslav resistance who emerged, Draža Mihailović. Neither submarines for landing British liaison parties (there were three exceptions) nor aircraft, other than two Liberators at Malta, could be spared for such operations. Quite apart from the aims of Mihailović himself, the underlying purpose of S.O.E. support was restricted to keeping his ill-defined force in being. As the Chiefs of Staff had stated in October 1941: 'From our point of view the revolt is premature.'[18]

The appearance of nebulous but more resistant and rival Yugoslav Partisans did not improve the situation, in the eyes of the British military leaders. The Chief of the Imperial General Staff reported to the Prime Minister on 2 June 1942. 'Although the activity of these wilder elements in the country will always necessitate considerable Axis garrisons, the policy of Mihailović is to curb their activities [a nice euphemism for engaging in civil war] in order to conserve his potential forces for civil war and to wait until his time is right.'[19]

From the beginning S.O.E. operations in this 'test case' of Yugoslavia (and later in every area of revolt in Europe) inevitably implied political issues and not simply temporising aid and liaison with a view to ultimate military enterprise, which would pass from its control to the planning of more regular expeditions.

By their nature the activities of S.O.E. operations were of a holding kind, and represented a substitute for eventual landings. Whatever form these might take would be conditioned by the opportunities opened by the main conduct of the war. Such a situation was only created after the North Africa landings, and with the possibility of moving considerable Allied forces into the Mediterranean.

The issue of future moves in the Balkans now became an integral part of Allied planning to knock Italy out of the war, and of the general shape of operations in the Mediterranean theatre – a subject of major controversy between the British and American Chiefs of Staff which dominated, throughout 1943, the whole conduct of the war against the Axis.

It is necessary to examine, with strict attention to essentials, the documentation now available on the role, actual and potential, of the Balkans in these summit discussions throughout the year 1943.

D. FROM CASABLANCA TO TEHERAN

At the Casablanca Conference (13–18 January 1943) the decision was taken to occupy Sicily, the ultimate target being the elimination of Italy from the war. It was hoped that this operation would bring in Turkey as an active ally – a move which would be an essential prerequisite for any substantial action in south-east Europe.

In preparation for the conference, the Combined Chiefs of Staff produced a background paper on 'American–British strategy in 1943'.[20] They recommended increased assistance 'to the insurgents in Yugoslavia, and sabotage in Greece, since in both countries the garrisons are largely Italian.' The planners based their future hopes of disorder in the Balkans on the assumption that 'Germany will be unable to undertake the two new commitments of garrisoning both the Balkans and an Italy in a state of collapse.' In the event, Germany did both.

The significance of the Balkan theatre for the war effort was outlined in this report. Action might result in: bases for attacking the Rumanian oil fields, and 'for fanning the already glowing embers of revolt in the Balkans: We should be able (i) to interrupt the Danube supply route to Germany; (ii) create a threat to the southern lines of communication to south Russia; (iii) cut the Axis sea communications between the Mediterranean and the Black Sea.' Above all, Germany would be deprived of vital supplies of copper and chrome (if Turkey came in).

As Churchill wrote in a paper sent to the President and given to the Turks at the Adana Conference with their leaders: 'The breaking down of Italy would lead to contact with the Western Balkans, and with highly hopeful resistance both by General Mihailović in Serbia and the Partisans in Croatia and Slovenia.'[21]

This last sentence is the first formal mention of the existence of resistance elements in Yugoslavia apart from Mihailović. On his way to Adana from North Africa Churchill sought a briefing from the Middle East Command of General Wilson on the general situation in the Balkans. In particular, he sent for Colonel Keble, Chief of Staff of S.O.E. (Cairo), who handed to him a memorandum (30 January 1943) which, while denying that Mihailović had been compromised with the Germans, stressed the importance of support for other resistance groups in Croatia and Slovenia, who were independent of Mihailović but could not be accurately termed Communists. Keble was convinced that if we did not act quickly we should be forestalled by the Russians or the Americans. Keble proposed that British officers should be sent to both sides and permitted to handle matters by withholding supplies according to the local situation.[22] This memorandum was coupled with a plea for an increase in the number of aircraft to enable S.O.E. to carry out such operations.

On his return to London, Churchill minuted to Major Morton (12 February 1943): 'Please show Lord Selborne the report I had from the S.O.E. Section (Cairo) dealing with Yugoslavia. I agree with this report in general terms. I consider it a matter of the greatest importance to establish the desired closer contacts with the Yugoslav leaders.'[23] (Note: Tito's name was not mentioned in any document.)

This report was endorsed within a week by the Foreign Office, who appear to have been stirred by the recent recognition of the Partisans by the Soviet Union. In a paper dated 20 February 1943, it was suggested that one should aim at 'the establishment in the areas previously occupied by the Yugoslav state of one or more independent units capable of joining any federal scheme or of contributing a stable settlement in the Balkans'.[24] The Foreign Office agreed that help should be sent to both sides.

The Chiefs of Staff considered this proposal on 4 March. They recommended the allocation of four Halifax aircraft to S.O.E., but nothing more. They also stated that they favoured backing Mihailović rather than the Partisans.

No immediate action was however taken in London for the next two months, but the stand taken by the Prime Minister and the Foreign Office enabled S.O.E. Cairo to begin the planning of special operations to contact the Yugoslav Partisans. Any extension of British activity in the Balkans must depend on the results of Sicily (operation *Husky*) and the attitude of Turkey.

Churchill's imagination was, however, caught and held by the prospects which might now be opened. On 2 April he minuted to Ismay:

> ...It must be considered a most important objective to get a footing on the Dalmatian coast, so that we can foment the insurgents of Albania and Yugoslavia by weapons and supplies, and possibly commandos.
>
> I believe that, in spite of his present foxy attitude, Mihailović will throw his whole weight against the Italians the moment we are able to give him an effective help. Evidently great possibilities are open in this theatre.[25]

The origin of this suggestion of seizing a foothold in the Eastern Adriatic was directly bound up with the study of how to exploit the anticipated collapse of Italy, and the ensuing position of the Germans. The strategic debate on this central issue took place at the Washington Conference in mid-May.

On 14 May the Combined Chiefs of Staff proposed in a memorandum, after the successful conclusion of *Husky*, a bridgehead might be established at Durazzo from which 'supplies and long-range penetration groups' should rally and support the guerrillas. The Dodecanese should also be seized. 'We should be prepared to exploit any weakening of the German position in the Balkans.'[26]

The clash at the summit between Churchill and Roosevelt and their planning staffs on *Overlord* versus operations in the Mediterranean, which had been masked at Casablanca, came into the open at Washington.

At no time was there, as that post-war 'legend' of British intentions implies, any suggestion of an alternative Balkan landing operation. All that was ever intended was the use of

Anglo-American forces in the Mediterranean to exploit the collapse of Italy on a flexible short-term basis.

The British planners in April and May proposed limited action at Durazzo and the Dodecanese, to be followed up if the Germans started to withdraw from the Balkans to reinforce the Italian front (an assumption which proved to be incorrect) and also if Turkey came into the war. These proposals were endorsed by the Combined Chiefs of Staff (see above), and the British Chiefs of Staff instructed General Wilson in Cairo to submit proposals for the capture of the Dodecanese, in anticipation of Turkish intervention and as a base from which to bomb Ploeşti, and also for the invasion of Crete and Greece as well.[27] For a fleeting moment, the outlines of a Balkan 'grand design' emerge, only to be finally rejected in Washington.

On 8 May General Wilson signalled to the Chief of the Imperial General Staff that the Dodecanese operation (*Accolade*) should be regarded as a preliminary to

> possible major operations based on Istanbul and Salonika with objectives up to the line of the Danube... Such operations would not only offer prospects of a decisive defeat of [the] enemy but [the] presence of powerful British forces in conjunction with Turkish forces in Eastern Europe would strengthen our hand in reaching [a] final settlement with the Russians.[28] Whether or not such far reaching operations are accepted as our policy for [the] future conduct of the war, Middle East must be prepared to open the Aegean and support Turkey.[29]

This proposal, which was never the subject of detailed planning, implied (a) the willingness of the Allied Commanders of Allied Forces Headquarters to release forces *and* landing craft for such an operation; (b) the entry of Turkey in the war; (c) the inability of the Germans to maintain their position simultaneously in the Balkans and Italy, and above all the agreement of the Combined Chiefs of Staff to a campaign of this importance, which would involve the postponement of the date of *Overlord*. None of these conditions were fulfilled.

The Washington decision was final and absolute. In their final report of 18 May the Combined Chiefs of Staff recommended that: 'Operations in the Mediterranean subsequent to

Husky should be limited to the air offensive, because any other operations would use resources vital to *Roundup* and present the risk of a limitless commitment of United Nations resources to the Mediterranean vacuum, thus needlessly prolonging the war.'[30]

The case for limited operations was, however, not dismissed. Churchill's own conception of the scope and nature of any Balkan diversions was clearly expressed in a paper ('Background' Notes) which he circulated at the end of the Washington Conference (31 May 1943).[31]

> The occupation of the southern parts of Italy...would give us access to the Adriatic and the power to send shiploads of munitions to the Adriatic ports, and also agents and possibly small Commando bands. *We should not have the troops to engage in any serious operations there, and H.M.G. do not contemplate the provision of any organized armed force for the Balkan theatre, either this year or in any period in which we are now concerned* [my italics].[32]

The successful Sicily landings were followed by the fall of Mussolini. These developments immediately revived the issue of exploiting the Italian situation across the Adriatic, and raised at the same time hopes of Allied action in the minds of Greek and Yugoslav leaders and consequent fears at Hitler's headquarters.[33]

Already on 12 July the British Joint Planning Staff returned to the Durazzo bridgehead project:

> (Its) establishment...would enable us to increase our assistance to the Resistance Groups and so extend German internal security commitments; we could also threaten Germany with the loss of vital raw materials. Possession of airfields in the Balkans and Turkey would enable us to increase interference with German resources especially Roumanian oil supplies.
>
>   The diversion of German divisions to meet the increased threat in the Balkans would indirectly contribute to the success of *Overlord*, but the denial of raw materials would not exercise an immediate effect on the German war economy. Nor could we hope for a decisive success in the Balkans in time to influence the cross-Channel invasion of the Conti-

nent, and we might well find ourselves involved in an exhaustive and indeterminate campaign. At the same time the collapse of Italy will enable us to give a greater degree of assistance to guerrillas in the Balkans even without establishing a bridgehead at Durazzo.

From this analysis, the planners concluded that if Italy collapsed, operations in the Balkans should be subsidiary to those against northern Italy, 'as resources permit; we should, in any case, increase the degree of assistance to guerrillas to the greatest possible extent.'[34] The pending collapse of Italy raised the whole issue of future Anglo-American strategy in the Mediterranean, which formed the subject of summit talks at Quebec and Washington in early August.

In a telegram of 14 August General Wilson returned to his constant theme of the strategic significance of the Balkans, and the immediate opportunities to exploit this theatre: 'Mideast should have force available to follow up on axis Rhodes–Athens and eventually Salonika...Subsequent forces would depend on extent [a] follow up [was] considered advisable in order to harass the enemy and accelerate his further withdrawal by making contact with and reorganizing the large partisan and Četnik forces in Yugoslavia...'[35]

The opposition of Eisenhower and Allied Forces Headquarters, however, to any removal of forces and landing craft from the Italian front to the eastern Mediterranean prevailed at the summit conferences. In a paper on 'the Strategic Concept for the defeat of the Axis in Europe' (19 August 1943), a clear directive was proposed and accepted. 'Operations in the Balkan area will be limited to supply of Balkan guerrillas by air and sea transport, and the bombing of Ploeşti and other strategic objectives from Italian bases. The Balkans are unsuitable for large-scale offensive operations, due to terrain and communications difficulties.'[36]

As has been stated, the feasibility of any landing operations in Greece and the Aegean islands, as bases for a mainland invasion, rested on the attitude of Turkey.

During the previous five months intensive negotiations at Ankara failed to achieve any result, and this situation, coupled

with the refusal of the Americans to divert the vital resources in
landing craft from Italy, drastically limited any moves available
to General Wilson.

The Italian surrender of 8 September was negotiated by
Allied Forces Headquarters in such a form as to preclude any
anticipatory operations by Wilson in the area of the Middle East
command. The Germans moved first, and with speed, against
the Italian garrisons throughout the Balkans.

British operations against Rhodes and the Dodecanese ended
in disaster. The British liaison missions in Greece and Yugoslavia received no prior warning of the Italian armistice, probably in part for security reasons (a decision which caused sharp
ill-will on the part of the local guerrilla leaders). Valuable
opportunities were missed. The absence in Washington of the
British Prime Minister and the Chiefs of Staff may have played
some part in this omission.

Churchill was conscious, at a distance, of the immediate
possibilities of exploiting the position. In a paper addressed to
Roosevelt of 9 September he wrote: 'We are both acutely conscious of the great importance of the Balkan situation. We
should make sure that the Mediterranean High Command,
absorbed in its present battle, does not overlook the needs of the
Patriot forces there...the utmost efforts should be put forth to
organize the attack upon the Germans throughout the Balkan
peninsula and to supply agents, arms and good direction.'
Churchill stated his intention of studying the available forces in
the Middle East, 'hoping that improvised expeditionary forces
and garrisons may be provided for various minor ventures.'[37]
The only immediate concrete action, but one which had positive implications, was the dispatch of a senior mission under
Brigadier Fitzroy Maclean to Tito, to recommend directly to
the Prime Minister the extension of decisive aid to the Yugoslav
Partisans.

On 14 October, the Chiefs of Staff informed the Prime Minister that they were suffering from 'a feeling of uneasiness...
that the rigidity imposed by the *Quadrant* decisions on our
military dispositions is hampering the proper exploitation of
our successes in the Mediterranean.' On the 19th, the Prime
Minister accordingly asked them to embark on a study of the

situation in that theatre, with particular reference to the resistance to Germany which was growing throughout the Balkans. On the same day, he held a Staff Meeting which discussed the position. All agreed that the operations hitherto conceived might fail to contain the necessary forces in the south, before and during the first three months of *Overlord*. Even if they succeeded in the earlier period, the danger still remained; for there was no plan of containment for the summer, to prevent a later concentration by the enemy against the forces that would then have landed in northern France. If both dangers were to be avoided, the connexion between the two campaigns must be re-examined. Strategy in the Mediterranean must be more flexible, and the date of *Overlord* itself should not be considered sacrosanct.

Unfortunately, we could not take a unilateral decision regarding the future strategy of the Allied nations. A further meeting with the Americans would therefore be necessary...[38]

In the meantime, Brigadier Maclean had submitted his first comprehensive report (6 November 1943) recommending a substantial increase in aid to the Yugoslav Partisans, and that support to Mihailović should be discontinued.[39]

The Chiefs of Staff reported on 11 November: 'There was general agreement that operations by the guerrillas in the Balkans had assumed so large a scale, and that the results of these activities were tied up so closely with our military operations in Italy, that it was essential to establish them on a regular military basis as soon as possible.'[40]

This appreciation prompted Churchill to press for the extension of such aid. In a paper dated 20 November he listed as the fourth priority for action in the Mediterranean theatre the seizure of

a port or ports and establish[ing] bridgeheads on the Dalmatian Coast, and carry[ing] a regular flow of airborne supplies to the Partisans. Use the British First Airborne Division and all the Commandos available in the Mediterranean, together with the 'Plough' force [a British force specially equipped and trained for mountain warfare], to aid and animate the resistance in Yugoslavia and Albania and also to capture islands like Corfu and Argostoli. Establish air domination of the Southern Adriatic, and maintain sea superiority there.[41]

This minute followed the draft submitted by the Chiefs of Staff on 11 November which contained the phrase: 'If necessary, we might form a limited bridgehead on the Dalmatian or Albanian coasts.'

At a meeting on 23 November, the Chiefs of Staff discussed the Prime Minister's minute and informed him that

> We do not favour the establishment of a bridgehead on the Dalmatian Coast, because it would take up too much of our resources. It was the one point in our Mediterranean proposals which General Alexander did not like. We think that we can do just as much, and, at the same time, avoid an unlimited commitment, by smuggling in material at many points on the coast and by air. The successful prosecution of operations in the Balkans depends much more on good organization...[42]

The Prime Minister thereupon amended his minute, which was not in fact used further and which appears, in its modified form and with the 'proposals for action' deleted, in Volume v of his memoirs.[43]

These operational proposals, now limited and more closely defined, still required American consent. The opportunity to discuss them within the general frame of Allied strategy came at the meeting of Churchill, Roosevelt, and the Combined Chiefs of Staff at Cairo (*Sextant*), prior to the Teheran Conference with the Russians.

Churchill's memorandum for Cairo was a chronicle of missed opportunities in the Mediterranean since the Italian surrender.

> We have been overtaken and in a sense outrun by our own success... We have failed to give any measure of support for the Partisans and Patriots in Yugoslavia and Albania... The Germans have weathered the difficulties caused by the Italian collapse and desertion... We are now faced with the prospect that a fixed target date for *Overlord* will continue to hamper and enfeeble the Mediterranean campaign, that our

affairs will deteriorate in the Balkans and that the Aegean will remain firmly in German hands.[44]

The military conference in Cairo agreed 'that the Partisans in Yugoslavia should be supported by supplies and equipment to the greatest possible extent, and also by Commando operations.' This decision marked both the end of the Anglo-American controversy on Mediterranean strategy in 1943, and defined, for the immediate future, the scale of Allied operations into the Balkans. At the Teheran conference this wording was adopted without alteration. The three Allies thus formally endorsed military aid on these lines to the Yugoslav partisans of Tito. Subsequent operational measures were taken, within the frame of this directive, during the course of 1944.[45]

The purpose of such operations remained a subject of lively debate between the British and American leaders. The Teheran meeting provided one such interchange. Somewhat surprisingly, Roosevelt suggested, in conversation with Churchill, a move 'from the Adriatic to the head of the Danube' as an alternative to the proposed landings in Southern France (*Dragon*).[46]

In a formal session, Churchill tried out this suggestion on Stalin. As he expressed it, some of the twenty-two divisions which might be left over after the Italian campaign 'could be used either for an operation against Southern France or for moving from the head of the Adriatic towards the Danube. Both these operations will be timed in conformity with *Overlord*.' There is no record of Stalin's comment.

Churchill's attraction for this proposal, which never in the event reached the planning stage, remained till the end of hostilities in Europe. As he told Roosevelt at the time of Teheran, he was taken with the idea of a 'right-handed move by Istria and Trieste, with the ultimate design of reaching Vienna through the Ljubljana gap'. But Churchill commented: 'All this lay five or six months ahead.'[47]

CONCLUSION

Churchill himself, when writing his account of the Second World War, was aware of the historical controversy which has stimulated this paper. 'It has become a legend in America that

I strove to prevent the cross-Channel enterprise called *Overlord* and that I tried vainly to lure the Allies into some mass invasion of the Balkans or a large-scale campaign in the Eastern Mediterranean which would effectively kill it.'[48] The leading British historians, who have studied these events, have demolished this Balkan theory, and a study of the documents now available reinforces their view.

Howard makes it clear that there was never any question, in British strategic thinking, of such a Balkan operation. The Chiefs of Staff never wavered from pressing for a maximum support for the Italian front. Any raids across the Adriatic were 'a continuation of the battle of attrition in Italy'.

Howard also contests the judgement of General Mark Clark (a central quotation often used by the protagonists of the Balkan front theory): 'the weakening of the campaign in Italy in order to invade Southern France was one of the outstanding political mistakes of the war.'[49]

Ehrman has summarised the position in the following terms:

It has often been asserted – and despite the evidence to the contrary, seems still to be widely believed – that the British, either under Churchill's influence or through him as their spokesman, wished in the second half of 1943 to develop a campaign in the Balkans towards the north, if necessary at the expense of *Overlord*, for strategic or diplomatic reasons, or for a combination of both. Whatever may have been the case later, this was not so at that time. There was, in the first place, no real difference of opinion between the Prime Minister and the Chiefs of Staff as to what should be done. Churchill's policy in 1943 was not that of Lloyd George in 1916. Whatever his dreams – and there were dreams – when faced with the realities he saw well enough the impossibility of a Balkan campaign involving substantial British or American forces; and while he was undoubtedly more enthusiastic than the Chiefs of Staff or their Planners over a policy in the Aegean that all acknowledged to be necessary, there was no need or occasion for him to urge on them a course of action which they adopted without serious hesitation from the first. The issue in the Eastern Mediterranean, in the autumn and winter of 1943, was not in fact whether the Allies should land in force on the mainland of south-east Europe, but whether they could and should bring Turkey into the war. Strategy, like politics, is the art of the possible. British plans centred on the Aegean, where in their view a limited force could produce the greatest effect in support of the main strategic object, and not on operations by the Allies on the mainland for which none of the necessary conditions existed. So far as 1943 is concerned, the Balkan campaign with substantial Allied forces is a myth.[50]

As early as 1944 Churchill seems to have been aware intuitively that such a legend would emerge. At a conference of the Dominions' Prime Ministers on 3 May he remarked that

He was bound to admit that if he had had his own way, the lay-out of the war would have been different. His inclination would have been in favour of rolling up Europe from the southeast, and joining hands with the Russians. However, it had proved impossible to persuade the United States on this view. They had been determined at every stage upon the invasion in north-west Europe...He himself had opposed the opening of this campaign in 1942 and 1943, but now he was in favour of it, and all his military advisers supported him in this. Russian pressure, too, had been very severe. Meanwhile, in Italy we must strike and prevent the enemy drawing his forces away...

In answer to a query later in the same meeting he said that

there had never been any question of major action in the Balkans. It was merely a question of assistance by commandos and air action. Due priorities must prevail in the application of resources...The Americans had all along said that we were leading them up the garden in the Mediterranean. His reply had been that, in return, we had provided them in the garden with nourishing vegetables and refreshing fruits. Nevertheless, the Americans had remained very suspicious, and thought that he was entertaining designs for dragging them into the Balkans. This he had never contemplated doing. He had merely hoped to be able to give adequate help to Tito, and he had viewed the whole Mediterranean problem from a purely military point of view.

There was no doubt that the obstinate and recurring British insistence on diversionary raids into the Balkans, after early 1943, roused atavistic suspicions, not of a strictly military nature, in the minds of the American political and military leaders, and that these lie at the origin of the post-war legend. The word 'Balkan' itself seems to have had a strong emotive content. 'The area to the east of the Adriatic was regarded by American strategists with something akin to the superstitious dread with which mediaeval mariners once contemplated the unknown monster-infested reaches of the Western Ocean.'[51]

In spite of such suspicions, widely held in high places in Washington, Churchill's Balkan 'policy', generally endorsed by the British Chiefs of Staff, was in effect no more than strategic opportunism, and devoid of conscious political motivation.

But perhaps the significance of the controversy, here briefly reviewed, lies not so much in a rational analysis of the evidence now available – which disproves the theory in question – as in the reality attributed to British strategic intentions in the Balkans in 1943 by Hitler and the German General Staff, and equally by Marshal Tito.

The former was convinced that the British intended to effect a major landing in south-east Europe after the collapse of Italy both for reasons of an obsessive personal analysis by Hitler of Churchill's psychology and the failure at the Dardanelles, and the strategy of Salonika in the First World War. The capture of the French General Staff documents at La Charité in June 1940 which revealed the Anglo-French plans for an Eastern Front confirmed to Hitler his historical interpretation. The deception plans of April–May 1943 (Operation *Mincemeat*) seemed to offer a decisive confirmation.

As to Tito, his analysis ironically followed closely that of Hitler, but its confirmation, in his eyes, lay in the '50–50' so-called agreement in October 1944 between Churchill and Stalin. He was convinced that a political division of Yugoslavia had been decided on this occasion and would be implemented, before the end of hostilities, by the advance of the Red Armies from the east, and the landing of Anglo-American forces from the west. In spite of the military evidence discussed in this paper, the 'political' legend persists in certain quarters.

NOTES

1. L. Morton, 'World War II. A Survey of Recent Writings', *American Historical Review*, LXXV (1970) 1987–2007.
2. See Conclusion below.
3. PRO. CAB 66/1.
4. PRO. CAB 66/1.
5. PRO. CAB 65/2.
6. PRO. CAB 65/2 WP (39) 159.
7. PRO. CAB 66/4 WP (39) 165.
8. PRO. CAB 80/12 COS (40) 438.
9. *Ibid.*
10. CAB 65/10 WM 295 (40) 5.
11. Michael Howard, *The Mediterranean Strategy in the Second World War* (London, 1968) p. 7.
12. J. M. A. Gwyer, *Grand Strategy* (London, 1964) III (i) pp. 42 ff.
13. Ibid., pp. 334–5.
14. According to an S.O.E. estimate in July 1941.
15. PRO. CAB 79/55.
16. The German attack on Yugoslavia extended to Greece and with it a threat to the whole British position in the eastern Mediterranean. This paper is not concerned with the ensuing Greek operation, which raised the fleeting mirage of a Balkan front.

But it was decided – and the controversy as to the justification continues – to send an expeditionary force to the mainland of Greece as a harbinger of things to come. As Churchill put it in a telegram at the time to the Australian Prime Minister: '*Lustre* [the Greek operation] in its true setting [is] not an isolated military act but a prime mover in a large design.' *Second World War* III (London, 1950) p. 152.
17. John Ehrman, *Grand Strategy* (London, 1956) V, p. 77.
18. PRO. CAB 79/15 COS (41) 354, 15 Oct 1941.
19. Quoted in Howard, *Grand Strategy* (London, 1972) IV, p. 386.
20. PRO. CAB 88/8, 3 Jan 1943.
21. Churchill, *The Second World War* (London, 1951) IV, p. 634.
22. See Howard, op. cit., pp. 389–90.
23. Churchill, *The Second World War* IV, p. 828 and Howard, op. cit., pp. 389–90.
24. Howard, op. cit., 390.
25. Churchill, op. cit., IV.
26. PRO. CAB 88/11.
27. See details in Howard, op. cit., p. 383.
28. The only mention, in 1943, in the British records of this argument.
29. Quoted in Howard, op. cit., p. 383.
30. *Ibid.*, pp. 659.
31. Churchill, op. cit., IV, pp. 736–7.
32. This and similar references to the Prime Minister's statements at the time do not feature in the writings of the protagonists of the 'Balkan invasion' theory.

33. On the Allied deception plans and their effect in convincing Hitler of the reality of Allied Balkan invasion plans, see Ewen Montagu, *The Man Who Never Was* (London, 1953) *passim*.

34. Ehrman, op. cit., pp. 80–1.

35. General Wilson to COS, Concrete telegram No. 188 (14 Aug 1943). Quoted in Howard, op. cit., p. 491.

36. PRO. CAB 88/15. CCS 303.

37. Churchill, *The Second World War* v, p. 121.

38. Ehrman, op. cit., pp. 106–7. In summing up this meeting the Prime Minister proposed that 'we should agree *to enter the Balkans*.' This remark must be taken in context. As Ehrman points out, this phrase was used at the start of the investigation (into future strategic possibilities in the eastern Mediterranean and before they were examined in detail) and before the campaign in Italy had clearly reached a stalemate. The 'entry into the Balkans' was not defined at all exactly, but would depend on the implications of reinforcing Italy 'to the full'.

39. The stages of British attitudes towards Mihailović do not form part of this paper.

40. PRO. CAB 88/20.

41. Ehrman, op. cit., Appendix VI, p. 555.

42. Ibid., p. 111.

43. Churchill, *The Second World War*, v, pp. 291–4.

44. Ibid., p. 291 ff.

45. Balkan Air Force was set up in June 1944 under Air-Marshal Sir William Elliot as co-ordinator of trans-Adriatic operations with Land Forces Adriatic (four commandos) and naval units under his command. Supply arrangements were organised by S.O.E., whose early role of experimental missions was now completed.

46. See Churchill, *The Second World War*, v, pp. 308, 312, 358.

47. *Ibid.*, p. 358.

48. *Ibid.* p. 304.

49. Quoted in Howard, *Mediterranean Strategy*, pp. 67–8.

50. Ehrman, op. cit., p. 112.

51. Richard M. Leighton, 'Overlord Revisited', *American Historical Review*, LXVIII (1963).

5 Summer 1943: The Critical Months

C. M. WOODHOUSE

I

In the six months between March and October 1943 two almost diametrical reversals of policy towards the Greek Resistance were made by the British authorities. The result was that at the end of the critical period the orientation of British policy was much the same as at the beginning, but in the meantime a serious crisis had occurred, from the consequences of which there was never to be a full recovery. Put in its simplest terms, in March 1943 British policy was friendly towards Zervas (E.D.E.S.)* and hostile towards E.L.A.S.†; by the end of June it had reached a point of careful balance between being pro-Zervas and pro-E.L.A.S.; but by the end of September it had reverted to the position held in March, of friendliness towards Zervas and hostility towards E.L.A.S., in an even more extreme degree.

During the same period there was also a profound change in British policy towards occupied Yugoslavia, with the difference that the change was entirely in one direction, from being friendly towards Mihailović and negative towards Tito into the exact opposite. The outcome of the two reversals of policy in Greece combined with the single reversal in Yugoslavia was just what might have been expected. Whereas at the beginning of the critical period the orientation of British policy in both countries was roughly the same, at the end of the period it was totally

* *Ethnikos Dimokratikos Ellinikos Syndesmos* – National Republican Greek League.
† *Ethnikos Laikos Apeleftherotikos Stratos* – National Popular Liberation Army.

different. So far as I know, no one gave consideration at the time to the long-term consequences of arriving at diametrically opposite policies in Greece and Yugoslavia. In May 1944 Churchill defiantly made a virtue of the contrast when he declared in the House of Commons: 'In one place we support a King, in another a Communist – there is no attempt by us to enforce particular ideologies.'[1] It is clear that at the time the decision in Yugoslavia was based on the simple consideration of military effectiveness: Tito was fighting the Germans and Mihailović was not. The military consideration was decisive, and political considerations were eventually assimilated to it. In Greece there was never an effective reconciliation of military and political considerations, nor did either decisively and finally prevail over the other. The first reversal of policy (June 1943) was determined primarily by military considerations, the second (September 1943) entirely by political considerations. Only for a very brief period in between did it seem possible that the two could be reconciled.

It is easy to see the reasons for the position in March 1943. On the one hand, British policy could hardly fail to be pro-Zervas. He was the only major leader in the Balkans who took the field at the express request of the British; he was the victor of the Gorgopotamos operation (code-named *Harling*) a few months before; he had an attractive, buccaneering personality, together with a natural flair for guerrilla operations; and he was unreservedly co-operative. In March 1943 he actually carried his co-operativeness to the extent of openly conforming to British policy on the monarchy – a controversial step within his ostensibly republican organisation (E.D.E.S.), but one which naturally made him more acceptable to the British authorities. On the other hand, at the same time the conduct of E.A.M.*–E.L.A.S. was becoming increasingly unacceptable and hostile. It is known in retrospect, though it was not known at the time, that in December 1942 the Greek Communist Party (K.K.E.)† held a Panhelladic Conference in Thessaly, which (it was later claimed) 'completely orientated the whole Party for the development of the guerrilla movement'.[2] This was only a few weeks after the principal leader of E.L.A.S. in the field,

---

* *Ethnikon Apeleftherotikon Metopon* – National Liberation Front.
† *Kommounistikon Komma Ellados.*

Aris Veloukhiotis, had co-operated with Zervas and the British
in the Gorgopotamos operation – a decision which almost certainly Aris took on his own initiative, against the advice and
perhaps against the orders of the leadership of E.A.M. Immediately after the Panhelladic Conference, in the last week of
December 1942, Aris made his first aggressive move against
Zervas, his comrade in battle only a few weeks earlier, and an
armed clash was only narrowly averted.

After that, acts of aggression by E.L.A.S. were frequent, and
were clearly aimed at establishing a monopoly of the resistance
movement. Two regular officers of comparable seniority with
Napoleon Zervas – Stephanos Saraphis and Dimitrios Psaros –
attempted to form armed bands with the support of the British
and in co-operation with Zervas. Their supporting organisations were known as A.A.A.* and E.K.K.A.†. One of the two
– Saraphis – was actually the first progenitor of the scheme for
forming a national network of forces to be known as the
'National Bands', which would serve as a kind of challenge to
E.L.A.S. either to conform to the same pattern or to wither
away for want of support. But this proved to be wishful thinking.
E.L.A.S. attacked both Saraphis (in early March) and Psaros
(in May, and again in June), in each case successfully. Other
potential National Bands in many parts of Greece – the Peloponnese, Macedonia and Thessaly in particular – were also
routed by E.L.A.S. Zervas almost alone survived. He claimed
that if he had sufficient support from the British, he could not
only survive but destroy E.L.A.S. But in the judgement of
Myers and myself, he certainly could not have succeeded.

There was in any case another reason why such an attempt
could never have been supported by the British authorities.
Neither the Foreign Office nor even the Special Operations
Executive (S.O.E.) was satisfied that Zervas was a man who
deserved unqualified support. His pre-war reputation was, to
say the least, unsatisfactory; and the circumstances in which he
had been induced to take the field were little short of blackmail.
In the early days after the Gorgopotamos operation, it was
evidently suspected that both Myers and myself had fallen
unduly under his influence. The first officer to be dropped into

* *Apeleftherosis Agon Arkhigia* – Liberation Struggle Leadership.
† *Ethniki kai Koinoniki Apeleftherosis* – National and Social Liberation.

Greece after the Gorgopotamos operation, the New Zealand
Major William Jordan, was provided with secret code-phrases,
unknown to us, to indicate to S.O.E. whether or not Myers and
I were actually being held under duress by Zervas. Even after
he had reported in our favour, other officers were dropped in
other parts of Greece to report on E.L.A.S., despite an explicit
undertaking by S.O.E. that no new missions would be put in
to Greece without consulting us. These new ventures did not
much help to clarify the picture, because very different reports
emerged. In Thessaly, Colonel Rufus Sheppard reported that
E.L.A.S. was virtually faultless; in Macedonia, Colonel
N. G. L. Hammond reported much more realistically; and
somewhat later in the Peloponnese, the British mission under
Colonel John Stevens went overboard in the opposite direction
to Sheppard. These discrepancies made the task of assessment
from the outside difficult, and should be borne in mind when
criticising the vagaries of British policy.

On balance, it was hardly possible to be other than extremely
critical of E.A.M.–E.L.A.S. from a British point of view at the
beginning of the summer of 1943. Both their short-term and
their long-term aims were plainly in conflict with ours. Their
long-term aim was unmistakably to achieve political control of
Greece at the end of the war. Their short-term aim was to fight
the Occupation only in their own way, whether or not that
coincided with ours. The question is why, during the early
summer of 1943, British policy veered from one of strongly
resisting these aims to one which appeared to come very near
to conceding them? The answer seems to lie partly in military
considerations, partly in politics, and partly in personalities.
Different weight might be given to them by different historians,
but perhaps only those who were there at the time would
appreciate fully the importance of the individual characters.
The most decisive factor was undoubtedly the balance of military and political priorities. But the balance was also affected
from time to time by the interaction of personalities.

II

Up to the middle of July 1943, when the landings in Sicily had
begun and were clearly succeeding, military considerations

predominated. It had been assumed at the beginning of the year that eventually an opposed landing in Greece would be necessary and that guerrilla support for it would be helpful. Thus after the success at the Gorgopotamos bridge in November 1942, the plans of S.O.E. were changed. It had been intended that most of the British party of twelve which had been dropped for the operation should be withdrawn from Greece, leaving only two officers and two wireless operators to maintain contact. In the event it was decided that there should be no evacuation, and that Brigadier E. C. W. Myers should be put in charge of a British Military Mission which would develop guerrilla forces, assisted by British Liaison Officers (B.L.O.s), all over the country.

These were considered to be purely operational decisions. The Foreign Office was not informed either of the original infiltration of Myers' party or of the change in his mission, though there is clear evidence that senior officials of the Foreign Office were aware that a British party was in Greece before the attack on the Gorgopotamos bridge took place. This fact emerges from telegrams exchanged between the Minister of State in Cairo and Sir Alexander Cadogan at the Foreign Office in mid-November.[3] But although the Foreign Office did not dispute S.O.E.'s right to maintain secrecy on operational matters, there were later severe recriminations over the failure to report decisions which were bound to have political consequences.

The decision to establish a British Military Mission in Greece was followed by a series of military directives to Myers in the first five months of 1943, of which succinct details can be found in Myers' *Greek Entanglement*. They were received by Myers on 3 January, 2 February, 21 February and 30 May respectively.[4] Although all were drafted in realistic terms, only the last of them correctly envisaged the fact that there would be no allied landings in Greece during 1943. All of them assumed that large and active guerrilla forces would be necessary, though their location and effective control would be much more important than their size. Myers accordingly drew up his first plans in January and amended them as later directives followed. At the same time I went to Athens to make contact with the leadership of E.A.M. and other clandestine organisations and to see how far their co-operation could be relied on. My visit to Athens was the

first occasion which removed all doubt that E.A.M. was effectively dominated by the Communist Party of Greece (K.K.E.),
some of whose leaders I met for the first time: Georgios Siantos,
Andreas Tzimas, Ioannis Ioannidis and Petros Roussos.

Our main object at the time was to induce the leaders of
E.A.M. to come out of Athens and take the field in the mountains, where we believed that the control of the guerrilla war
must be located. Two interesting facts of the time came to my
knowledge only long afterwards. One was that Aris Veloukhiotis, who also visited Athens in February and whom I met on my
way out, was offering exactly the same advice. Tzimas reports
him as quoting to the Central Committee Danton's advice:
'De l'audace, et encore de l'audace, et toujours de l'audace' –
which he interpreted as 'underlining the necessity for the whole
leadership of the Party to take to the mountains'.[5] Tzimas
clearly agreed with Aris; but the second interesting fact is that
the K.K.E. leadership was sharply divided on this point. Some
Communists, including Siantos (who was then the Acting
Secretary General of the Party), believed that the mountains
were a relatively insignificant arena in the struggle for power,
which would be won in the cities. Evidence of this division came
out at the end of the occupation, when the Yugoslav leader,
Svetozar Vukmanović (Tempo), told a British journalist that
in 1943 he had met Siantos 'on a frontier peak', and heard him
say that 'while his forces controlled the countryside, the key to
absolute power lay in the centres of population; he who ruled
Athens ruled Greece. The Athenian workers would be organised
into military formations, so that at the moment of liberation,
they could seize the city.'[6] Tempo himself recorded the same
conversation, including Ioannidis in it as well as Siantos, when
he wrote a severe attack on the policies of the K.K.E. in 1949,
which was published in English as *How and Why the People's
Liberation Struggle of Greece Met with Defeat*. Tzimas as well as
Aris seems to have shared Tempo's view that Siantos was
wrong in his judgement of the relative priority of the cities and
the mountains.

The division of views in the K.K.E. was unknown to us at the
time. But given that there was such a division, it is not surprising
that we should find ourselves more in sympathy with Tzimas
and Aris than with Siantos and other members of the Central

Committee. For our orders were to make preparations for military operations on a nationwide scale; and by the spring of 1943 E.A.M. had forcibly created a situation in which the military requirement could not be fulfilled without E.L.A.S. It was therefore necessary to devise a way of harnessing E.L.A.S. to the allied effort without yielding entirely to the K.K.E.'s ambition to secure complete control of the resistance, and hence of Greece after the war. The method devised was to establish a network of independent 'National Bands' throughout the country; to lay down ground rules for their co-operation; to link them through British Liaison Officers; and to insist that E.L.A.S. should conform to the pattern as the price of obtaining supplies. In essence, it was the scheme suggested to Myers by Saraphis in February; but early in March Saraphis's embryonic force was dispersed and he himself captured by E.L.A.S. The first draft of the National Bands Agreement, prepared by Myers and myself on 14 March, was therefore intended incidentally also to help in securing the release and re-instatement of Saraphis.

Its ten brief clauses were thus summarised by Myers:

> ...its signatories merely bound themselves to allow all bands, to whatever organisation they belonged, to exist unmolested by them, and to be free to carry out operations against the enemy, in accordance with instructions from the Middle East Command, through me or any of my officers. In return they would be supplied with arms, ammunition and other essentials by the Allies, so far as was within their means.[7]

There was no doubt in our minds that the agreement would be acceptable to Zervas, who in fact signed it at once, as well as to any other nationalist officers who were allowed to survive: for example, Psaros (E.K.K.A.). But it would be much more difficult to make it acceptable to E.A.M. Although each successive member of the hierarchy of E.L.A.S. who saw the text said that he personally found it acceptable, each had to refer it to higher authority, which meant ultimately the Central Committee in Athens. The difficulty was aggravated by an unexpected event early in April. Saraphis was released by E.L.A.S. and immediately invited to become its Commander-in-Chief. He informed Myers, who had hastened to rescue him from his presumed peril, that he intended to accept provided that the

Central Committee of E.A.M. and his own associates in Athens were agreed. Consequently he was no longer interested in his own scheme for National Bands. Psaros, on the other hand, rejected Saraphis's suggestion that he should follow the same course, and his force was eventually reconstituted.

III

With Saraphis's adherence to E.L.A.S. began the long and tortuous negotiations which ended in the signature of a much modified form of the National Bands Agreement, more correctly renamed the Military Agreement because E.A.M. objected to the term 'National Bands'. The agreement was signed by E.A.M. and E.L.A.S. on 5 July, though they had already agreed to respect it as if it had been signed some weeks earlier. Zervas signed it a few days later, with some reluctance in view of the changes in the draft; and Psaros on 21 July. The most important changes, for which E.A.M. struggled tenaciously and in the end successfully, were essentially two: that there should be a Joint General Headquarters, responsible directly to the Commander-in-Chief, Middle East, in Cairo; and that the function of the British Liaison Officers should be limited to liaison, without any power of issuing orders. The Communists correctly saw that the British intentions for the guerrilla movement had been quite different from their own. Tzimas later put the point, with some exaggeration, like this: '[Our British allies] did not want the development of a mass patriotic movement in Greece in any circumstances...They wanted to limit the guerrilla movement to a few hundred men in the whole country, who would be under the guidance of Greek officers whom they could rely on, if not of British officers.'[8] Saraphis described the disagreement in substantially similar terms. On this fundamental point a struggle of attrition took place between the British Military Mission (B.M.M.) and the E.A.M. leaders: was the resistance to consist of small, basically British-controlled guerrilla bands, or of a large, E.A.M.-controlled popular army?

The Greek Communists had a number of assets in this struggle. One was that they were probably less dependent on us for supplies than we thought at the time. It has even been stated, on good authority, that in June 1943 E.L.A.S. acquired 'the greater part of the light arms which the Greek Army had avoided handing over to the Germans and Italians, and hidden in the countryside'.[9] Another major asset was the adherence of Saraphis to E.L.A.S. His conversion was probably genuine and not, as we thought at the time, due to coercion; and his own account of it, corroborated on many points by Tzimas, is on the whole convincing.[10] His motives were partly patriotic, for he did not wish to see the resistance controlled by foreigners, however friendly; and partly egoistic, because he wanted to resurrect his ruined military career by becoming Commander-in-Chief of a regular army, not (as he saw Zervas) as a mercenary brigand-leader. He therefore helped enthusiastically not only in strengthening E.L.A.S. but also in supporting Tzimas in the negotiations with Myers.

A third major asset for E.A.M. was the increased need on our side for planned military operations. By the early summer it had become unlikely that the Allies would attempt an opposed landing in Greece, and on 30 May Myers was informed that the next target after North Africa would be Sicily. Operations in Greece would be needed mainly to distract the enemy's attention from the real target and to create the impression that the target would be the southern Balkans. Myers drew up the plan of what was called Operation *Animals*, the details of which need not concern us now. It is sufficient to record that Operation *Animals* was launched throughout Greece on 21 June and lasted until 14 July, when the landings in Sicily had been successfully lodged. The deception plan to which Operation *Animals* made a small contribution was successful, as appears from the German records.

An appreciation by a German staff officer in Greece, dated 19 June, concluded that: 'The guerrillas are preparing for the expected landing by the allies. The strong concentration of guerrilla bands in the area Arta–Pindus indicates that it is at this point that the springboard for the support of the landing operation must be looked for.'[11] A further German appreciation dated 3 July summarised indications which 'make it possible that a landing operation by the allies is imminent on the west coast of Greece with the support of the guerrillas'.[12] Even after the landings in Sicily, the Germans continued to expect landings in Greece. Hitler's War Directive No. 48 of 26 July is particularly revealing. It stated that:

> The enemy's measures in the Eastern Mediterranean in conjunction with the attack on Sicily, indicate that he will shortly begin landing operations against our strong line in the Aegean, Peloponnese–Crete–Rhodes, and against the west coast of Greece with the offshore Ionian islands. Should the operations of the enemy extend from Sicily to the mainland of Southern Italy, we must also reckon with an assault on the east coast of the Adriatic, north of the straits of Otranto. The enemy's conduct of operations is also based on the bandit movement, which is increasingly organised by him in the interior of the South-east area.[13]

The same directive added that the most important task for the German Commander-in-Chief in south-east Europe was 'to make defensive preparations for the coast of Greece, on the islands and the mainland'; and that 'an essential preliminary is to destroy the bandit gangs in Greece, Serbia and Croatia, and thus open up the supply lines, in particular the main railway lines, to ensure to our forces the necessary freedom of movement in rear areas.'

Hitler's sensitiveness about the railway line can be explained by the fact that it had twice been dislocated during the last eight months by major demolitions for periods totalling at least three months in all. But his reactions were grossly exaggerated in relation to the real threat. He sent Rommel to reorganise the defences of Greece and then recalled him a few weeks later when Mussolini fell. He also proposed to move six divisions from the eastern front to reinforce the protection of the Belgrade–Larisa railway line. It seems that this force never materialised; nor have I seen any evidence to support Churchill's claim that two German divisions were diverted to Greece from Sicily.[14] The *Official History* states, however, that the German strength in the Balkans as a whole was increased from eight to about sixteen divisions between May and August 1943, due to the deception Operation *Mincemeat*.[15] It is self-evident that the activities of the guerrillas must have contributed to the credibility of that deception.

Although, as F. W. D. Deakin has shown in Chapter 4, there

never was a plan for a Balkan invasion, the Germans' fear that there might be persisted through the following year. It seemed the only logical explanation of the Allies' continued support of the resistance movements. According to Hermann Neubacher, the German Foreign Office's special plenipotentiary in south-east Europe, he assumed in 1944 that the reason why the British continued to support Zervas in Epirus and Abas Kupi in Albania, and even to tolerate their recent inactivity, was the importance of being in a position to control the straits of Otranto.[16] The scale of counter-guerrilla operations is also significant: between October 1943 and August 1944, apart from purely punitive reprisals, nine operations serious enough to warrant codenames were launched, all in northern Greece.[17]

Except for the last case (in August 1944), all these operations took place at a time when the guerrillas were under instruction not to undertake offensive operations, so that they were in a sense gratuitous. They were mainly directed against E.L.A.S., because the Communists ignored the instruction of General Headquarters Middle East to refrain from offensive operations; whereas Zervas took advantage of it to make a temporary un-authorised truce with the enemy.[18] But in spite of what the Germans called Zervas's 'loyal attitude', the pattern of destruc-tion of villages in these and other operations throughout the Occupation shows the heaviest concentration in Zervas's terri-tory – that is to say in the coastal region of Epirus, northwards from Preveza where landings from Italy would presumably be attempted.[19] As late as September 1944 Hitler's war directives show that the fear of Allied landings in the Balkans still per-sisted; and this seems to have been the reason for continuing to hold Crete even after that date.[20]

The strategic consequences of the deception plan to which Operation *Animals* contributed could not, of course, be foreseen in the middle of 1943, but they tend to validate the judgement of the military planners that such operations were required. This requirement was itself an asset to the E.A.M. negotiators in their arguments with Myers. On the other hand, there were also constraints limiting their freedom to negotiate success-fully. Chief among them was the fact that the Communist leadership was itself divided on the question whether to co-operate with the British at all. They were perhaps as much beset by divided counsels as the British authorities were, though neither side knew it of the other. The British were in the dark about two constraining factors on E.A.M. One was the extent and depth of the K.K.E.'s anxiety to acquire respectability by gaining recognition for E.L.A.S. as an allied force approved by General Headquarters Middle East. The other was the pressure on E.L.A.S. by the Yugoslav Partisans to co-ordinate its policy with them.

In connection with the second point, it should be noted that the pressure came entirely from the Yugoslavs, not from the Bulgarians. The two Slavonic Communist Parties were already at cross purposes, and Macedonia was a bone of contention between them. But the Bulgarians played no significant role at this date in relation to the K.K.E. The only genuine trace of contact between them is perhaps that in May 1943 guerrillas were seen by Hammond in Greek Macedonia wearing the symbol of the Bulgarian-sponsored I.M.R.O. (Internal Macedonian Revolutionary Organisation) on their sleeves. On the other hand, the story that a secret agreement to establish a Balkan Federation, including a united autonomous Macedonia, was signed by Ioannidis with the Bulgarians, at Petrich on 12 July 1943, is a complete fabrication.[21] The K.K.E. had no reason to be beholden to them.

IV

On the first point – E.L.A.S.'s need for recognition – it had already been noticed that the leaders were constantly pressing the B.M.M. for publicity for their operations. It was alleged that Zervas's forces were often publicised by name, but never E.L.A.S.; and even that the Gorgopotamos operation had been ascribed to Zervas by the B.B.C. without mentioning Aris or E.L.A.S., though of this no evidence has ever been forthcoming.[22] Saraphis regularly pressed Myers for some statement of approval from General Wilson, the Commander-in-Chief in Cairo, and finally obtained it on 22 June.[23] He and Tzimas were acutely conscious of the bitter hostility felt towards E.L.A.S. by a large segment of Greek public opinion, which they judged it imperative to remedy. The extent to which they were under pressure from their own Central Committee only became apparent long afterwards, when Tzimas wrote that:

...our people in Athens were demanding that I sign the Agreement as soon as possible because we needed it. Signature was very necessary politically in the cities, to neutralise the campaign of reactionary bourgeois circles and collaborators, to the effect that we were contributing no military service worth mentioning to the allies by the guerrilla movement, only inflicting on the population the torments and reprisals of the occupation.[24]

In particular, it was only by gaining the respectability of British recognition that E.L.A.S. could hope to attract the large number of officers whom Saraphis needed in order to turn the guerrilla bands into a regular army. This advantage on our side was perhaps not as fully exploited as it might have been.

The other principal constraint on the E.A.M. negotiators was the pressure of the Yugoslav Partisans, to which Tzimas was particularly sensitive, being the only major leader of the K.K.E. who was fluent in Serbo-Croat and Macedonian, and who felt a close sympathy with Tito. It is not certain when the first contacts between the K.K.E. and the Partisans were formed, though it should not be forgotten that when Tito returned to Yugoslavia in 1940 he passed through Salonika. Early in 1943 he appointed the Montenegrin Svetozar Vukmanović (Tempo) to take command of the Partisans in Macedonia, a region which the Yugoslavs did not regard as terminating at the Greek frontier. Whatever the steps by which links were established between the Greek and Yugoslav Communist Parties, it is certain that they first emerged into the open at a conference held at the end of June 1943 at Tsotyli in Greek Macedonia. This important occasion was attended by Tempo, Tzimas, Myers, and a representative of the Albanian Partisans, but not apparently by any Bulgarian. It was followed a week later by a similar gathering at Kastania in Thessaly, which was attended additionally by Saraphis and Aris Veloukhiotis. Apparently Siantos was also in the neighbourhood at the time, though he did not reveal himself to Myers, whose reports were based on the statements made by Tempo and Tzimas. These reports contained what must have been among the earliest clear indications that the Yugoslav Partisans had no intention of being submissive dependents of the Soviet Union after the war. Myers's conclusion was to detect among them, as well as in E.A.M., a 'determination to set up independent regimes [at] end of war unfettered to or by any (repeat any) major power'.[25]

During these conferences, though only in private session, a proposal was advanced by Tempo that a Balkan General Headquarters should be formed of the Communist-led guerrilla forces. It was rejected by E.L.A.S. on the grounds that they had already agreed in principle to place themselves under the command of General Headquarters Middle East. The military agreement was in fact about to be signed, and Operation *Animals*, covering the imminent invasion of Sicily, was already under way. The argument of the Greek leaders profoundly shocked Tempo, who later wrote a severe criticism of their policy; but it should not have entirely surprised him, because it is clear in retrospect (as was perhaps suspected at the time by the K.K.E.) that Tempo's ulterior object was to create conditions favourable to the eventual absorption of Greek Macedonia within the Yugoslav Federation.[26] His only success was to persuade the K.K.E. to allow the Slavophones, who had their own National Liberation Front (S.N.O.F.), to form separate units within E.L.A.S. – a concession which the Greeks later bitterly regretted.

On the other hand, the British had reason to believe at this stage that their tactics were succeeding. The rebuff by E.L.A.S. of Tempo's proposal of a Balkan General Headquarters was as welcome to them as it was infuriating to Tempo. One account of Myers's reception of the news ends with the remark that 'as a good Oxonian' he appreciated to the full 'the flavour of the Communist dialectic'.[27] It seems that Tzimas himself favoured the idea of a Balkan General Headquarters, but as it was irreconcilable with that of placing E.L.A.S. under the command of General Headquarters Middle East, Siantos and Ioannidis overruled him. This was perhaps just as well for Tempo, since later in the year both Tito and Stalin expressed disapproval of his scheme; but the post-war denunciations of the K.K.E.'s policy by both Zakhariadis and Tempo suggest that the British policy was on the right lines and had achieved a substantial success.[28] There is no evidence however that any serious attention was paid either in Cairo or in London to Myers's reports on the conferences at Tsotyli and Kastania.

V

It remains to say a word about the impact of personalities on the issues at stake. Here too E.A.M. gained a psychological advantage through the emergence into the field of Andreas Tzimas (known as Evmaios or Vasilis Samariniotis), who stood out above all the rest. Aris Veloukhiotis was a brilliant but unpredictable maverick; Saraphis was a capable staff officer without independent initiative; Zervas was handicapped by the general assumption that he would accept anything the British demanded. Tzimas, by contrast, seemed to be a man in equal measure intelligent, flexible and reliable. One could make agreements with him which would be respected, at least until circumstances drastically altered. He alone seemed to have a thoroughly Western mentality.

He had his faults, of course. He was capable of cheating, though he did so with an engagingly ironic smile. He made errors of judgement, like Saraphis, though for different reasons. Both men assumed that they could manipulate Myers: Saraphis because Myers was, like himself, in the full sense a regular officer, which put both of them in a superior category to Zervas or myself; and Tzimas, oddly enough, because he discovered that Myers was a Jew, which put him, like Tzimas (who was a Slavophone), in the category of an oppressed minority. Despite such misconceptions, Tzimas had a strong and persuasive personality which certainly played a part in the negotiations. He was the only leading Greek Communist with whom it was an intellectual pleasure to argue. I see him as something like a Milovan Djilas with a sense of humour. But it is admittedly difficult to be objective in judging a man who has saved one from the Gestapo.[29]

Tzimas's superior in the party, Georgios Siantos, on the other hand, was a dim figure in the background during the months of negotiation. I had met him in Athens in February 1943, but Myers and he did not come face to face until early August. Undoubtedly he exercised a deadening influence on Tzimas from behind. Writing in 1967, Tzimas implied that they were not on good terms. It is interesting that Tzimas describes as 'the greatest mistake of the period' the failure to get sufficient officers for E.L.A.S. out of Athens in time, for this was precisely the mistake for which Zakhariadis blamed Siantos in the aftermath of the 'third round' (1946–9).[30] Tzimas was evidently handicapped by Siantos's lack of confidence in the mountains as an arena of action. Equally clearly Tzimas gained prestige by his apparent ability to manage the British; but there was anxiety lest he should carry co-operation too far. When relations turned sour later in 1943, Tzimas rapidly lost credit and was entirely superseded by Siantos. Later still Siantos himself was discredited by the failure of the co-operative policy which he had allowed Tzimas to pursue. He was bluntly described by Zakhariadis and other leading Communists as a traitor and a 'British spy'.[31]

Zakhariadis, who resumed the post of Secretary General of the K.K.E. when he returned from a German concentration camp at the end of the war, wrote in 1950 that during the occupation the K.K.E. failed to give correct guidance to E.A.M., and consequently E.L.A.S. was in effect subordinated to British policy. He continued: 'The leadership of the K.K.E. in reality understood the common allied struggle against Hitlerite Fascism in terms of unreserved support not for the common allied cause but for British policy and British imperialist aims in the Mediterranean and South-east Europe.'[32] He listed five major blunders made by the K.K.E. under the occupation, one of which (the earliest chronologically) was 'the subordination of E.L.A.S. to G.H.Q., Middle East'. He went on to denounce many others as traitors, including Tito, Siantos, and Aris Veloukhiotis, though curiously enough he did not name either Tzimas or Saraphis.

Although Tempo naturally could not agree with Zakhariadis's denunciation of Tito, he endorsed the substance of these criticisms of the K.K.E. He wrote in 1949 that E.L.A.S. had 'constituted an auxiliary army of the Anglo-American allies', and that the military agreement with the British Military Mission in 1943 had only helped the British and 'Zervas's Quisling forces'.[33] The wider theme of his criticism was that the K.K.E. was not truly a Communist party at all but no better than a bunch of Social Democrats.[34] He was indignant over their refusal to conform with the policies of the Yugoslav Partisans in the summer of 1943. The conclusion seems to be that British policy had gained a greater success than was appreciated at the time. In addition to the military success of Operation *Animals*, a new political situation had emerged. These were not spectacular results in comparison with Yugoslavia, but I mention them because both the military and the political results were more substantial than we originally supposed.

VI

It can be argued that the co-operativeness of E.A.M. was purely superficial, temporary and opportunistic. This may have been true, but it did not necessarily follow that the co-operation was unreal, because E.L.A.S. itself had reasons for seeking to continue and sustain it. Between March and July, E.A.M. had achieved a good deal of what it wanted, but not everything. It had established E.L.A.S. as a conventionally organised army, no longer a loose collection of guerrilla bands; and it had obtained recognition as an allied force under the nominal command of General Wilson in Cairo. It gave much prominence to General Wilson's telegrams of recognition and congratulation on 22 June and 18 July.[35] It had obtained a right to an allowance of two sovereigns a month *per caput* (one for each guerrilla and one for his family), apparently with no specific ceiling on recruitment. It had achieved the creation of a Joint General Headquarters with an E.L.A.S. component equal to the rest combined, and it had eliminated the British Liaison Officers from any formal right to exercise command or give orders; though in practice both these changes were less substantial than they might have appeared. On the other hand, E.A.M.'s plans had gone awry in at least two important respects. First, they had failed to eliminate all their nationalist rivals, particularly Zervas and Psaros; and the establishment of a Joint General Headquarters was itself an acknowledgement of that failure. Secondly, they were embarked on a very different course from their comrades in Yugoslavia, who were a year ahead of them in development and owed nothing to the British.

The chief characteristics of the situation in July 1943 were therefore as follows. There was an uneasy equilibrium between the rival guerrilla forces in Greece; there was a better relation than there had hitherto been between E.L.A.S. and the British; there was a puzzled coolness between E.L.A.S. and the

Yugoslav Partisans; and there was still strong feeling against the British among the Partisan leaders. Within a few weeks all these relationships were drastically changed. The arrival in Yugoslavia of Deakin at the end of May, followed by Fitzroy Maclean in September, led to a reversal of policy towards the Partisans. The visit of Myers and a delegation from the Greek Resistance to Cairo in August led to a sharp quarrel between the Greek and British authorities on the one hand, and the Greek Resistance (not confined to the Communists) on the other. Only the second of these events is properly the subject of this paper, though it deserves a passing comment that no one seems to have given much thought to the implications of the conjunction of events in Yugoslavia and Greece. For my part, I can only say that I never even knew of the existence of Deakin or Maclean until a year later.

VII

So far as Greece was concerned, the changes set in with the completion of Operation *Animals* on 14 July. From that moment the balance of military and political considerations in British policy-making began to be reversed. Political pressures had of course never been absent even when they were taking second place. The importunities of King George II of the Hellenes over his right to be restored to his throne, if necessary by British arms, were regularly transmitted through the Foreign Office, and they affected the directives sent to the field. But it was only in March 1943 that the Foreign Office became aware of the political significance of what was happening in Greece under the authority of S.O.E. When they did so, they complained angrily about having been kept in the dark.

Two kinds of complaint need to be distinguished. One was that the Foreign Office had been neither consulted nor informed by S.O.E. about the original infiltration of Myers's party (Operation *Harling*) in September 1942, nor about the change in its mission in January 1943. This was true, though, as I have already shown, the Foreign Office had been informed by the Minister of State in Cairo that there was a British party in Greece in mid-November, before the attack on the Gorgopotamos bridge took place.[36] The other complaint was that S.O.E. withheld from the Foreign Office important material of a political character reported from the field. This complaint was strongly made in March 1943, and repeated in August, particularly by Reginald Leeper, the ambassador to the Greek government in Cairo. The extent to which it was valid can be judged from the dates and the circumstances.

No substantial reports of any kind could be made from the field before January 1943, because wireless communication was extremely imperfect and Myers's party was constantly on the move. Myers had adequate wireless contact for the first time only in the first week of January. Even then, for operational reasons, contact had to be brief and telegrams very succinct. The first reports of any substance were naturally concerned retrospectively with the Gorgopotamos operation. The first situation report of any political significance was sent on 13 January. It was received and deciphered in Cairo on 20 January and subsequent days, and relayed to S.O.E. in London on 24 January.[37] There followed an exchange of questions and answers between Cairo and Myers to clarify certain points. This was protracted by circumstances which S.O.E. never explained to the Foreign Office, such as Myers's serious illness, a running battle with the Italians, and much other operational traffic. During the process, new material came to hand in February, including particularly the first reports from Rufus Sheppard in Thessaly and from me on my visit to Athens. These confused the picture, because although my report bore out those of Myers, Sheppard's reports presented a very different and much more sympathetic view of E.A.M. and E.L.A.S.

In the event, a consolidated appreciation, drawing on all this material, was submitted to the Foreign Office early in March, under the title, *Political Aspects of the Greek Resistance Movement*.[38] It was followed a few days later by a paper on E.A.M., dated 12 March. The compilers of the two reports had made somewhat half-hearted attempts to reconcile the rival views, which was really impossible. But at least they were reasonably up to date and scarcely suggested any deliberate procrastination. The earliest material embodied in them was less than eight weeks old, and the most recent was less than two weeks. It was believed in the Foreign Office however that they would never have got the information at all from S.O.E. if they had not peremptorily and persistently demanded it.

Pierson Dixon, the first Foreign Office official who studied the first S.O.E. report on *Political Aspects*, found it 'quite interesting'; but he also found it difficult to keep his temper when reading it. Apart from the delay in receiving it, there were two other reasons. The first was that it showed Zervas to be an adherent of Plastiras, a revolutionary republican general then living in France, whom S.O.E. had already urged the Foreign Office, against its will, to 'build up'. The second reason, not unrelated to the first, was that all the reports on which the S.O.E. appreciation was based showed hostility to the King. Dixon minuted:

> ...it is intolerable that Colonel Myers, who is specifically stated to have no special knowledge of Greek politics, should have been entering into negotiations destined to bring the various groups together on the basis of a political programme apparently of his own devising. The salient feature of this programme is the holding of a plebiscite at the end of the war. Here then we have the genesis of the plebiscite idea which has been launched at us by S.O.E. and the Minister of State's Office as the sovereign remedy for the internal Greek situation.

Just over two weeks later, in a letter signed by Dixon, the Foreign Office put a series of questions to S.O.E. in London: was Myers the first British officer to be sent into Greece on a sabotage mission; what instructions had he been given on his dealings with the guerrilla leaders; where were the other British officers in Greece; and under whose overall command did they come?[39] There followed a protracted wrangle, in which S.O.E. displayed a good deal of obstinacy, before the questions were answered.

The upshot was a strenuous effort by the Foreign Office to regain control of policy towards the Greek Resistance. Their difficulties were compounded by the need to consult the Chiefs of Staff and the Commanders-in-Chief in Cairo, who tended (particularly General Wilson) to support Myers and to favour good relations with E.L.A.S. for operational reasons. On 18 March the Chiefs of Staff in London telegraphed to the Middle East Defence Committee that 'Agreement on policy has now been reached with S.O.E.'[40] But in fact the dispute was still

going on several weeks later. The Chiefs of Staff directive to
S.O.E. for 1943, dated 23 March, contained the following sentence:[41] 'Besides close contact with Commander-in-Chief
Middle East, S.O.E. should also be closely guided by the
Foreign Office in view of the dangers of entanglement with
opposing political groups and risk of action contrary to the
policy of H.M.G. and of conflict with the Soviet Union.' The
Joint Operational Staff of the Commanders-in-Chief in Cairo
reacted critically to these words, on which they commented in
April: 'While we appreciate that S.O.E. must have political
guidance and cannot be allowed to do anything which conflicts with H.M.G.'s policy in any particular country, we feel
that operational rather than political considerations are at present paramount and that our primary aim should be to organise
the maximum resistance to the Axis.' They also invoked in their
support for this argument a recent directive from the Prime
Minister himself, dated 18 April, in which the crucial sentence
read:

> In view of operational importance attached to subversive
> activities in Greece, there can be no question of S.O.E.
> refusing to have dealings with a given group merely on the
> grounds that political sentiments of the group are opposed to
> the King and Government, but subject to special operational
> necessity S.O.E. should always veer in the direction of groups
> willing to support the King and the Government and further-
> more impress on such other groups as may be anti-monarchi-
> cal the fact that the King and Government enjoy the fullest
> support of H.M.G.

The dispute can thus be seen to be one between short-term
considerations, mainly military, and long-term considerations,
mainly political, both of which were valid. Inevitably it was
also a dispute between the Foreign Office and the staff of the
Commander-in-Chief, which it was left to S.O.E. to reconcile in
practice. This was the more difficult because in effect Churchill
supported both sides. He wanted the maximum military effort
against the Germans, and had instructed the first Minister responsible for S.O.E. to 'set Europe ablaze'; but he was also
determined to retain British influence in Greece and to restore
King George to his throne.[42]

The final form of the first politico-military directive to Myers, which he received in the last week of April, was a compromise.[43] It said that the King's position must be maintained, but that all forces prepared to fight the Axis must be supported. It added, rather desperately, that in the circumstances civil war after the liberation of Greece was almost inevitable. This was a view that S.O.E. had already expressed as early as September 1942, even before putting Myers's mission into Greece. On both occasions the Foreign Office had taken a less pessimistic view, relying chiefly on British arms and prestige.[44] Myers's response was also less pessimistic than that of S.O.E., but on different grounds. He argued that if the King could be persuaded to state publicly that he would not return to Greece until a plebiscite had been held, civil war would not be inevitable because 'the bottom could be knocked out of E.A.M.'s basket of propaganda.'[45]

The Foreign Office reacted adversely to any suggestion that the King's status should be put in question, and also doubted the value of the resistance anyway. Sir Orme Sargent, who succeeded Cadogan as Permanent Under-Secretary of the Foreign Office, suggested early in 1944 that the activities of the guerrillas were a figment of S.O.E.'s imagination.[46] Although such an extreme view was not yet held in the summer of 1943, Dixon minuted on 21 June that 'There has never been any doubt that our long-term political interests would be better served by an inactive sabotage policy.'[47] Despite such reservations, express approval was given by the Foreign Office for the signature of the military agreement with E.L.A.S., and by Eden personally for the launching of Operation *Animals*.[48] But in both cases agreement was given only reluctantly, with an implication that the Foreign Office had been edged unwittingly into a position where it was impossible to take any other decision.

This was no doubt among the reasons why Eden decided to send into Greece a Foreign Office emissary, Major David Wallace, to report personally to him on the situation in the mountains. Wallace arrived at the end of June, but first met Myers only in mid-July. It is worth noting that during the same weeks in which he was forming his impressions of the Greek Resistance, which were decidedly unfavourable to E.L.A.S., Deakin was simultaneously forming his impressions of the Yugoslav Resistance, which were decidedly favourable to the Partisans. This coincidence helped to widen the gap between the policies adopted in the two countries. In both cases S.O.E. was held severely to blame for having misreported or concealed the facts, though in an opposite sense in each case.

VIII

The mutual distrust between the Foreign Office and S.O.E. came to a climax in August 1943, when Myers took advantage of the lull in operations after the landings in Sicily to propose a temporary visit to Cairo by himself, Wallace, and three representatives of the resistance (one each from E.L.A.S., E.D.E.S. and E.K.K.A., the three signatories of the military agreement). The episode of the resistance delegation to Cairo, and its conduct and treatment there during the five weeks between its departure on 9 August and its return on 16 September, is a complex story which I do not intend to examine in detail (see Chapter 6). I shall comment only on a few points of fact, and in particular on the three features of the resistance delegation which caused consternation. These were its size, its political character, and the lack of adequate forewarning. In all three cases S.O.E. was held to blame, particularly by Reginald Leeper, British ambassador to the Greek government-in-exile.

The unexpected size of the delegation was due to a manoeuvre by the K.K.E. It had been suggested to me in Athens in January that an emissary from E.A.M. should go to Cairo, but the arrangements were not made until a landing-ground was constructed in Thessaly in July. Then Myers invited Tzimas to accompany him, with the approval of S.O.E., and soon afterwards, as a natural corollary, Komninos Pyromaglou of E.D.E.S. and Georgios Kartalis of E.K.K.A. were added to the party. On 8 August, the eve of departure, Siantos arrived at the landing-ground with three other members of E.A.M. who, he insisted, must go too. These were K. Despotopoulos, Petros Roussos, and Ilias Tsirimokos, of whom the first two were Communists and the third was not. Siantos claimed to have received a telegram in Athens, through Cairo, from Myers's own headquarters – that is, from myself as Myers's deputy – to the effect that 'there would be room in the aeroplane for as many representatives as the Central Committee chose to send.'[49] He produced the telegram in Greek, which Myers found (when it was translated into English) could conceivably be taken to mean what Siantos claimed. Myers very reluctantly gave way, since otherwise Siantos would not allow even Tzimas to go. The delegation therefore included four representatives of E.A.M., E.L.A.S. and the K.K.E. instead of one. Even Leeper conceded, 'It is clear that Myers could not have refused, even if he had wished, to bring these Greeks with him without causing suspicion and ill-will, and although it came as a surprise to me, it was obviously the right thing for him to have done.'[50]

As the original English text of the telegram used by Siantos has survived, it is worth quoting in full:

> Following from Evmaios to Central EAM from Chris. Means visiting Cairo assured. Imperative EAM representatives arrive KARDITSA repeat KARDITSA soonest. If possible send runner to me with instructions. My journey Cairo will take place. Ends. Please send above EAM their morning sked 25 without repeat without fail. Ends.[51]

My interpretation of this text would be not only that it did not support Siantos's claim, but also that Tzimas himself, in sending it through my wireless link, had been assuming that he would go to Cairo alone to represent E.A.M., and wanted the others to come up to the mountains only to brief him. If my interpretation is correct, it implies that Siantos did not trust Tzimas to represent the party line on his own, because he had shown himself too co-operative with the British. Siantos therefore insisted that Tzimas should be accompanied by three other representatives, including two more members of the K.K.E.

This interpretation has a bearing on the second cause of consternation in Cairo, which was the political character of the delegation. The six Greeks included three Communists (Tzimas, Despotopoulos and Petros Roussos) and three republicans who were not Communists (Kartalis of E.K.K.A., Pyromaglou of E.D.E.S., and Tsirimokos of E.A.M.). What caused consternation was that all of them proved to be men of political substance, not simply respectful *kapetanioi* as had been expected; and still worse, they were unanimous in calling for a drastic clarification of the King's position. Another fact about them was so surprising that at the time it was not recognised at all. This was that the non-Communist republicans (Kartalis, Pyromaglou and Tsirimokos) were more insistent than the Communists that the King must not return to Greece without a plebiscite. Earlier accounts, particularly those by Leeper and myself, assumed that it was Tzimas who took the lead in demanding such a declaration from the King, but Pyromaglou explicitly corrects this error, attributing the leading role to Kartalis and himself, and stating that the Communists were relatively more willing to compromise.[52] The reason why the non-Communist republicans were more uncompromising on this point than the Communists was presumably the same as that suggested by Myers in April: that to foreclose the constitutional question would remove the main prop from the Communists' propaganda. But the King, supported by Churchill, Smuts and Roosevelt, refused to give way. He had lately given an undertaking, on 4 July, that within six months after the liberation free elections would be held for a constituent assembly. He refused to go further, even though his own government supported the *démarche* of the resistance delegation.

The question why all this came as such a shock leads to the third complaint of the Foreign Office against S.O.E.: the lack of adequate forewarning. Here the crucial point concerns Wallace's reports from the field, which had not yet been received by the Foreign Office or by Leeper in Cairo even when Wallace arrived back with Myers and the resistance delegation. Leeper was convinced that S.O.E. had deliberately withheld Wallace's telegrams: he was still asserting this to me personally a year later. Examination of the file of Wallace's telegrams preserved in the Foreign Office shows that the differences between the dates of despatch and receipt vary from six to sixteen days, the longest delays being at the beginning of the series.[53] The dates of despatch (meaning encipherment in the mountains) range from 23 July to 8 August; the dates of receipt (meaning, presumably, decipherment in Cairo) from 3 August to 10 August. Two or three of the earliest in the series were in the hands of the Foreign Office by 10 August, but the bulk of them seem not to have reached London until the end of the month. None of them, according to Leeper, reached his hands in Cairo until 22 August. As a minute in the Foreign Office remarked on 31 August, 'it is incredible that SOE Cairo should not have passed all these tels on to Mr Leeper'; but it was true. The only question is whether the delay was deliberate. It seems to me clear that in fact it was due rather to gross inefficiency and muddle. Conceivably someone in S.O.E. thought that as Wallace was already back in Cairo to speak for himself by 10 August, his telegrams from the mountains no longer mattered. Such stupidity is less improbable than bad faith. The telegrams could not have been deliberately delayed before decipherment, because at that stage there was no way of knowing which were from Wallace. To hold them up after decipherment would have been a wanton folly which could not have escaped detection. Moreover, it would have been pointless, because Wallace's telegrams said nothing new.

This is the most important point about them. Myers recorded that he saw them all in advance: 'They were accurate and on the whole I fully agreed with the views he expressed.'[54] In substance they said nothing that had not been said by Myers or myself during the previous six months. This was especially so on two matters: the true character of E.A.M., and the need to clarify the King's position. Eden and Leeper were both impressed by Wallace's reports, particularly over the King, though Churchill remained adamant in supporting the King. But while Wallace's reports were welcomed as cogent and well-balanced, Myers, who had been reporting in the same sense ever since January, was not regarded as vindicated. The accusation that he had virtually invented the campaign for a plebiscite on the monarchy was never withdrawn. More serious still, the Foreign Office continued to believe that he held views on E.A.M. which were totally different from those which he had actually expressed. It was mainly for these reasons, coupled with the personal antipathy of the King and Leeper, that Myers was not allowed to return to Greece. The decision was nevertheless not taken easily: it was opposed by General Wilson and even by some members of the Foreign Office, and it was not finally notified to me until mid-November.[55]

Meanwhile the six Greeks were sent back with nothing accomplished, and in high dudgeon, on 16 September. Civil war followed within a month – the 'first round' of the armed struggle, of which the second was the rising in Athens in December 1944 and the third was the renewal of guerrilla war in the mountains from 1946 to 1949. An agonising reappraisal of British policy took place in London. The two most significant results of it were that even more stringent measures were taken to bring S.O.E. under control, and that the official attitude towards E.A.M. and E.L.A.S. reverted to one of extreme hostility. But the hostility was not universally shared. Many senior officers, including General Wilson, and some even in the Foreign Office, including Eden, doubted whether it would be right to make a final break with E.A.M. and E.L.A.S. for the sake of salvaging the King of the Hellenes.

IX

The confused wrangle over the resistance delegation in August and September 1943 still needs deeper examination than I can give it. I shall not pursue the story further, though I must express sympathy with Leeper's lament to Sargent: 'I have never, as you know, been happy at the way His Majesty's Government have found themselves pursuing one policy in Greece and another policy in Cairo.'[56] He might well have added: 'and two more in London'. I find it impossible to fix the responsibility for these undoubted contradictions, though some of the blame must certainly be attributed, in the broad sense, to failures of communication, both physical and personal. For these failures S.O.E. cannot be held guiltless. While the Foreign Office was touchy and short-sighted, S.O.E. was arrogant and secretive to an excessive degree. S.O.E. had also the faults as well as the merits of its amateur status. Its administration in Cairo was not equal to emergencies, and its judgement was often unwise. For example, it created unnecessary difficulties for itself by trying to establish independent missions in Greece early in 1943 without consulting Myers, and above all by choosing for the first such mission a rather naive officer who knew little Greek. But there were some handicaps which seemingly could not be overcome in any case. The most noteworthy was that the Foreign Office would only believe what it was told when the source was one of its own; and it was unwilling to accept any advice that did not fit in with its own preconceptions. Eden, however, was much better in this respect than any of his officials.

I do not think it can be disputed that the episode of the resistance delegation made civil war certain. I cannot say that civil war would not have come in any case, however. I do not see how it could ultimately have been avoided except either by conceding victory to the K.K.E. without a struggle, or by changing the revolutionary character of Greek Communism. The preference of many Greeks and most of the Foreign Office, that no British mission should ever have gone into Greece at all during the occupation, would only have been another way of conceding victory to the K.K.E. without a struggle. It is just possible that the alternative of changing the revolutionary character of Greek Communism might have been achieved if the King of the Hellenes could have been induced in the spring of 1943 to make the concessions which he was ultimately forced to make at the end of 1944. I would once have argued that such a change in the character of Greek Communism was unthinkable; but I have been struck in recent years by the evidence that both Tempo and Zakhariadis feared that it had actually happened.

NOTES

1. House of Commons Debates, 5th Series (H.M.S.O., London) (24 May 1944) col. 778.

2. Andreas Tzimas, 'Pos kai pote o Stephanos Saraphis proskhorise ston ELAS', *Pyrsos*, no. 6 (1967) p. 20, col. 2; D. G. Kousoulas, *Revolution and Defeat. The Story of the Greek Communist Party* (London, 1965) pp. 153–4.

3. FO 371/33177, R 2657: Minister of State to F.O., 14 Nov 1942; and Dixon's minute and Cadogan's draft telegram, 15 Nov 1942.

4. E. C. W. Myers, *Greek Entanglement* (London, 1955) pp. 97–8, 113, 121–2, 202.

5. Tzimas in *Pyrsos*, op. cit., p. 20, col. 3.

6. Kenneth Matthews, *Memories of a Mountain War – Greece 1944–1949* (London, 1972) p. 79; cf. Svetozar Vukmanović (Tempo), *How and Why the People's Liberation Struggle of Greece met with Defeat* (London, 1950) pp. 14–16.

7. Myers, op. cit., pp. 130–1. Texts of the first and final drafts in C. M. Woodhouse, *Apple of Discord. A Survey of Greek Politics in their International Setting* (London, 1948) pp. 298–300.

8. Tzimas in *Pyrsos*, No. 1 (1967) p. 18, col. 3; cf. Stephanos Saraphis, *Greek Resistance Army* (London, 1951) p. 58.

9. Komninos Pyromaglou, *O Doureios Ippos* (Athens, 1958) p. 96.
10. Saraphis, op. cit., pp. 37–43; Tzimas, op. cit., 20–1.
11. P. K. Enepekidis, *I Elliniki Antistasis, 1941–1944* (Athens, 1964) p. 41.
12. *Ibid.*, p. 42.
13. Walter Hubatsch, *Hitlers Weisungen für die Kriegsführung, 1939–1945* (Frankfurt, 1962; English translation ed. H. R. Trevor-Roper, London, 1964) pp. 142–4.
14. Michael Howard, *Grand Strategy* (London, 1972) IV, p. 480; W. S. Churchill, *The Second World War* V (London, 1952) pp. 472–3.
15. Howard, op. cit., pp. 462, 480.
16. Hermann Neubacher, *Sonderauftrag Südost, 1940–1945* (Göttingen, 1957) pp. 146–7.
17. D. M. Condit, *Case Study in Guerrilla War: Greece during World War II* (Washington, 1961) p. 259; Hugh H. Gardner, *Guerrilla and Counterguerrilla Warfare in Greece, 1941–1945* (Washington, 1962) pp. 156–61.
18. André Kédros, *La Résistance grecque, 1940–1944* (Paris, 1966) pp. 346–9; Heinz Richter, *Griechenland zwischen Revolution und Konterrevolution* (Frankfurt, 1973) pp. 340–71; Condit, op. cit., pp. 162–4; Gardner, op. cit., pp. 143–4.
19. See map in Condit, op. cit., p. 266.
20. Hubatsch (ed. Trevor-Roper), op. cit., pp. 194–5.
21. Evangelos Kofos, *Nationalism and Communism in Macedonia* (Thessaloniki, 1964) pp. 134–5; cf. Elisabeth Barker, *Macedonia: Its Place in Balkan Power Politics* (London, 1950) pp. 87–8. Text of Petrich Agreement in Stylianos Khoutas, *I Ethniki Antistasis ton Ellinon, 1941–1945* (Athens, 1961) p. 324; Costa de Loverdo, *Les Maquis rouges des Balkans* (Paris, 1967) p. 185.
22. Richter, op. cit., p. 258; Dominique Eudes, *Les Kapetanios* (Paris, 1970; English translation, London, 1972) p. 22.
23. Saraphis, op. cit., pp. 81–2; cf. Myers, op. cit., p. 199.
24. Tzimas in *Pyrsos*, No. 6 (1967) pp. 19–20.
25. *S.O.E. Records* (private collection), Mobility to Cairo 91, 1 Jul 1943; cf. Loverdo, op. cit., p. 178; Vukmanović, op. cit., p. 14.
26. Saraphis, op. cit., p. 85; Stephen E. Palmer and Robert R. King, *Yugoslav Communism and the Macedonian Question* (Hamden, Connecticut, 1971) pp. 97–9; Eudes, op. cit., p. 70.
27. Loverdo, op. cit., p. 179. Myers was a graduate of Cambridge.
28. Palmer and King, op. cit., pp. 104–5; Nikos Zakhariadis, *Deka khronia palis* (Nicosia, 1950) pp. 9–10; Vukmanović, op. cit., pp. 31–8, 43–4.
29. On 2 February 1943, a busy day for Tzimas, on which he also arranged a meeting for me with members of the Central Committee of E.A.M., and got married. See Eudes, op. cit., pp. 45–8; Kédros, op. cit., pp. 176–9; Tzimas in *Pyrsos*, No. 6 (1967), p. 22, col. 2.
30. Tzimas, op. cit., p. 23, col. 3; cf. Zakhariadis, op. cit., pp. 34–5.
31. Zakhariadis, op. cit., pp. 10, 30; Dimitrios Vlandas' unpublished typescript, 'Exartisis kai antidimokratikotis' (1972) pp. 44–51, and his article in *Acropolis*, 1 Apr 1973.
32. Zakhariadis, op. cit., p. 9.
33. Vukmanović, op. cit., pp. 31, 43–4.

34. *Ibid.*, pp. 61, 66, 68–9.

35. *E.A.M. White Book, May 1944–March 1945* (Trikkala, 1945; English translation, New York, 1945). Documents 34 and 37.

36. See note 3.

37. *S.O.E. Records*, Cairo to London, 24 Jan 1943; cf. Myers, op. cit., pp. 124–7.

38. FO 371/37201, R 2050, 7 Mar 1943; R 2702, 12 Mar 1943. Dixon's minute, quoted in the following paragraph, is under the first reference.

39. FO 371/37201, R 2636, 23 Mar 1943; R 3348 (Sargent's minute) 23 Apr 1943.

40. FO 371/37201, R 2598, 18 Mar 1943.

41. For this and the following quotations, see *S.O.E. Operations in Greece and the Aegean Sea* (unpublished typescript, Cairo, 1945) App. II (A).

42. Hugh Dalton, *The Fateful Years* (London, 1957) pp. 366–7. See also FO 371/37203, R 5552 (Churchill's minute of 15 June on Minister of State's telegram of 26 May); and Churchill's minute to Eden of 15 June 1943 (under the same reference): 'Why should his Kingship be called in question at this stage? He should go back as he left as King and General.'

43. Myers, op. cit., p. 189.

44. *S.O.E. Operations*, op. cit., App. II, p. 4; cf. FO 371/37202, R 5306 (D. S. Laskey's minute) 21 Jun 1943.

45. Myers, op. cit., p. 190.

46. FO 371/43676, R 1127, 23 Jan 1944.

47. FO 371/37202, R 5396, 21 Jun 1943.

48. FO 371/37203, R 5029; F.O. to Leeper, replying to his telegram 115 of 7 Jun 1943; Bickham Sweet-Escott, *Baker Street Irregular* (London, 1965), p. 161.

49. Myers, op. cit., pp. 241–2.

50. FO 371/37204, R 7884: Leeper to Sargent, 13 Aug 1943.

51. *S.O.E. Records*, Lemon to Cairo, 294, 24 Jul 1943. Evmaios = Tzimas; Chris = Woodhouse.

52. Pyromaglou, op. cit., p. 160, correcting Reginald Leeper, *When Greek meets Greek* (London, 1950), p. 32, and Woodhouse, op. cit., p. 152. See also E. Tsouderos, *Ellinikes Anomalies sti Mesi Anatoli* (Athens, 1945) pp. 65–6.

53. FO 371/37204, R 7532, 10 Aug; and R 8088, 23 Aug and 31 Aug.

54. Myers, op. cit., p. 217.

55. Field-Marshal Lord Wilson, *Eight Years Overseas* (London, 1948) p. 180; FO 371/37205, R 8766, 17 Sep 1943; R 9679, 6 Oct and 8 Oct 1943.

56. FO 371/37204, R 7864, 19 Aug 1943.

6   The Andarte Delegation to Cairo: August 1943*

BRIGADIER E. C. W. MYERS

Early in March 1943 I had been told by S.O.E. Cairo 'to prepare for two eventualities; the first, not before June, when we might be called upon to cut communications, either to prevent enemy reinforcements travelling south through Greece, or to act in conjunction with an Allied attack elsewhere in the Mediterranean; the second, not before August, to cut all communications, neutralise all aerodromes, attack important nerve centres and organise and control civil revolt throughout Greece in conjunction with an invasion of the mainland'.

On 30 May I received instructions to finalise our preparations for widespread demolitions during the last week in June and the first week in July in conjunction with an Allied invasion of Sicily. In reply to my immediate enquiry when Greece was likely to be liberated, I was told this would be 'at least 3 months after the capture of Sicily, but that the enemy would be constantly fearing invasion as a result of various deceptions.'

On 21 June I requested further elucidation, signalling, 'If possibility Greeks having to undergo another winter please tell me now.' After stressing the risk of serious grain shortage in the mountains, my signal continued, 'If it is felt inside Greece that freedom is being delayed in order to postpone political issue end of war, or if for any other reason there was loss of confidence in G.H.Q. Middle East plans, further controlled andarte effort might become impossible. Request directive for intermediate period soonest.' I urgently repeated this request on 30 June. A few days later I was told that, after our widespread demolitions

* See also my *Greek Entanglement* (London, 1955) pp. 228 ff. This account includes hitherto unpublished original material and impressions of meetings recorded shortly after they occurred.

in conjunction with the invasion of Sicily, we were to lie low and concentrate on training and re-equipping the andartes until Greece was invaded, which might not be until the end of 1943 or early 1944.

I immediately pointed out to S.O.E. Cairo that it appeared to me we had brought the andarte effort to a peak prematurely, and that we would be faced with considerable difficulties in maintaining the morale of the civilian population and in keeping the rival andarte political movements from fighting each other until early 1944. I expressed the desire to visit Cairo, to report personally on the many problems which now faced me and to co-ordinate our future plans as far as possible with those of General Headquarters. I was told that they would be delighted to see me in Cairo, but they considered it too risky to come out by caique to Turkey, the then usual method. They would send an aircraft for me as soon as we had completed an airstrip, the site of which I had already selected near Neraida.

On 10 July I told Andreas Tzimas, the E.A.M./E.L.A.S. representative at my joint andarte headquarters in the mountains, that I hoped to be going to Cairo at the end of the month. He asked if he might accompany me. Cairo readily agreed. On 24 July, shortly after Komninos Pyromaglou had joined my headquarters as Zervas's representative, I told him about my intended visit. He immediately asked if he might also come, subject to Zervas's permission. Both Zervas and S.O.E. Cairo agreed. On 30 July Colonel Psaros, in command of E.K.K.A., arrived at my headquarters with Georgios Kartalis, whom he planned to leave with me as his representative. Psaros asked if Kartalis might come too. Once again Cairo agreed, subject to there being room on the flight, which was then planned for the night of 8 August. David Wallace, my political adviser, who had arrived a month earlier, was also to accompany me. This, I thought at the time, completed the party.

By the evening of 7 August we were all assembled at Neraida with the exception of Tzimas, who had gone off to meet a representative of the Central Committee of E.A.M. sent out from Athens at his request with instructions for his visit. Late in the evening of 8 August, after the flight had been postponed for twenty-four hours on account of Tzimas's delay, he arrived at Neraida with Georgios Siantos, acting Secretary of the Greek

Communist Party, Ilias Tsirimokos, leader of a pre-war small Social Democratic Party and two other Communists, Petros Roussos and K. Despotopoulos, all of them members of the Central Committee of E.A.M. All except Siantos thought they were coming with me to Cairo. This confusion was possibly due to the misinterpretation of Tzimas's signal sent to Athens on our wireless link via Cairo.* Siantos refused to let Tzimas go alone. Eventually I agreed to take all four E.A.M./E.L.A.S. representatives, if the pilot agreed. Otherwise I would do my utmost to arrange a later aircraft for them. I signalled Cairo accordingly. There was no time for a reply.

In the small hours of the morning of 10 August 1943 the whole delegation arrived safely in Cairo. I had no illusions about the serious problems we had to solve. An extract of my signal of 28 July to Cairo read, 'Consider whole future of Greece may be bound up with forthcoming visit, but we have it in our power to prevent civil war.'

Before I left my headquarters I had many lengthy discussions with Woodhouse and Wallace about the recommendations I should submit to S.O.E. Cairo, with the object of making it possible for the andarte movements to continue without civil war breaking out.

The most effective solution would have been to keep the andartes busy fighting the enemy. But General Headquarters Middle East required them to maintain a state of relative inactivity in order to make surprise and widespread sabotage again possible when Greece was invaded. To achieve this, we agreed that both a moral and a material stimulus were necessary and to recommend development in three ways. Firstly, we considered that the andartes should be recognised by the Greek Government as part of the armed forces of Greece; that they should be provided with light artillery and other supporting arms, and that the Greek General Staff should be asked to accept liaison officers from them. Thus the status and quality of the andarte army would be improved without increasing its size, and a stimulus to train would be provided. Secondly, we considered that, with the raising of the status of the andarte army, it was desirable to remove from my Joint Headquarters

* See also pp. 139–40 above.

in the mountains the responsibility for as many civilian administrative and political matters as possible, and therefore to divide
it into separate military and civil components. It was agreed to
recommend to General Headquarters Cairo to accept civil
liaison officers to advise on the problems and needs of the
civilian population. Lastly, in view of the unrepresentative
character of the existing Greek government-in-exile, and the
extent to which it was out of touch with and lacked the confidence of 'Free Greece', it was agreed to recommend that one or
two officials of the Greek government should in due course be
transferred to the mountains. They would smooth the way for
the return of the government, by providing a measure of continuity of civil order and a means whereby the andarte civil
organisation in 'Free Greece' could be progressively absorbed
within the national structure.

On the morning of 9 August I had a satisfactory discussion
about these proposals with Siantos at Neraida, following successful ones a few days previously at my headquarters with Pyromaglou and Kartalis. I then held a meeting with all the delegates together. My proposals were adopted without any major
alteration.

When we arrived in Cairo, I discovered that no plan had
been made about the conduct of the delegation. Lord Glenconner, head of S.O.E. Cairo, fully agreed with my outline
plan. I met Reginald Leeper, the British Ambassador to Greece,
on my first day in Cairo. We had a long, frank and cordial discussion about the anti-monarchical swing of opinion inside
Greece since the end of the Metaxas regime. He told me that
the arrival of the Republican andarte representatives was most
opportune, because it gave the Greek government-in-exile
something new to think about. For, at that time anti-Royalist
disturbances in the Greek Army in the Middle East, coupled
with the virtual failure of all attempts to date to make the
government more representative, had resulted in a serious risk
of the resignation of a number of its members. He facilitated
early meetings between the delegation and the Prime Minister,
Tsouderos. King George of Greece also met them unofficially.

On 11 August, my second day in Cairo, Leeper took me to
see the Greek King. He told me to speak frankly about the
anti-monarchical feeling inside Greece. Shortly after this meet-

ing I wrote, 'During an hour-long talk I explained to the King that, should he return to Greece at the head of his army, I thought E.A.M. would separate themselves from the fragile National Group of andartes which I had formed, and declare themselves openly against him. Zervas would align himself alongside the King. There would probably be civil war immediately and the King's life would be in danger unless heavily protected by British forces. Should he return to Greece protected by the British Army, E.A.M. would regard this as interference in purely Greek affairs and this, again, would cause open revolt by them.'

On 13 August, after a dinner party at the house of Lord Moyne, Deputy Minister of State, I had a further two-hour talk alone with the King. I recorded, 'I asked him if he would consider paying a short visit to the andartes in the mountains in order to help re-establish confidence of the people in him. He thought he was too old for that sort of thing. But it was his duty to go back to Greece at the head of his Army. When I suggested that he might stay outside Greece as ambassador until a plebiscite as to his future had been held, he replied, "How can I ever go to London, not having returned to Greece? I know too many people there who would call me a coward. I should never be able to face them." '

Two days after the arrival of the delegation they had been eagerly received by their government. They had cast aside our agreed proposals and had raised the political issues uppermost in their minds. They had demanded a statement from the King that he would not return to Greece until (and as a result of) a plebiscite in his favour. Within four days, fully supported by Georgios Exindaris who had arrived independently from Athens as representative of the old Venizelist Liberals, they had obtained not only the ears but the support of practically the whole of their government, except Tsouderos, and they were further emboldened to suggest that the andarte movements be given three seats in the government.

Leeper did not stand in their way. In one of our daily conferences with Lord Glenconner, I recorded that 'Mr Leeper told us he was unable to advise the King to remain adamant about his return to Greece and that it was up to the King himself to do what he thought right.' In fact I believe it then appeared to both S.O.E. Cairo and the British embassy to Greece that, if the King made a suitable declaration, there was an immediate prospect that the government could be broadened and strengthened by making it more representative of current opinion inside Greece.

It was at this stage that I subsequently learnt the King had sought the advice of Roosevelt and Churchill regarding his future action. It also appeared to me that on or about 17 August Leeper must have received firm instructions from the Foreign Office to support the King's position and on no account to acquiesce in the andarte delegation's request for three seats in the government.

From then onwards Leeper's attitude to S.O.E. Cairo and to me personally changed completely from one of cordial cooperation to one of suspicion and unjust accusations. He accused me of bringing out the delegation without any warning and of meddling in political affairs beyond my terms of reference. He accused S.O.E. of following a policy of its own towards Greece which was not in accordance with that of the Foreign Office, and of deliberately withholding from him the signals from Wallace and me. In due course I was even accused by Tsouderos of having encouraged members of his cabinet to align themselves with the delegation, thereby risking his government's resignation. Fortunately Wallace or a member of Leeper's staff had accompanied me to every meeting I had been asked to attend with different members of the Greek government and they were able to refute this particular charge.

Within a few days the Greek political situation in Cairo had also completely changed. The King had received the personal support of Roosevelt and Churchill and had decided to stand firm by his previous declarations. Tsouderos, supported by a nucleus of Royalists in the Greek government, had rejected the delegation's other political requests; and Leeper had told S.O.E. Cairo to get the delegation back to the Greek mountains as quickly as possible.

I had originally thought that we would have been able to complete the discussions of our agreed proposals and to coordinate our future military plans within a fortnight. But the prospect of sending the delegation back to Greece in such a disappointed state of mind filled me with apprehension about my ability to retain their future co-operation. Moreover when I lunched with the delegates on 19 August, they told me that as a result of the impasse on political matters they had discussed with no one our previously agreed joint proposals, and that with their mission so incomplete they did not wish to return to Greece (their return was then planned in three days' time).

I had several lengthy and sympathetic meetings with the Minister of State, R. G. Casey, the Director of Military Operations, Brigadier George Davey, and the Commander-in-Chief, General Sir Henry Maitland Wilson, but to no avail. Regardless of my personal pleadings with Leeper, he insisted that the delegates should depart. Glenconner said he was in no position to order them to go. I was instructed by the Commander-in-Chief to do all I could to get them into such a frame of mind that they would depart peacefully over the weekend. But no one gave me any definite order to pass on to them.

On 21 August Glenconner arranged for the delegates to see Casey in the hope that this might result in their leaving Egypt in a more satisfactory frame of mind. I attended this meeting with him and Leeper. 'At the end of an hour and a half', I recorded, 'not one of the six delegates had voiced what was uppermost in their minds, their objection to returning to Greece with their political views so rudely rejected and all overtures for government reconstruction refused. They were due to leave the following afternoon. No one had told them to go. No one had said they might stay. Mr Casey got up, shook hands with them and said goodbye.'

Whilst we were all standing, I acted in desperation. I asked if I could say a few words on behalf of the Commander-in-Chief. Mr Casey readily agreed. I then spoke out in front of the delegates. I told Mr Casey that three days previously the Commander-in-Chief had instructed me to tell them that if they stayed on in Cairo they might cause the resignation of their government. Mr Tsouderos might not be able to form another government and a purely military cabinet might have to be resorted to. The Commander-in-Chief wished the Greeks to return temporarily to Greece, pending the King's decision about their recommendations regarding his future movements and their ideas for broadening the Greek government by including Republican elements from the mountains.

This gave the delegates the opening to unburden their minds. In fairness to them, I should add that prior to the meeting I had warned them against overstating their case. For the next twenty minutes, whilst we were all standing ready to leave, they gave their reasons why they wished to stay until they could take back decisions regarding their political recommendations. They stressed that they had postponed all other discussions pending decisions on these matters, regarding which they had been asked by their government not to press for an immediate answer. Mr Casey listened sympathetically but was not in a position to make any helpful suggestion. 'Well gentlemen', he concluded, 'You have heard the wishes of the C-in-C. I advise you to act accordingly and I thank you for the most interesting talk I have had with you.' The delegates filed out.

With Mr Leeper and Lord Glenconner still present, I rapidly explained to Mr Casey the disastrous effect the return of the delegates in so disappointed a frame of mind would have upon any future military contribution by the andartes. Lord Glenconner supported my apprehensions. But Mr Leeper considered the political factors more important. Mr Casey saw no way out and so we parted.

Immediately afterwards, I asked Lord Glenconner if I might try to arrange a final interview the following morning between the delegates and the Commander-in-Chief, in the hope that he might feel able to reverse the decision on military grounds. It was suggested that they might be sent on a battlefield tour pending the political decisions. Lord Glenconner allowed me to try. From Mr Leeper's own flat that evening after dinner I arranged the meeting, and late into the night I prepared a short brief for the Commander-in-Chief summarising the delegates' arguments and the dangers regarding the future.

At this meeting, attended also by Leeper and Glenconner, the delegates again cogently presented their reasons for wanting to stay. I recorded,

> They ended up by reminding the C-in-C that no-one in their own Government had expressed to them any desire that they should return to Greece so prematurely. In fact they believed the majority wanted them to stay. They were Greek subjects. How could they face their leaders inside Greece with their

tasks unfulfilled and so frustrated? They tactfully hinted at British interference with Greek affairs. Their return now might cause loss of confidence of the andartes in them and in the British. At one moment I thought that the C-in-C would postpone their departure. But Mr Leeper's views prevailed. I could do no more; and Lord Glenconner and I, who had been instructed by S.O.E. Headquarters in London to report personally to them, bade them farewell.

Their final request, I think, to Lord Glenconner was that they might visit Mr Tsouderos on their way to the airport. They were told that, as Greek subjects, they could not be prevented from doing so, but that S.O.E. was in no position to advise them either way. They duly called on Mr Tsouderos. I never learnt the details of this meeting. But it resulted in Mr Tsouderos telephoning Mr Leeper to say that he now did not wish the delegates to return. Mr Leeper had to acquiesce and recall them from the airport.

The following week I held numerous meetings with the delegates and the necessary specialist officers in S.O.E. and General Headquarters on purely military and supporting matters affecting future training and operations by the andartes. By the end of the week we had dealt with them all, and during the second week in September the delegates returned to Greece.

On 7 September Glenconner and I – accompanied by Brigadier Davey, bearing plans for the reorganisation of S.O.E. Cairo under the Commander-in-Chief's control – arrived in London. The purpose of my own visit was to report personally on the situation inside Greece, as a result of which I hoped that my para-military and political directives would be made more compatible and achievable.

By 16 September I recorded,

I had had meetings with all the Departments in the War Office concerned with operations in the Balkans up to the level of the Directors of Military Intelligence and of Military Operations, but with no one in the Foreign Office. It was only on this day that I had my first interview with Mr Howard, head of the Southern Department, engineered at my request by Wallace, who, on Mr Eden's personal instruction, had come to London three days ahead of me. Howard's polite excuses for not having seen me earlier appeared thin. Instead of having a full discussion with him, as I had hoped, we only had five minutes together before I was taken in to see Sir Orme Sargent. During a frank fifty minute discussion he told me the Foreign Office thought that I had put up the delegates to the idea of asking for portfolios in the Greek Government. I believe I convinced him that this and a number of other Foreign Office contentions about S.O.E. and myself in particular were unfounded. We finally agreed that it would be helpful if the story of the Greek King's loyal support to the Allies was prepared for the benefit of my officers in Greece and that I should be given a clear political directive for them all to take back with me.

Two days later I saw the Chief of the Imperial General Staff, with whom I only discussed military matters. He seemed pleased with our efforts inside Greece and congratulated me.

On 27 September I gave a talk in the Curzon Cinema to a large and mixed Whitehall gathering of the three armed services, the Foreign Office and the Cabinet offices. I had been given no specific brief as to what to say. I carefully prepared not only the exciting story of my eleven months in Greece, but also an account of my progressive and inevitable involvement in political as well as para-military matters and an explanation of the present political situation. The evening before the talk I read my long speech through to Major Eddie Boxshall and Colonel Pearson, two S.O.E. London officers concerned with the Balkans. They commented favourably. But I subsequently learnt from General Gubbins that 'My talk had done S.O.E. no good.' The whole organisation was by then under serious fire from the Foreign Office for having become involved in Greek political affairs, and I was told I should have confined myself purely to an account of our successful operations against the enemy. It was a pity no one had told me so beforehand.

On 28 September I was summoned to Buckingham Palace. I recorded that

> I thought I was going to see the King. I arrived in a car driven by a woman M.T.C. driver in uniform. At the Palace gates no one asked me for my pass or my name. We drove

across the forecourt to the East Wing door. An A.R.P.
Warden outside took no notice of us. There was no bell and
no one else about. I opened the door and walked in. There
was no one in the passage. I found a door on the right, with
an official inside who did not know I was coming. He took me
along to Sir Alan Lascelles' study.

After the first five minutes it became apparent that I was
not going to meet the King. But I had an interesting hour long
talk with Sir Alan and another person who I believe was Sir
Godfrey Thomas. I found Sir Alan extremely well briefed.
He kept on asking me highly pertinent questions to draw out
the necessary information. I explained the situation inside
Greece and the prospects of the Greek King as I saw them.
We then discussed the visit of the andarte delegates to Cairo.
After I had evaded answering several particularly pointed
questions, Sir Alan said, 'You can say what you like to me. I
don't belong to the Foreign Office and I am completely
neutral here.' In reply to his further direct enquiries I eventually admitted, I hope with due diffidence, that I did not
think the situation had been well handled by Mr Leeper.

A week later I learnt from roundabout sources that the
Palace thought the future prospects of the Greek King returning
to Greece were remote.

On 29 September I had a further meeting with Howard at
the Foreign Office about the impracticability of the King
returning to Greece. By this date I had also had several discussions with representatives of the Ministry of Economic
Warfare, including Dingle Foot, on the serious food shortage
likely to occur in the forthcoming winter in the Greek mountains. From the War Office and the Joint Planners I had
gathered it appeared likely that virtually no Allied troops would
be available to accelerate the liberation of Greece and that the
country would only be freed from enemy occupation by their
withdrawal due to Allied pressure elsewhere, or by being out-
flanked by our progress up Italy. 'This', I recorded, 'made the
possibility of the return of the Greek King at the head of his
Army appear more than ever impossible.'

At noon on 30 September I was summoned again to Buckingham Palace, this time to see the King.

I spent half an hour alone with him in his study, both of us comfortably seated in fireside armchairs. After ten minutes of questioning by him on local colour and the general situation inside Greece, the King settled down quite freely to ask the questions he obviously wanted to put to me about the future prospects of his cousin King George's return to Greece. I told him frankly about the situation as I saw it. Amongst other things I explained to him how the Greek people did not look upon their King as we looked upon him. 'At the moment', I said, 'there is only a small Royalist group, virtually a political party, which favours his return. These Royalists regard the King more as the leader of their party, under whom they would attempt to intrigue, protected by British bayonets, in order to re-attain power inside Greece, rather than as we look upon you, Sir, as our constitutional King.' The King asked me if I had told his cousin about this when I saw him in Cairo. I replied that I believed I had done so, but that if I had not, I thought the Greek King realised that this was so. 'Ninety per cent of the people in Greece appear to be Republicans', I continued, 'and feared this intrigue by the Royalists. It was for this reason that they were so opposed to the return of the King until there had been a free expression of the people's will.' I explained the subtle difference between what the Greek King had suggested and what the great majority wanted. 'The King had suggested that he should come back to Greece at the head of his Army and he had assured his people over the B.B.C. that within six months free elections would be held. The Republicans feared that during those six months clashes would break out between them and the Royalists protected by the British Army and that the leading Republicans would be locked up, particularly the more leftist ones. The King had said that the elections would be for a Constitutional Assembly, which would then decide about his future. The people mistrusted this, as they thought these elections would be rigged after the arrest of their leaders. They wanted all the people to vote first of all about the return, or not, of their King.' He asked me if I had seen his Secretary of State. I replied that I had not. He said, 'I saw my Secretary of State yesterday and told him he ought to see you. He must get this sort of information first-hand

from the people who have seen for themselves. Obtaining it
from subordinates who have seen you is not good enough.'
Shortly before I departed he said, 'See that you see my
Secretary of State.' I replied, 'It is a little difficult for me to
arrange such an interview. I feel it ought to be done from the
other end.' He agreed: 'Yes, I suppose that this is so.' We
parted with a joke.

In my record of this meeting I noted that I was impressed by the
King's deep interest and obvious sincerity; also by the relaxed
way in which we talked to each other after the first few mo-
ments.

The next day, 1 October, I was summoned to see Eden, but
only for twenty minutes. I recorded that 'he was short of time,
but all smiles, polite and certain that he was perfectly briefed,
but obviously ill-briefed by his subordinates.' He told me about
the Greek political situation and what he wanted done. He
omitted to tell me how it could be achieved. I hardly opened my
mouth during the whole interview.

I was deeply shocked and frustrated by the generally prejudiced attitude in the Foreign Office and their refusal to face up
to unpalatable facts. 'One exception', I noted,

was Mr Dixon, who unfortunately was too busy with Italian
affairs to devote enough time to the Balkans, which he
understood well. It was not until I got to Chequers that I
found a great man, to whom I could talk as a man and who
was prepared to listen.

I arrived at Chequers shortly after 1:15 p.m. on 2 October.
At about 1:30 Mrs Churchill joined me. Churchill's personal assistant, a naval commander and Churchill's brother,
a nice old country gentleman, were also there. At about a
quarter to two, the Old Man having at last got out of bed,
where he had been working all the morning, dressed in his
one-piece dungarees, joined us with his Secretary, Peck. He
greeted me and immediately entered into quite a long one-
sided conversation, which was carried on as we straightaway
walked into the dining room. 'Ah, yes, your organisation has
been meddling in the work of my Foreign Office and, if it
had not been for me, they would have gone under. They

must not try to run things their own way. We are the people to do that. Don't you get mixed up in politics. Leave that to the politicians.'

I sat down to lunch between Mr and Mrs Churchill. Whilst Mrs Churchill talked to me socially on one side, Churchill often simultaneously talked on the highest level about the most confidential matters on the other, even with the servants in the room. I found myself having to talk to Mrs Churchill about the A.T.S., the contribution of the women of Britain to the war effort and gardens, whilst listening to Churchill as well. Every time Churchill and I got into a deep discussion, Mrs Churchill would try to steer the conversation away onto some more social subject. But as the Old Man appeared quite at ease talking about confidential matters in front of the servants, I soon lost no opportunity to put in my say too. I said that I felt certain that our policy towards Greece was a just one, but that we had left all public announcements to the Greek King and Government and that our silence, particularly as a result of the return of the andarte delegation with their aims so unfulfilled, would be interpreted by those inside Greece as determination on our part to enforce the return of the King. Although I knew this to be false, those inside Greece did not, and I felt it was up to us, by tactful and truthful propaganda, to explain our policy.

After lunch, sitting round the table, smoking a good cigar – Churchill insisted that I pocket another to take away with me – I showed him photographs which had recently come out of Greece of the Italian General Infante and his surrender with seven thousand of his troops. I also showed him a pair of stereoscopic aerial photographs of the Asopos railway viaduct lying at the bottom of the gorge it had spanned, after we had blown it up shortly before our other widespread demolitions in conjunction with the invasion of Sicily. He chuckled delightedly.

I told him I thought that his recent speech at Quebec, in which he had said he looked forward to the Greek King's return to Greece, had made my job more difficult. 'Surely', I said, 'what happened to their King is a Greek affair and it is not for us to interfere.' He asked me what he had said at Quebec and I produced an extract of his speech out of my

attaché case, which he looked through. He politely said that
he agreed with what he had said; so I left it at that.

I then produced a draft of the broadcast over the B.B.C.
which I was proposing to make to the andartes before I left
London in a few days time. It contained a message of good
cheer from Mr Churchill. It was entirely non-political and
had already been approved by S.O.E. and the Foreign
Office. Churchill read it through in silence and at the end
said, 'Well, that's alright, perfectly harmless. Would you like
me to add a bit of pep to it?' I said I would be very pleased
if he would. Whereupon he got out his fountain pen filled
with red ink and slowly started scratching away. Afterwards
I was given what he had written to read and comment. I
found that he had added a paragraph almost exactly on the
lines I had suggested at lunch, affirming and justifying our
policy towards Greece. He had written words to the effect
that 'we have no intention whatsoever of restoring the Greek
King against the will of the Greek people. Whatever form of
Government they elect when the time comes, we will respect.
We do not wish to interfere with Greek affairs.'*

He gave the amended draft to his Secretary to be re-typed
and went off to his study whilst I took a walk around the
garden with Mrs Churchill.

It was then about half past three. About half an hour later
I returned to Mr Churchill's study. The re-typed draft of my
broadcast was brought in. Mr Churchill read it through. He
soon started altering it a little bit and eventually became
firmer and called for his blue pencil. He then began striking
out whole sentences of what he had written. 'No', he said,

* Churchill's handwritten amendment to my draft broadcast can be seen
amongst his recently released operational papers in the Public Record Office
in a file entitled *Brigadier Myers*. (PREM. 3 211/5) and reads as follows:
'The Greek people must be masters of their destinies. They alone can decide
their future form of Government. England, always their friend, will never
interfere in their home politics and will always champion their sovereign
rights. We have obligations of honour to King George because he fought
for the Allied cause. These we must discharge. They do not in any way
affect the full freedom of the Greek people to settle their own affairs once
conditions of tranquility and orderly politics are re-established.'

'It is too risky. I don't want to say anything in the wrong way.' I said that, if he could allow me to make any statement which would give confidence to the Greek people that we had no intention of interfering with their affairs, it would be of the greatest help to me. 'Yes', he replied, 'but I don't like it being done in this way. The Americans are very interested in this and I don't want to say anything unconstitutional over the heads of my colleagues. No, I don't like any of this, it's too risky.' And his blue pencil went through all he had written. 'No', he said, 'I'll say this in the House in the proper way. You just say what you have written.'

I did not argue further and my draft again went out to be re-typed, almost as it had been originally, but with a few words of Churchill's added here and there, improving the English and deleting superlatives, which, he said, weakened the force of good English, not realising that the whole speech was to be translated into Greek.

One point I could not get into Churchill's head was that the andartes were not just 'bandits', but that they represented all types of Greeks, as well as many Republican leaders. Sarafis had been Military Attaché in Paris. Tzimas had been a Communist Deputy. Kartalis had been Finance Minister in more than one Greek Government. Colonel Psaros was one of the most capable soldiers I have ever met. There were many such others. They were not just 'Tom Wintringhams',* which Churchill had more than once called them. I could not convince him that I was in touch not only with the andartes and the mostly poor people in the mountains, but with virtually every element and every thinking body inside Greece, including those in all the big towns.

When I said earlier that I thought between eighty and ninety percent were Republicans and not Royalists, he replied, 'Yes, that's what you say or think. I am not sure you are right.' I told him that I had already been accused, behind my back, of political prejudice and that this was entirely false. Everything that I had said was based upon considerable evi-

* Churchill was presumably referring to Captain Tom Wintringham, military correspondent of the *Daily Worker* and commander of the Saklatvala Battalion of the 15th International Brigade during Spanish civil war. During World War II he wrote articles on guerrilla warfare in the *Picture Post*.

dence and what I knew to be true. During our discussions he treated me with respect and as his equal, and I found that I could speak to him in a straight-forward manner, in spite of the fact that he wanted to do a lot of the talking himself. He congratulated me on our work in Greece and, before I finally departed, he twice rose to say goodbye to me. He respect-fully gave me God's blessing. 'Don't let them pre-judge the issue about the King,' he concluded. 'I want to see him have a fair deal. I won't be stampeded by a lot of Tom Wintring-hams.' When I replied that our silence as to our policy might be interpreted as weakness or an attempt at interference to restore the King and that the more leftist of the Republican elements might turn towards Russia for support, he retorted, 'I won't be blackmailed by these bandits! If they want to go to Russia, let them. When Greece is freed, who is going to save them from starving? We are. And they oughtn't to for-get that. You see that the King gets a fair deal.' I replied that I would do my best.

As I went out with Churchill's personal assistant through the front door, he said, 'The Old Man is a bit muddled.' I asked him if he thought I had made my points clear. He replied that he thought that I had done so. I asked him to do his best to put over to Churchill once again that the andartes were not just Tom Wintringhams, but that they represented a large section of the people of Greece today.

I left at 5 o'clock, already late for an appointment in Lon-don. I was pleased with my visit. I had almost achieved a tremendous success. I felt that my failure had only been one of a temporary nature and that I had sown the seeds for future developments on the lines I knew to be right in the interests of all brave Greeks.

On 8 October, with Wallace as my interpreter, I broadcast a message of good cheer to the andartes. In this speech, at Chur-chill's request, I said that 'in the near future we would be help-ing them more and more' and concluded 'Let nothing spoil your united battle with us against our common enemy. Death to the huns!' There was no word about Greek politics or their King.

My records continue:

On 10 October, with the understanding that a new Foreign Office directive would shortly be following me, I arrived back in Cairo. I learnt from S.O.E. Headquarters that the situation inside Greece had deteriorated and that everyone was fearing the outbreak of civil war. I had appreciated that E.A.M. would not take any action until they had heard the result of my visit to London. I sent a confidential signal to Monty Woodhouse to keep the situation as fluid as possible and at the same time I wrote personally to him, saying that I was delaying my return for a few more days in order to come back with some fruits as a result of my past two months' work. I felt that in a very short time the Foreign Office would accept the reality of the swing of Greek opinion against their King and, in order to obtain the maximum further contribution by the andarte movements towards winning the war, would give me a frank statement of H.M.G.'s policy on the lines of Churchill's withdrawn amendment to my B.B.C. broadcast.

On 12 October I was married and went off to the Lebanon on a week's leave. On my way through Haifa I met a S.O.E. officer who had just arrived from Cairo. He told me the staggering news that I was probably not returning to Greece. I had read the previous day that civil war had broken out in Greece. When I got back to Cairo I discovered that, although my recent letter to Monty Woodhouse had got through, my confidential signal to him had been withheld at Mr Leeper's request. Instead, Woodhouse had been told that I was probably not returning, and he was invited to give his own personal and candid views on the political situation, regardless of 'my' past policy.

'Monty's reply must have disappointed Mr Leeper,' I recorded. 'It was a long manuscript which came out by air. He said he entirely supported my past policy and would continue to act in accordance with it in the future, whether I came back or not, it being the only possible one to follow.'

I then learnt from Brigadier Keble that Glenconner was not coming back, that Keble was shortly leaving S.O.E., and that Colonel Tamplin, next on the list, was also departing. Eden had demanded their withdrawal because of 'political taint'. 'In my opinion', I wrote at the time, 'these three officers have done nothing more than their duty and they have done it well. They are being removed because they have stated facts which are distasteful to the Foreign Office. What an example of democracy! What harm to the war effort!'

At my request I was granted an interview with the Chief of Staff, General Ronald Scobie, in the temporary absence of the Commander-in-Chief. I told him that I considered my position to be most difficult. I owed allegiance and loyalty to my officers and the andartes. I thought that the removal of the three senior officers from S.O.E. Cairo was a narrow-minded action, harmful to the war effort in the Balkans. I, for one, was not going to be sabotaged by the Foreign Office. Rather than that, I would prefer to go back to regular soldiering. I told him how I had been shattered by some of my encounters with Foreign Office people in London.

General Scobie told me that, when the Commander-in-Chief returned to Cairo, it was likely that I would be asked to return to Greece immediately, in order to stop the civil war, because all the andarte organisations had confidence in me. I told him that I could only go back if the Foreign Office also had complete confidence in me. I would need to know what they and the Commander-in-Chief wanted, and I would like to be given a free hand in deciding how to achieve this. If not, I considered it my duty to tell the officers who originally went into Greece with me the reason for my resignation and to give them the opportunity to be re-employed elsewhere.

General Scobie was sympathetic. He gave me encouragement by saying that he was practically certain the Foreign Office was only looking for a face-saving way of approaching the Greek King to advise him to make a public statement that he would not return to Greece until the free expression of his people's will in his favour, and to advise the Greek Government to get in touch again with the new Republican leaders inside Greece.

Unfortunately civil war had already broken out in the mountains on 7 October, and my broadcast from London had therefore been too late to have any effect. I recorded on 30 October:

It appears to me the immediate bloodshed has already passed its peak. E.A.M. started the civil war for various reasons. The

Germans put out clever propaganda indicating that Zervas had been co-operating with them and that they were leaving Greece. This, coupled with the fact that the Greeks believed that we, by our silence, intended to enforce the return of the King, led E.A.M. to think that the time was ripe to strike. As a result of the treatment of their delegation to Cairo and the fact that I, whom they all trusted, have not returned, they have lost confidence in the British. The Axis have not left Greece and E.A.M. are feeling a bit stupid. If in the next few days we can adopt a firm line, the civil war will peter out. But it is too early to say whether we will be able to reform those bands of E.D.E.S. which have been so shamefully attacked, and whether we will be able to reform our joint headquarters in the mountains.

I continued,

Although Zervas' conduct has been exemplary – and he has at last been given the one opportunity he always sought, even if only temporarily, of justifying unilateral British support – such little confidence that E.A.M. had in the British has been lost. It has been lost only because the Foreign Office for the past two and a half months have been exaggerating the Communist menace in Greece to suit their own policy and have refused to face the facts as they really are. They will eventually come round to my way of thinking, but perhaps too late.

I fought on to obtain a realistic and achievable political brief with which to return to Greece. But the Foreign Office and the Greek King remained adamant. Eventually, towards the end of November 1943, after receiving much sympathy from Lord Selborne and a direct order from General Gubbins, I was forced to give up my struggle to be of any further help to the Greek people and the war effort in their country. Long afterwards Monty Woodhouse said to me, 'You only made one mistake in Greece and that was to accompany the andarte delegation to Cairo. I feared at the time that you might never be allowed to come back to Greece.' But so much was at stake that, even now, I believe I was right to have reported personally on the many problems, para-military, civilian and political, which faced me as a result of the unexpected delay in the liberation of Greece.

7 'Pearls from Swine': the Foreign Office papers, S.O.E. and the Greek Resistance

RICHARD CLOGG

I should make it clear that I do not intend in this paper to give a systematic analysis of the development of British policy towards the Greek resistance during the period I particularly want to look at – roughly the period from October 1942, when the *Harling* mission was parachuted into Greece, until the signing of the Plaka agreement at the end of February 1944, which patched up the civil war within the resistance that had begun during the previous October. Sir Llewellyn Woodward has already performed this task competently in his chapter on British policy towards Greece in his recently published *British Foreign Policy in the Second World War*,[1] and it would be pointless to try to duplicate his efforts. Sir Llewellyn himself made the point that his account is told from the Foreign Office point of view and that he has not made use of Special Operations Executive documents which might put S.O.E.'s case and which remain inaccessible, apparently for the indefinite future. This is a little puzzling for there is a considerable amount of S.O.E. material available in the Foreign Office papers, some of it in the form of *pièces justificatives* written specifically to counter Foreign Office criticism. What I mainly want to do is to fill in some of the gaps in previously published accounts and in particular to chart, as far as is possible on the basis of the available documents, the disastrous course of the Foreign Office's relations with S.O.E., which reached their nadir during the visit of the delegation of six Greek guerrillas to Cairo in August 1943, after which S.O.E. in the Balkans was brought under the direct control of the Commander-in-Chief Middle East.

Before looking at British policy after October 1942 I want to look briefly at the way in which the British government became so enmeshed in the cause of King George II of the Hellenes – a commitment against which a number of major initiatives to change the direction of British policy foundered. The seeds of the Foreign Office's stubborn and ultimately disastrous rearguard action on behalf of the King were sown at an early stage. Within a matter of weeks of the fall of Crete, Edward Warner of the Southern Department, who was later to become an adviser on Greek affairs to the Minister of State in the Middle East and subsequently to Reginald Leeper when the latter became ambassador to the Greek government-in-exile in Cairo, minuted:

> It must be remembered that it does not in the least matter if we offend extreme Veniselist opinion by backing the King and giving honour where honour is due to Metaxas. What matters is that we should not offend 'Royalist opinion'. The Germans can never win over the extreme Veniselists; but they may be able to make something out of some of the Royalist (or right wing) elements, as in the last war.[2]

It is somewhat unfortunate that Warner, who was to play a fairly important role in the formulation of British policy, both in London and Cairo, should have had a rather unsympathetic view of Greek politicians and their aspirations. In December 1941 he wrote off 'most of the upper class Greeks' as 'self-seeking Levantines...quite unworthy of the rank and file',[3] while on 18 April 1943 he wrote to Pierson Dixon of the Southern Department that the political mess in Cairo was unbelievable and that he very much sympathised with King George 'in letting Metaxas go ahead' on 4 August 1936.[4] Warner was certainly aware however that the hold of the King on the affection of his subjects was somewhat precarious and believed that the Foreign Office's policy should be one of 'selling the King and Government' to the Greek people.[5]

The Foreign Office's strong commitment to the cause of the King, who, they felt, had more or less single-handedly held the Greek government together during the crisis caused by the German invasion in April/May 1941, went beyond mere propaganda to an active involvement in the King's manifold intrigues and obsessions. In the autumn of 1941, for instance, the Foreign Office became deeply implicated in King George's efforts to have six Greek Republicans expelled from Egypt. This, in the King's eyes, at least, was the *quid pro quo* for his dismissal from the government-in-exile of Konstantinos Maniadakis, who as Metaxas's Minister of the Interior had been as unpopular as he was efficient in hounding opponents of the dictatorship. Sir Orme Sargent, the deputy permanent under-secretary at the Foreign Office, later conceded that it had been a mistake to get involved in this particular intrigue,[6] and it is a significant indication of the extent of the failure of both the King and the Foreign Office to appreciate the trend of Greek opinion that one of these six purported undesirables, Vyron Karapanayiotis, was to re-appear as Minister of War in the Greek government-in-exile in 1943, while there was considerable embarrassment in the Foreign Office when it emerged that the six for the most part had unimpeachably pro-British records.

The Foreign Office did however draw the line at an early stage of the war when it received a request from the King and Tsouderos which ultimately envisaged a restoration of the monarchy by force. The document in which this request was made has been withdrawn, but that such a request was made is clear from a minute by Warner of 21 November 1941. He wrote: 'we have now been asked by the Greek Prime Minister to co-operate in the execution of a policy which foresees, as a last resort, the restoration of the King by force.' But, he added that 'we cannot for one moment contemplate helping to restore the King by force,' and that this should be made plain to the King and his Prime Minister, Emmanouil Tsouderos.[7] A few months later, during the course of a dinner conversation, an influential member of Tsouderos's entourage told Warner that the Greek government intended to use the Greek army in the Middle East to impose a regime of its own choosing 'when we return'. In a memorandum of 11 February 1942 recording this conversation, Warner added that the Foreign Office had 'the uneasy feeling that this was the position'.[8]

King George of Greece emerges from the documents as a person with an almost boundless capacity for self-deception. On 21 April 1943 he wrote personally to Churchill from Cairo that the latter's March directive urging all-out support for the King and government-in-exile was 'starting to produce excellent results and will lead to an enormous improvement in conditions regarding Greek affairs in this part of the world'.[9] Moreover, King George did not always reciprocate the warmth of the Foreign Office's support for his cause. In March 1942 the King complained to the Director of Naval Intelligence that the Foreign Office was 'Republican and anti-King', a charge described by Warner as 'quite absurd' and by Dixon as 'ridiculous'.[10] At about the same time a close personal friend of the King told Harold Caccia of the Foreign Office that the King felt that if he failed to return to Greece 'the blame would very largely attach to the Foreign Office and their agents'.[11] Given attitudes such as this it is not altogether surprising that the Foreign Office's patience with the King's obduracy, although very considerable, was not boundless. Eden minuted on 30 March 1944 that 'I have had many dealings with the King in recent years and I fear that I am forced increasingly to the conclusion that he is little, if any, more to be relied upon in his records of opinions or events than the Greeks he abuses so freely.'[12] A few days later on 3 April 1944, he minuted: 'the King is not wise and he is obstinate. It is in my judgement increasingly unlikely that he will ever return to Greece as King, and stay there.'[13]

Only in 1943 did questions of policy towards the resistance involving the Foreign Office arise, for as late as March 1943 the Foreign Office claimed to have had no knowledge of the existence of a British military mission on Greek soil. But the 1942 documents do raise a number of interesting points in connection with the resistance, and particularly the extent to which the Foreign Office was aware of political developments in occupied Greece, and how far this knowledge was also available to S.O.E.

Colonel C. M. Woodhouse, in a recent article, has stressed the complete absence in the briefing by S.O.E. of the *Harling* party at the end of September 1942 of any mention of E.A.M., E.L.A.S. or the K.K.E.[14] Yet the documents make it clear that the Foreign Office, and indeed other British organisations, were at this time not only aware of the existence of E.A.M. but had evidence that it was by far the largest secret organisation in

Greece. As early as February 1942, for instance, M.I.3 passed
to the Foreign Office an appreciation of the situation existing
within Greece which listed among the main anti-Axis groups
'the so-called Popular Front', which I take to be a reference to
E.A.M. M.I.3 had reports of some twenty-two secret organisations, which appeared to be resolving into four main groups.
These were the Venizelists, the constitutional monarchists,
'scattered ex-Royalist groups now with conservative or Republican sentiments' and 'the so-called Popular Front, consisting
of Left-wing groups under certain revolutionary officers and the
two Communist parties. The Popular Front is Republican and
economically far to the Left.' The appreciation concluded that
'party differences seem at the moment to have fallen into the
background' and that 'the two Communist parties are known
to have received instructions from Moscow to desist from
ideological activity for the duration of the war and to combine
with the other parties against the Axis forces.'[15] On 31 August
of the same year, Dixon wrote to Warner in Cairo stressing the
need to build up the 'Action Committee' in Athens 'as a magnet
for the various organisations constituting the Popular Front'.[16]
More significantly, Warner was reporting back to London
within a matter of days of the *Harling* briefing about the political
significance of E.A.M. On 5 October 1942 he reported that he
was preparing a lengthy report on Greek secret organisations,
which was to include an appendix on E.A.M. Warner wrote
that, according to his sources, E.A.M. was 'much the largest
secret organisation in Greece' with 100,000 members in Athens
alone, who were organised on a cell system. Warner's source
considered that E.A.M. was 'not outwardly communist' but
was rather 'non-political and purely patriotic'.[17]

It is difficult to believe that S.O.E. in Cairo during the last
week of September knew less about E.A.M. and its potential
significance than the Foreign Office. Presumably the absence
of any mention of E.A.M. or E.L.A.S. in S.O.E.'s briefing of
the *Harling* mission was a consequence of the reorganisation of
S.O.E. Cairo in 1941 on functional rather than geographical
lines. This reorganisation had been reversed in the summer of
1942, but it presumably took some time for the newly reconstituted country sections to function efficiently. Again at the
time of the *Harling* briefing, it is Woodhouse's clear recollection

that Panayotis Kanellopoulos, Deputy Prime Minister and Minister of Defence in the government-in-exile, made no mention of the K.K.E. as an active force in the Greek resistance. Yet Kanellopoulos informed Warner at the beginning of October 1942 that he thought the organisers of E.A.M. were 'probably communists' although the membership was 'most diverse'.[18] A month later, on 2 November 1942, Warner wrote to Dixon from Cairo that according to a Greek officer in Athens the 'old gang' politicians were quite discredited with the younger generation, 'who looked to E.A.M. as the only political organisation worth supporting'.[19] Further, in a telegram of 4 November the Minister of State Cairo described E.A.M. as 'the only important political organisation in Greece'.

Incidentally, the documents do enable us to dispose fairly, if not absolutely, conclusively of one canard put about in recent analyses of the Greek resistance. This concerns the B.B.C.'s treatment of the blowing up on 25 November 1942 of the Gorgopotamos viaduct on the Salonika–Athens railway. André Kédros, Dominique Eudes and most recently Heinz Richter have claimed that when the B.B.C. broadcast the news of the destruction of the Gorgopotamos viaduct, praise was lavished on Zervas, but no mention was made of the participation of the E.L.A.S. contingent or of its leader, Aris Veloukhiotis.[20] Eudes portentously adds that this signified that the British had already made their political choice, i.e. to back E.D.E.S. and not E.A.M./E.L.A.S.

Unfortunately, the actual script of the Gorgopotamos broadcast is apparently no longer preserved in the B.B.C.'s archives. But a study of P.W.E. directives to the B.B.C. for this period make it extremely unlikely that the broadcast did take the form that these historians claim. While stressing that 'we must never neglect the question of Greek resistance even when we have no fresh news', the directives emphasise that 'no names of places or leaders must be given' (30 October–5 November and 20 November–27 November). The first explicit references to Gorgopotamos occurs in the directive for 11 December to 18 December, and it was presumably during this week that the news was first broadcast. Here the directive read, '...in exceptional cases, such as the blowing up of the Gorgopotamos bridge, on which we have completely reliable evidence, we can give details of acts of resistance, but in no case, unless otherwise advised, should we give the names of guerilla leaders...'[21] It is true that in a minute of the previous February Warner had written that most of the energies of Dilys Powell of P.W.E. were being 'consumed in internecine warfare, *owing to the refusal of the B.B.C. Greek section personnel to accept P.W.E. guidance*', and that, as a result, she was thinking of resigning.[22] But it is highly unlikely that the B.B.C., at this particular juncture, would have wilfully disregarded such clear directives for the treatment of the Gorgopotamos affair.

What I principally want to do in this paper is to trace the stormy history of relations between the Foreign Office and S.O.E. after the possibilities of large-scale guerrilla warfare in Greece had become apparent, although of course there had been much friction at an earlier stage of the war between the Foreign Office and S.O.E. or its antecedent organisations. In December 1941, for instance, Warner had complained of the 'quite incredible bias and lack of judgement prevailing in our various intelligence [sic] organisations'.[23]

What is rather surprising is the extent to which the documents reveal the depth of the bitterness, already known from other sources, felt by the Foreign Office for S.O.E., as presumably those of S.O.E., if they were made available, would reveal similar attitudes on the part of S.O.E. towards the Foreign Office.* There are innumerable references to the 'ramps' being perpetrated by S.O.E.,[24] to telegrams from S.O.E. being 'Pearls from Swine',[25] to S.O.E.'s inevitable preference for the 'cranky and unorthodox',[26] to the purported lack of political finesse of their operatives. Leeper, for instance, described Brigadier Myers as 'a complete disaster', 'a very dangerous fool' and a 'fanatic' 'with a very strong streak of megalomania',[27] while he found General Gubbins to be 'a very difficult man'.[28]

Sometimes the contempt felt by some members of the Foreign Office for S.O.E., at least as far as its Greek operations went, reached almost incredible proportions. As late as 23 January 1944 Orme Sargent minuted:

The truth, of course, is that the whole guerilla movement in Greece has been largely fiction created by S.O.E. to justify a

---

* See, for instance, p. 226 below.

vast expenditure of money and raw material in that country. As long as they kept the whole management in their own hands we never knew whether this investment was producing any dividends, but for the last six months, since when the Commander-in-Chief has been in control, the military have discovered that the movement is a complete fake, as far as resistance to the Germans is concerned, (even if we succeed in putting an end to the actual civil war), and are increasingly inclined to write it all off.[29]

Eden himself, who was not over-solicitous of the reputation of S.O.E., wrote against this passage: 'I really think that this is exaggeration.'

There is no evidence, however, that Sargent was ever convinced of this, and indeed in this minute he was merely repeating views he had advanced almost exactly a year previously, when, in January 1943, the Southern Department were discussing the operational value of S.O.E.'s activities in Greece. Douglas Howard, the head of the Southern Department, minuted only a couple of months after Gorgopotamos that 'S.O.E. have nothing very impressive to show as yet in Greece.' Sargent added:

Nor do I think there will be in the future. The achievements of S.O.E. are sadly out of proportion with the vast sums of money which, during the last year and a half, have been spent in Greece, chiefly on subsidising communist organisations in opposition to the Greek Government, which we are supporting.[30]

It was in March 1943 that matters first seem to have come to a head between the Foreign Office and S.O.E. over questions related directly to the guerrilla movement in Greece. This first crisis was prompted by the receipt by the Foreign Office of the first political reports from within Greece sent by Myers, Woodhouse and Colonel Rufus Sheppard, the British Liaison Officer in Thessaly.* The Foreign Office was incensed to learn that Myers had, in their view, been meddling in internal Greek political affairs. As for the idea that a plebiscite be held before the King's return – a proposal commended by Myers – Dixon

* See p. 120 above.

minuted on 7 March 1943 that it was 'plain that this idea has its origin in one or two self-interested groups of guerillas in Greece, who cannot possibly claim to represent the general feelings of the Greek people.'[31] The consolidated Myers–Woodhouse–Sheppard report, Dixon minuted, strengthened 'the case for suspending S.O.E. activities in Greece and making a constructive effort to build up our official policy'.[32]

Some of the wind was taken out of the Foreign Office's sails by the receipt of 13 March of Zervas's message of 9 March in support of King George II. Howard minuted on the 14th:'Sir C[harles] Hambro [head of S.O.E.] seized the opportunity yesterday morning of ringing me up to ask if I had digested the telegram. He was, of course, delighted with it, and said, somewhat smugly, that it was the perfect answer to the Foreign Office's accusations that S.O.E. encouraged nothing but anti-King movements. (I was busy, in fact, at that very moment drafting a letter to him repeating the same accusation! It had to be toned down as a result of the telegram.)'[33] The Foreign Office pressed ahead, however, with their efforts to curtail S.O.E. operational activities in Greece, on the grounds that they involved supporting elements hostile to the Greek government. Eden wrote to the Chiefs of Staff to this effect, but an agreement was patched up after the Middle East Defence Committee had sent to the Chiefs of Staff on 18 March a spirited defence of S.O.E.'s activities in Greece. The Middle East Defence Committee regarded 'the sabotage which Colonel Myers has organised and is continuing to organise and direct in Greece, as an important element in our plans. We believe that it is effectively disrupting the flow of enemy reinforcements, and supplies, and materially facilitating the eventual re-occupation of Greece. We should like to see it maintained at the maximum which resources permit.'[34]

The Foreign Office did not get its way over the suspension of S.O.E.'s operational activities, although Hambro agreed that S.O.E.'s operatives would now be instructed to say that 'while they don't mix in politics, they knew that H.M.G. support the King and his Government.'[35] The Foreign Office was still unhappy about the way in which, 'as far as [they] remembered', the project of sending Myers into Greece had not been discussed in advance. On 23 March Howard wrote formally to

Colonel J. S. A. Pearson, of S.O.E.'s Balkan section in London, requesting information about Myers and the British Military Mission.[36] To this Pearson sent a curt answer, which Sargent considered to be 'frankly impertinent', provoking Sir Alexander Cadogan, the permanent under-secretary in the Foreign Office, to speak to Hambro personally about it. Pearson sent a more pacific reply on 9 April to the effect that Myers had been sent in on the instructions of General Headquarters Middle East for the specific purpose of cutting the Salonika–Athens railway line. He added that 'as this operation was of great secrecy, it was not considered by the Anglo-Greek Committee in Cairo, although M. Canellopoulos himself was privately told that it was to be undertaken.' Following the success of the operation, Myers was asked by the Commander-in-Chief Middle East to stay on in Greece and 'attempt the co-ordination of the guerrilla bands on a non-political basis for resistance to the Axis'. Pearson concluded that 'all these officers are in uniform, and are therefore responsible, through S.O.E., to the control of G.H.Q. Middle East, and are amenable to general army instructions.'

This reply was still considered unsatisfactory by the Foreign Office. On 23 April Sargent minuted,

> . . . the introduction of British officers into Greece to organise resistance movements and direct guerilla warfare represents a very important new development not merely from the military but from the political point of view. In spite of this we were told nothing about it and only succeeded in extracting the necessary information from S.O.E. when Sir A. Cadogan personally intervened with Sir C. Hambro. The decision to introduce British officers into Greece ought obviously to have been reported by S.O.E. at their monthly meeting with the F.O. under Sir A. Cadogan's chairmanship. Nothing however has ever been said on the subject at any of these meetings.[37]

Why Sargent should have written in these terms is unclear. For Cadogan, at least, was certainly aware of the presence of a British party on Greek soil as early as November 1942. For it was Cadogan who initialled the reply, dated 15 November, sent to the Minister of State in Cairo, who had sought permission, following a request from Myers, for leaflets to be dropped over

Greece threatening counter-reprisals if the Axis occupation forces carried out reprisals after the Gorgopotamos operation.[38]

During the protracted negotiations leading up to the National Bands agreement in July 1943* the Foreign Office, if worried about the implications of the Joint General Headquarters agreement, were by and large content to accept S.O.E.'s handling of the matter, and indeed were appreciative of Myers's successful handling of the negotiations.[39] In concurring in the final instructions sent by Lord Glenconner, head of S.O.E. Cairo, to Myers, authorising the latter to agree to the establishment of the Joint General Headquarters, the Foreign Office stated that they agreed with S.O.E. 'that their policy should be to increase the number of British Liaison Officers as much as possible including the despatch of naval and air force representatives to the joint Headquarters. Our aim must be so to increase our influence on the guerrilla bands that, by the time the King returns to Greece with the British Commander-in-Chief of our army of liberation, British influence will so far have swamped the political aspirations of E.A.M. that they will be unable to organise an effective opposition to the King.'[40] Leeper during this period strongly advocated a showdown with E.A.M. But the Foreign Office, while agreeing with Leeper that the influence of E.A.M. must be diminished or broken, feared that a showdown might involve 'a very real risk of provoking civil war, and that at a time when circumstances were not altogether favourable to us'.[41]

Relations between the Foreign Office and S.O.E. were to reach a stage of total breakdown during the critical confusion surrounding the visit of Myers, Major David Wallace and the delegation of six representatives of the guerrilla organisations to Cairo in August 1943. As Reginald Leeper who, as ambassador to the Greek government-in-exile found himself in the very eye of the storm, put it in a letter to Sargent of 25 August: 'There have really been two crises running at the same time: (i) the crisis with the Greek Government: and (ii) the crisis with S.O.E. The latter has been so unpleasant that in comparison I could almost take the members of the Greek Government to my bosom.'[42]

* Described in Chapter 5.

As Colonel Woodhouse and Brigadier Myers emphasise in chapters 5 and 6, the Cairo visit marked a crucial turning point in the history of the resistance in Greece. As a result of its failure any hope of a co-ordinated resistance movement vanished, if indeed it had ever been anything other than a chimera, in a welter of mutual recrimination and bitterness. After Cairo, civil war within the Greek resistance moved from the realm of possibility into the realm of probability.

I want to look in some detail at this episode, as the Foreign Office documents do amplify in a number of important respects the previously published accounts of participants, those of Leeper, Myers, Field-Marshal Lord Wilson and Komninos Pyromaglou,[43] while Sir Llewellyn Woodward devotes only a summary paragraph to this crucial encounter, in itself perhaps an indication of the Foreign Office's failure to grasp the significance of the opportunity that had presented itself.

As early as 21 February 1943, following Woodhouse's meetings with members of the E.A.M. Central Committee in Athens, Myers reported that E.A.M. wanted to send representatives to Cairo, a proposal which Myers strongly supported, adding that he had arranged provisional details with Evmaios (the *nom de guerre* of Andreas Tzimas).[44] The Foreign Office was informed of this proposal on 6 March in a digest of S.O.E. telegrams from Greece forwarded by Pearson to Dixon,[45] although in the digest 'representatives' became 'a representative'. On 23 March Pearson wrote Dixon that the Minister of State had agreed to such a visit as useful. In his covering letter Pearson emphasised that the attached paper on E.A.M. should be taken as only an interim report, pending the arrival of the E.A.M. representative.[46]

Cairo was clearly expecting an imminent visit, but the proposal seems to have lapsed, presumably due to the difficulties of organising transport, until early May. On 6 May Myers was asked to use his influence to get certain political leaders in Greece to send representatives to Cairo.[47] In reply Myers promised to exert the utmost influence but urged, as Leeper expressed it, 'that the Greek Government and the Foreign Office should consider Greek political parties as they are now and not as they were in 1940. The realities should be faced and representatives of the present "Peoples' Parties" be got out; namely E.A.M., Communists and Plastiras Party.' Myers was told in

reply by Leeper that his telegram was difficult to reconcile with
a policy of splitting the E.L.A.S. bands from E.A.M., that
E.A.M. and the Communists should in no way be encouraged
and their adherents should be attracted into the National Bands.
There was, however, no objection to a visit of an E.A.M.
representative along with the politicians.[48]

On 24 May, Leeper, in a letter to Sargent, urged the need
for further statements by the King and the British government
on the constitutional question, the importance of making the
Greek government more representative and that means be
found of 'getting people out of Greece both from the politicians
and the resistance groups'.[49] Clearly then, Leeper, whatever he
may subsequently have thought, had no apparent objection to
guerrillas being brought out of Greece and being incorporated
in the government-in-exile. He must also have assumed that
these guerrillas would be political animals; otherwise there
would be little purpose in engaging them in an attempt to
broaden the basis of the Tsouderos government.

Closely linked with the question of the six Greeks was the
Wallace mission to Greece, for Major David Wallace, after a
short visit to Greece between the end of June and the beginning
of August, returned to Cairo with Myers and the guerrilla
delegation. From an early date Leeper had urged that a
Foreign Office representative be sent to Greece as political
adviser to Myers. He secured the ready agreement of Lord
Glenconner, the head of S.O.E. Cairo, to this arrangement on
14 April and, in informing the Foreign Office, Leeper wrote that
'the appointment of a proper political adviser is a matter of
urgency. Myers is purely a soldier. As such he is doing excellent
work but we cannot leave him on his own without our own man
there.'[50] Leeper was particularly anxious that Wallace be appointed political adviser, as he duly was. The Foreign Office's
suggestions for the guidance of Wallace arrived shortly after he
had left for Greece, but are none the less of interest, for Leeper's
own briefing covered the same points. Wallace's instructions
were to insist on the implementation of His Majesty's Government policy and to keep H.M.G. informed about political
feeling in Greece. He was to bear in mind that the main essentials of British policy were (a) full support for the King and
government, (b) approval of the various undertakings given by

the King and the Greek government and particularly that of 4 July, by which the King promised to respect the will of the people over the constitutional issue and guaranteed general elections for a constituent assembly, which would be held within six months of liberation, (c) the King's return to Greece in a military capacity along with the invading army. In the meantime premature discussion of constitutional issues was 'to be deprecated since it will detract from the war effort,' while any direct conflict or breach with E.A.M. was to be avoided. Wallace was also to assess the possibility of broadening the government with politicians from within Greece and with representatives of the National Bands.[51]

There is little doubt that the Wallace mission was regarded by Leeper, who had implicit faith in Wallace's judgement (Wallace was not a professional diplomat, although he had served in the information department of the British embassy in Athens at the beginning of the war), as essentially a means of double checking the reports he was receiving from Greece via S.O.E. For Leeper had already expressed serious doubts as to Myers's political judgement. On 12 May, for instance, he wrote to Sargent that Myers 'has no political acumen and does not see beyond his nose or, should I say the noses of his guerillas. He is not astute enough in dealing with E.A.M. and I am sure he exaggerates their political importance.'[52] He was particularly incensed by Myers's report of the reaction within Greece to the King's 4 July declaration, in which Myers said that 'the King is prepared to make any sacrifices except in anything concerning himself. Although it is not my business as a soldier, once again I strongly recommend that the sooner the King states he will not set foot in Greece, until asked for by common vote of the people, the better. I lay a 100 to 1 bet that Wallace will agree when he sees the position for himself.' Leeper, however, was not amused by this and asked Glenconner to rebuke Myers as he appeared 'to be completely under the thumb of E.A.M.'.[53]

This view that Myers was a tool of E.A.M. or, conversely, that E.A.M. was the virtual creation of Myers was widely held in the Foreign Office, and was subscribed to, indeed, by Churchill himself. In a minute of 24 February 1944, Churchill described 'General Myers' as 'the chief man who reared the cockatrice brute of E.A.M.–E.L.A.S.'. Somewhat uncharacteristically, Sargent came to Myers's defence but only to make a further attack on S.O.E. 'The hand that reared the cockatrice was that of S.O.E. who fed it sedulously for two years in spite of our repeated warnings and protests. All that Brigadier Myers did was to attempt to introduce a little discipline and order into the tyranny and inefficiency of E.L.A.S. when he went into Greece last spring.'[54] How these opinions of Myers received such wide circulation is inexplicable. Long before Leeper asked Glenconner to rebuke Myers there was plenty of evidence available to the Foreign Office that Myers was under no illusions as to the long-term objectives of E.A.M./E.L.A.S. In a S.O.E. report for the week ending 15 May made available to the Foreign Office, for instance, Myers warned that 'Sheppard [the British Liaison Officer in Thessaly] and his mission are becoming E.A.M. yes-men, not troubling to investigate deeper than E.A.M. desire'. Here it was the compiler of the report who sprang to Sheppard's defence: 'It may be here pointed out that both Major Sheppard and his principal assistant, Captain Hammond, are thoroughly competent and have long experience of the Levant. They are both first-class officers fairly well known to the writer, and in his opinion it would be most surprising if they had in fact been hoodwinked by the E.L.A.S. leaders to whom they are attached, to the extent feared by Brigadier Myers.'[55] Again it was known to the Foreign Office that in May Myers had been considering the withdrawal of all B.L.O.s with E.L.A.S. if it became apparent that Aris Veloukhiotis had acted on the instructions of the E.A.M. Central Committee in disbanding Psaros's E.K.K.A. guerrillas, a threat which Cairo ordered on the same day that he must not carry out.[56]

The immediate circumstances of the departure of the guerrilla delegation from the Neraida airstrip and its arrival in Cairo are described in Brigadier Myers's *Greek Entanglement* and by Colonel Woodhouse in Chapter 5. In his book, *When Greek meets Greek*, Leeper maintains, and in this he is supported by Sir Llewellyn Woodward, that the guerrilla delegation was virtually sprung upon him: 'I had been told a day or two before that some Greek guerilla representatives were coming by air to discuss military questions with G.H.Q. Cairo, but I did not know who they were and I certainly did not expect them to be almost purely political.'[57] He made the same complaint, that he had no idea that the delegation would be political rather than military in character, in a letter to Sargent of 13 August.[58]

In fact, Leeper was by no means caught so unawares as he suggests. In a letter to Sargent of 21 July (almost three weeks before their arrival) he wrote that he had learnt from Glenconner and the Director of Military Operations that a plane was being sent to Greece to bring out Myers: 'The idea is that he would also bring with him in the same aeroplane Zervas and Evmaios (the well-known Greek Communist Tzimas)...it is absolutely vital that Myers and I should have a talk, and I would also welcome the arrival of these two Greek guerilla leaders.'[59] In the event, E.D.E.S. was represented not by Zervas but by his second-in-command, Komninos Pyromaglou, and indeed it seems that there was never any intention within Greece that Zervas should accompany Myers. But none the less Leeper, who had frequent occasion to complain of the politicised nature of the Greeks, should surely have realised that a guerrilla delegation of this calibre would have been quite as much concerned with political as military matters. In retrospect it was clearly a serious error on Leeper's part not to have forewarned the King and the Tsouderos government of the arrival of a guerrilla mission of considerable significance. Leeper was, given the circumstances, adequately forewarned of the visit and indeed shortly before the arrival of the delegation, as Bickham Sweet-Escott has recorded, 'appeared to be delighted at the prospect of meeting them all'.[60]

Leeper's enthusiasm survived his initial shock in discovering that Myers and Wallace had an entourage of six rather than two Greeks, and he acknowledged that Myers had clearly made the right decision in bringing them along. The morning the guerrilla delegation arrived Wallace spent closeted with Leeper and Warner. Wallace stressed that there was 'practically no support that you can trace anywhere for the immediate return of the King' and 'with even greater emphasis' that 'if the King were to return at once in the face of the very strong public opinion against it, there would certainly be disorders, and these disorders would be exploited by E.A.M., who would greatly increase their influence by being able to rally non-Communist elements against the King.'[61] As Leeper himself put it, Wallace was just as emphatic on this point as Myers, and Leeper was clearly persuaded of the critical importance of the constitutional question, and indeed had shown himself more aware than the Foreign Office of the need for further clarification of the constitutional issue even before the arrival of the six Greeks. The King's statement of 4 July, inadequate though it subsequently proved to be, was a direct consequence of Leeper's urgings on this score. Moreover, if Leeper needed any further persuading on the constitutional issue it was provided by a meeting just three days before the guerrilla delegation arrived with Georgios Exindaris, who had arrived in Cairo, quite independently of the guerrilla delegation and quite fortuitously, as a plenipotentiary of the liberal politicians in Athens. This was, by an odd coincidence, the first official contact during the war between the British government and party leaders in Greece. Exindaris made it abundantly clear that he had a mandate to try to persuade the King and the Greek government that the King should not return to Greece before a plebiscite had been held.

This demand, that the King submit to a plebiscite before his return, was in Leeper's view not an insuperable obstacle to a settlement, even if it did conflict with the existing policy of the British government.

Leeper was thus fully prepared for the similar demand made by the six Greeks. Four of these represented E.A.M., Andreas Tzimas, Petros Roussos, K. Despotopoulos and Ilias Tsirimokos, of whom the first three were Communists. Komninos Pyromaglou represented E.D.E.S. and Georgios Kartalis E.K.K.A.

In *When Greek meets Greek* Leeper claims that the guerrillas overreached themselves in demanding three posts in the Tsouderos government. He is rather ambiguous on this point in his book: 'Had these representatives been more moderate, I would have welcomed the opportunity to establish contact between the Greek Government and the guerillas and thereby to broaden the basis of the Government.'[62] It is by no means clear in this passage whether he thought that they should actually form part of a coalition. Yet it is clear from the documents that even before he had met the delegation, let alone learnt of their demand for a coalition, Leeper was keen to try and construct a representative coalition there and then. After his first meeting with Wallace, the day the delegation arrived, he decided to propose that same evening to S.O.E. that 'we should accept as our goal the attempt to form here and now an all-embracing coalition Government under the King,'[63] a proposal which Eden appeared to approve.[64] In his book, Leeper blames the E.A.M. representatives for making totally unrealistic demands about entering the government, but initially at least Leeper's fear, as expressed in a telegram of 11 August, was that E.A.M. might not join the coalition: 'E.A.M.', he wrote, 'can hardly afford to stay out of the coalition, as they need assistance both materially and morally.'[65] In a telegram sent next day, 12 August, Leeper reported that both the King and Tsouderos were 'fully prepared to examine all possibilities arising out of the arrival of the six Greeks.' He concluded on an optimistic note: 'I cannot help feeling that the appearance on the scene here of men who have been actively resisting the enemy at home cannot but have a refreshing and stimulating effect on the Greek Government and might in fact modify their present standpoint and that of the King also.'[66]

Tsouderos, on 12 August, made it clear to Leeper that he was trying to steer the King in the direction of a broad coalition to be formed then if possible on the understanding that the King 'would agree of his own accord not to return until the future of the régime had been settled'. In reporting this conversation to the Foreign Office in a further telegram despatched on 12 August, Leeper wrote, 'I fully realise that events have developed more quickly than we could have anticipated. We cannot ignore the facts as they are now, for the first time fully presented to us, and it is my duty to inform you that the case against the King's early return is strong and might well induce the King to accept it.' He asked for very early guidance as to whether he should let 'the King be swayed in his own interest by advice which M. Tsouderos has given him and will, I think, continue to give him even more definitely during the next few days'. Leeper was clear in his own mind that the British government should not advise King George to resist Tsouderos's advice. The King would, he believed, 'gain in estimation of all Greeks here including the new arrivals, and will enhance his future prospects if he helps to find a solution which shows him to be actuated purely by national interest. These six men will shortly be returning to Greece, and we can count on some of them, if not all, doing the King full justice on their return.' Things now appeared to be moving altogether too fast for Eden, who minuted, 'I am very doubtful about this. The King has proved himself our true friend. We must do the best we can for him.'[67]

The guidance which Leeper requested was contained in a telegram of 15 August (despatched 16 August). The Foreign Office, while reaffirming its wish that the Greek government be made as representative as possible, feared that the incorporation into the government of 'Left Wing elements represented by the six Greeks and by Exindaris without any corresponding representation of the Royalist elements in Greece would result in Republican Government paying temporary lip service to the King but resolved that he should not be given an opportunity to state his case or appeal to his adherents when Greece is liberated.' They took the view that Tsouderos would scarcely continue long as a member of such a government, let alone as its Prime Minister. 'As we see it,' the telegram continued,

> a Government formed on the basis now proposed would be overwhelmingly Republican if not Communist, and whatever professions its extremist members may now make, such a government would be more than human if it did not try to influence the Greek people against the absent King as soon as it got into Greece, and a plebiscite, if one were ever held, would in such circumstances be a foregone conclusion. In our view, if the King now pledges himself not to return to Greece until after a plebiscite he is in fact signing his abdication...
> We must be very careful therefore before we advise the King to take the big risk of placing himself at the mercy of an E.A.M. Government, on the assumption that they will play straight by him when established in Greece and allow a free plebiscite to be held when the time comes.

A possible alternative to the coalition proposal, as it now stood, was that Royalist elements should be got out of Greece to form part of a coalition. In this case the Royalist members, if supported by the British, might be able to safeguard to a certain extent the King's interests while he was out of the country.

The Foreign Office accurately predicted that the guerrilla representatives would press the King 'to decide immediately whether or not to pledge himself to remain outside Greece for an indefinite period when it is liberated'.[68] In fact just such a demand was made a day after Leeper received this telegram. The six guerrillas, together with Exindaris and Kanellopoulos, declared on 17 August, as 'representative of the greatest part of Greek public opinion', that the King should not return to Greece before the people had pronounced on the form of the constitution. On the 19th Tsouderos and the Greek cabinet issued a statement acknowledging that the demand of the eight represented the will 'of the great majority of the Greek people'.[69]

Leeper's enthusiasm for a coalition and for a concession by the King that he would not return to his country before the constitutional question had been settled rapidly waned on receipt of the Foreign Office's instructions on the 16 August.* His policy was to try to play for time, while King George received replies to his appeals for advice to Churchill and Roosevelt. These appeals, which referred to the six Greeks somewhat unfortunately as 'certain individuals from Greece who are supposed to represent various guerilla bands', was despatched on 18 August.[70] One of those who weighed in urging uncompromising support for the King was Lord Selborne, the Minister responsible for S.O.E., in a letter to Sargent on 19 August. He was disturbed by signs that Leeper appeared to be weakening in the face of the politicians and guerrilla leaders. It was impossible under existing circumstances to say who the politicians represented, Selborne wrote, while 'the leaders of the guerilla bands represent some 50,000 armed brigands. These gentlemen are heroes of great gallantry, but have no claim to speak for the whole of the people of Greece on a matter of this sort.'[71]

Leeper managed to gain some breathing space at a meeting on 20 August between the Greek government, the Minister of State, the Commander-in-Chief, Lord Moyne and Leeper, at which the Greek government were persuaded to defer taking any precipitate action over the King for at least a fortnight. To try to secure 'a solution acceptable to the King in a calm atmosphere' Leeper also decided to pack the six guerrillas back to Greece forthwith. Brigadier Myers, not unreasonably, assumed that in this matter the British embassy in Cairo was merely

* See p. 152 above.

passing on instructions from London.[72] But the documents make it quite clear that the decision to get rid of the guerrillas was Leeper's and that in this matter he was acting on his own initiative. In a telegram of 23 August Leeper wrote that despite the objections of S.O.E.,

> For political reasons I asked both the Minister of State and the Commander-in-Chief that we should send them back now on the ground of having myself the responsibility for these very delicate negotiations with the King and Tsouderos and knowing how much the presence of these six men would influence M. Tsouderos' colleagues, I was satisfied that it was essential for the Government to try to find a solution acceptable to the King in a calm atmosphere. I maintained that a settlement of the crisis here which if not found might lead to the disappearance of any Greek Government, was more important to His Majesty's Government than adverse effects in Greece anticipated by S.O.E.

The Commander-in-Chief 'reluctantly', as Leeper put it, agreed to see the six Greeks and tell them that 'in our opinion' they should return to Greece.[73]

The Foreign Office was agreed on condemning Leeper's handling of this particular matter. Sargent minuted on 25 August: 'I am afraid this is a bad business and that it was an error of judgement on the part of Mr Leeper to try and send them back to Greece straight away.' D. S. Laskey made precisely the suggestion that Myers makes in *Greek Entanglement*, namely that if they had to be got out of Cairo then rather than being returned to Greece they should have been sent on a tour of the battle front.[74] But Leeper had one powerful ally. Churchill, who was under the impression that the decision to send the Greeks back was 'the settled policy of all other British authorities', cabled to Eden on 30 August: 'I hold strongly that these six men should be sent back to Greece. We cannot allow decisions so carefully arrived at to be flouted. They cannot do so much harm in Greece as they will do in Cairo to the distracted Greek Government and unhappy King. Strict control should be kept on S.O.E.'[75]

The six Greeks received a last minute reprieve after a visit to Tsouderos on the way to the airport, a détour which Leeper

immediately suspected had been made at the suggestion of
S.O.E. It would be going too far to suggest that Leeper rounded
on S.O.E. only after his attempt to dump the six Greeks had so
badly misfired, but this undoubtedly contributed to his determination to bring S.O.E. to heel, and he certainly held S.O.E.
wholly responsible for what he regarded as a virtually inextri-
cable mess.

In a telegram of 19 August to Sargent, three days before the
airport fiasco, he had already made it clear that he intended to
try to exert much closer Foreign Office control over events in
Greece:

> This crisis has shown how imperative it is for the Foreign
> Office through Stevenson [British ambassador to the Yugo-
> slav government-in-exile] and me here to gain far greater
> control of the situation in the countries in which we are con-
> cerned. I have been placed in a position of acute embarrass-
> ment with the Greek Government by the arrival of these
> Greeks on a political mission about which I had no pre-
> liminary warning. Had I been consulted in advance I would
> not have agreed without the approval of the King and
> Tsouderos. I do not wish to make bad blood and I have
> covered up the situation with the Greeks without recrimina-
> tion but I have told Glenconner and Minister of State that I
> can no longer carry on under existing conditions and I must
> insist on receiving all S.O.E.'s information and that the
> political side of Myers' work be regarded as of equal impor-
> tance with the military. In fact the political aspect is more
> important.
>
> I have never, as you know, been happy at the way His
> Majesty's Government have found themselves pursuing one
> policy inside Greece and another policy in Cairo. For military
> reasons we have accepted the former though I have never
> been able to satisfy the King about it.
>
> So long as the two sides we were backing kept apart we
> could avoid a collision, but their presence together in Cairo
> has revealed to me how embarrassing for His Majesty's
> Government this double policy can become.

In a letter to Dixon of 21 August, Leeper again wrote 'that it
would be difficult to exaggerate the acutely embarrassing posi-

tion in which S.O.E. have placed me, the King and Tsouderos'.
He again complained about the lack of adequate forewarning
of the projected visit, a complaint which the Foreign Office did
not regard with much sympathy. On 2 September, for instance,
Howard minuted that 'I confess the case against S.O.E. for
bringing out these six Greeks is a poor one.'[76]

By an unfortunate coincidence it was only on 22 August, the
very day that the six Greeks were to be shipped back, that
Leeper received from S.O.E. the series of telegrams which
Wallace had radioed from Greece between 23 July and 2
August. This delay was more likely due to over-strained communications or incompetence than malice and indeed the first
telegram, dated 23 July, was forwarded by Pearson in London
to Dixon in the Foreign Office on 10 August,[77] twelve days
before Leeper, in Cairo, received any of the telegrams. But
Leeper not surprisingly saw this delay as affording further evidence of S.O.E. intrigue, and he complained to Eden on 23
August: 'You will appreciate that, if I had received these
telegrams in due time I should have been much better informed
at the opening of the recent negotiations with the politicians
who were brought out of Greece by S.O.E.'[78]

Yet even had Leeper received the reports before the arrival
of the delegation it is difficult to see that they would have made
much difference to his handling of the crisis, because there was
little, if anything, in them to which Myers could not and did
not subscribe. And Wallace, in any case, was able to brief
Leeper the moment he arrived. But Leeper was, in retrospect,
not happy with these initial meetings with Wallace. When the
latter first arrived in Cairo, he wrote to Sargent on 25 August,

> he must have been a little dazed, and certainly very tired,
> because he did not disclose to me the picture as he really saw
> it in Greece, and I had the impression that he was in full
> agreement with Myers. He may have felt it was improper for
> him to go against his senior officer, and I doubt if he grasped
> at once, as I assumed that he did, that on arrival he auto-
> matically became a member of my staff. Had I known the
> revelations which subsequently emerged, I would have taken
> a very much stiffer line in the first two or three days.[79]

Wallace fell ill soon after arrival and it was only when he

recovered that Leeper, as he put it, discovered 'the real enor-
mities of S.O.E.'s actions in Greece, conducted with an irresponsibility which simply appals me'.

But what was the picture as Wallace really saw it? This is
difficult to say, for he seems to have shifted his ground on his
arrival in Cairo. In a significant passage in his letter to Dixon
of 21 August, Leeper wrote, '...I have been able to convince
him [Wallace] that Myers' political outlook and the policy he
has been pursuing are quite mistaken. He naturally has been
anxious, in view of Myers' many sterling qualities, not to
criticise over much his chief, but David [Wallace] has far too
clear a political head not to realise the folly of allowing a policy
to be run inside Greece independent of the official policy of
H.M. Government.'[80] The only inference that can be drawn
from this is that until Wallace had become subject to Leeper's
persuasion he had in fact been more or less 'in full agreement'
with Myers. Illness prevented Wallace compiling a detailed
report during August but Leeper was able on 24 August to
cable a brief interim report, the gist of which had been given to
the Director of Military Operations in Leeper's presence on 23
August. There were two main points in this interim report. The
first was that the military capability of the guerrilla forces in
Greece was not nearly so great as had been claimed by S.O.E.

> They are, in fact, untrained and ill-disciplined: they are
> regarded with contempt by most of the British liaison officers
> who are highly sceptical about their ability ever to undertake
> serious military operations such as holding beaches or neu-
> tralising airfields, which tasks S.[O.E.] cheerfully assured the
> C-in-C they will be able to do on the day of invasion...In
> the recent series of operations against Greece's communica-
> tions which was part of Sicilian cover plan, it is admitted that
> the guerillas were 95 % cowardly, unwilling or inefficient, and
> that the whole job was done by the British officers themselves.

The second was that Zervas had been more or less browbeaten into signing the recent Joint General Headquarters
agreement which he regarded as highly detrimental both to his
own interests and those of the British. Leeper was concerned
that this reluctance was never apparently referred either to the
Middle East or to the Foreign Office when they were asked to

approve the terms of the agreement.[81] Leeper also claimed that
Pyromaglou had confirmed to him the way in which Myers had
made the Joint General Headquarters agreement work 'by
always forcing Zervas to give in to E.A.M.'.[82] The only conclusive evidence however as to whether or not Wallace really
did come to agree with Leeper that Myers's political outlook
and policy was quite mistaken is presumably contained in the
considered report which Wallace submitted to the Foreign
Office on his return. This document however has been retained
in the department of origin and is not available for consultation.[83]

It was presumably the fact that Brigadier Myers showed no
such readiness as Wallace to be convinced by Leeper as to what
was really going on in Greece that so aroused Leeper's ire.
Leeper certainly expressed himself extremely forcefully, even
violently, about what he regarded as Myers's obstinacy. Writing
to Sargent on the 25 August, he said:

> Myers has been to my mind a complete disaster. He is a man
> of most upright and obstinate character, which I find very
> boring as it is quite impossible to penetrate his skull. My
> blows seem to ricochet off his skull and disappear somewhere
> in thin air. He keeps on telling me that he must have hours
> and hours of conversation with me in order to convince me.
> I have avoided as many of these hours as possible, but even
> so I am completely convinced that he is a very dangerous
> fool, and being a fanatic for his own ideas, thinking that they
> provide the only means of winning the war in Greece, he runs
> around exposing them to all and sundry, British as well as
> Greeks. People of his kind naturally put their foot in it
> almost every hour, and his indiscretions, which are always
> frightfully well meant, came back and hit me in the face.[84]

Leeper's peremptory and abortive attempt to send the six
Greeks packing wrecked any chances there might have been of
bridging the vast gulf that had opened up between the resistance
and the government-in-exile, and in any case the uncompromising support given by Churchill, Roosevelt (then attending the
Quadrant Conference in Quebec) and Smuts to the King gave
him no room for manoeuvre. The Foreign Office and Churchill
were in complete agreement in this policy of total support for

the Greek King. Sargent had cabled Eden in Quebec on 20
August that 'our policy [is] still to give him all support we can
with a view to replacing him on his throne... Greece is and
always has been a vital British interest and... the King is
entitled to look to us for support, in return for the gallant role
he played in the early part of the war.'[85]

Despite their ready acquiescence in the guerrilla's demands
over the plebiscite, the members of Tsouderos's government
were incensed by the guerrillas subsequent demands that they
hold three portfolios within the government, those of the
Interior, War and Justice, actually on Greek territory.[86]
Leeper, despite his earlier enthusiasm for a coalition, was not
prepared to give any encouragement to such proposals. He was
further alarmed to hear from Tsouderos in early September
that the King was considering forming a non-political government on the Yugoslav model.[87] When one of the E.A.M.
representatives declared that they wanted the three portfolios
whether or not the King made the desired declaration on a
plebiscite, Leeper characteristically interpreted this as a sign of
E.A.M.'s inherent weakness. He considered it clear that the
Greek government 'counted for more in Greece than we had
been led to suppose if all these people were flocking into it as a
kind of Mecca'.[88] Moreover he felt vindicated when the Foreign
Office, following Churchill's 30 August telegram, joined in
calling for the immediate expulsion of the guerrilla delegation.

Clearly what most exercised Leeper during the latter phase
of the crisis was not so much the Greek government crisis as the
need to bring S.O.E. to heel, and in this he now of course had a
powerful ally in Churchill. He was also absolutely determined
that Myers should not go back to Greece, a determination
which he maintained to the bitter end. It has been claimed that
it was George II who prevented Myers from returning to Greece
by threatening to abdicate, but in fact the opposition to Myers's
return came in fact very largely from Leeper, although, according to Leeper, Myers had made a 'deplorable impression' on
the King and Tsouderos.[89] The Foreign Office certainly did
not share his strong feelings and were content that Myers should
return after his visit to London. As Howard put it in his minute
of 6 October, 'our case against Myers is weak. He was left
without guidance most of the time he was in Greece, and he

therefore evolved a policy of his own and carried it out heavily supported by S.O.E. This in fact led to our difference of opinion with S.O.E.'[90] It was the Commander-in-Chief Middle East who with Foreign Office encouragement decided in October that it would be inappropriate to send Myers back in view of the outbreak of open civil war in Greece, and in particular until the circumstances surrounding the death of the New Zealand B.L.O. Lieutenant Hubbard following an incident involving an E.L.A.S. detachment, had been clarified.[91]

Leeper, in the aftermath of the visit of the six Greeks, was determined that S.O.E.'s political activities should be totally subordinated to the Foreign Office. He told the Minister of State that it was imperative to get complete control over S.O.E. and, at the same time, he told Glenconner that he must issue 'the most stringent instructions to all his officers that they are to have no political conversations whatever with any Greeks, and they must leave the whole of this ridiculously complicated situation to me.' 'I hope', he added, 'that this will at least be partially obeyed, but I am far from confident that all S.O.E. officers understand what is and what is not a political conversation.'[92]

Leeper got quite a lot of what he was after. Certainly, it was the visit of the six guerrillas that precipitated what Sweet-Escott has called 'the annual August reorganization of S.O.E. in the Middle East'.[93] Lord Glenconner was forced to resign, Brigadier Keble (whom Leeper considered to be 'completely unscrupulous'[94]) was removed, Colonel Guy Tamplin died. Sir Charles Hambro, who resigned as executive head of S.O.E. in September, was a further indirect casualty of the Cairo shake-up. General Wilson despatched Brigadier Davey, his Director of Military Operations, to London to arrange with the Chiefs of Staff that Force 133, the section of S.O.E. concerned with the Balkans and the Near East, be brought under military control.*[95] Doubtless Leeper approved of this particular mission, although he considered Davey to be 'entirely in the hands of Keble'.[96]

Leeper was to some extent mollified by this new arrangement but his suspicion of S.O.E. remained firmly ingrained. On 7

* See pp. 266–268 below.

October 1943, for instance, he wrote somewhat cryptically to Sargent that 'S.O.E. telegrams destroy many little patriotic illusions'.[97] In a letter of 13 November 1943 to Sargent he complained that he found himself 'quite unable to understand the S.O.E. telegrams in their code form. It is not the vulgarity of the language in which they are couched, as I have picked up various vulgar expressions in the course of my life; it is not even the military abbreviations which defeat me; it is mainly the incomprehensible use of code words, scattered about here and there in every telegram just to make it more difficult for the Embassy.'[98]

I have dwelt at length with the Cairo crisis of August/September 1943 because this was clearly crucial in determining the subsequent course of British policy and because there the newly released documents do add a great deal to our knowledge. Leeper was aware of whispers emanating from some General Headquarters and S.O.E. circles that in his handling of the crisis he was in 'an excited mood about S.O.E.' and it is difficult, in fact, not to conclude this was in fact the case. But in fairness it should be pointed out that the British Embassy in Cairo was seriously handicapped by illness throughout the August crisis. Leeper, Wallace and Warner all spent several days confined to bed, the last in hospital, during August, while the King of Greece was also quite seriously ill during this period. This is clearly a factor that cannot be left out of account. Moreover, Leeper was clearly up against a formidable adversary in Brigadier Keble of S.O.E.*

After Cairo attitudes on both sides hardened, the six Greeks 'returned to Greece [in mid-September] disgruntled at their treatment and in a most disappointed frame of mind'.[99] The total failure of their mission and the ignominious treatment to which they had been subjected, coupled with the evidence they had received of the strong commitment of the British government to the support of the King, was certainly a factor contributing to the outbreak of civil war between the rival resistance groups in October.

In a minute of 7 October 1943 Howard referred to 'the disastrous effects of our dual policy in regard to Greece'.[100]

* See pp. 223–6 below.

This dual policy consisted of the Foreign Office policy of backing the King and government and S.O.E.'s of full support for E.A.M. There seemed to be, he considered, only two alternatives: either to drop British support of E.A.M. and concentrate on the King or to drop the King and concentrate on E.A.M. Following the outbreak of civil war in early October it was a modified version of the first alternative which was adopted and strongly advocated by Leeper, with the somewhat reluctant acquiescence of General Wilson, who was anxious to retain the cover that E.L.A.S. provided for British officers engaged in sabotage missions in Greece. In advocating a break with E.A.M. Leeper enjoyed the support of Churchill, who minuted on 3 November: 'E.A.M. and E.L.A.S. should be starved and struck at by every means in our power. But I fear that these means are small...'[101]

Leeper's zeal to destroy E.A.M. provides further evidence of his tendency to discount unpalatable evidence or views he disagreed with when supplied by on the spot observers. For when Woodhouse submitted a lengthy report from Pertouli, dated 19 October, shortly after the outbreak of civil war, in which he concluded that the Allied Military Mission would have 'to recognise the right of E.A.M.–E.L.A.S. to fight the war in its own way but may be able to achieve a good deal of your requirement by means of the personal popularity of individual British liaison officers'; Leeper commented on 4 November that 'I should point out that Woodhouse's report was written in the belief that Myers would be returning to Greece and that we were committed to an E.L.A.S. policy, whatever happened. I think we can take it that he would have expressed himself much more strongly against E.L.A.S. if he had thought there was any prospect of a change.'[102]

In mid-November 1943 Eden proposed to the War Cabinet that the British government adopt a policy of breaking with E.A.M./E.L.A.S.; General Wilson, again rather reluctantly, acceded to a modified version of this plan put forward by Leeper. By this plan support of E.A.M./E.L.A.S. was not to be renewed and, in an effort to wean the moderate rank and file from E.A.M./E.L.A.S., the King was to declare publicly that he would not return until invited to do so by a properly constituted and representative government. At the same time Zervas was to seek the incorporation of E.D.E.S. bands into the

Greek regular army, and propaganda was to be employed to induce the E.L.A.S. rank and file similarly to seek incorporation into the Greek regular army. Wilson was certainly conscious of the disadvantages associated with such a plan, not least the fact that the lives of 146 British personnel in Greece would be endangered, of whom 119 were in E.L.A.S.-controlled territory. He added that 'if British direction and energy were removed and then Civil War or complete control by E.A.M./E.L.A.S. supervened, [the] Germans might be able to withdraw a further 3 divisions from Greece'.[103] But despite the pleadings of Churchill and Eden, the King, backed up by Roosevelt, refused to give the desired assurances and the whole scheme foundered.

Following the collapse of this plan in November, the next initiative undertaken by the Foreign Office was to propose to the Greek government that they should appeal to Zervas (E.D.E.S.) and Sarafis (E.L.A.S.) to conclude an armistice and withdraw their bands to clearly specified areas. To give added strength to this appeal, it was suggested that the public approval of the British, American and Soviet governments should be sought. This plan was basically Leeper's and was outlined by him in a telegram of 14 December. The proposed plan was commended by Leeper on the grounds that it justified to the full the help given to Zervas if E.L.A.S. ignored the appeal, while at the same time it would undermine the authority of the leaders of E.L.A.S. if they did refuse. It brought in the three Allied governments and this, so Leeper thought, made it practically impossible for E.L.A.S. to ignore it. It would greatly strengthen the Greek government both in Egypt and in Greece, at the same time enabling the British government to avoid assuming any direct responsibility for taking sides in Greek internal affairs. Lastly it would increase the chances of renewed resistance to the Germans in Greece. The broad outlines of this plan met with the approval of the Foreign Office in London.[104]

Yet within a few days Leeper engaged in a characteristically volatile switch in policy. With the apparent concurrence of the Commander-in-Chief Middle East, Leeper advocated a virtually total British withdrawal from Greece and the complete dissolution of the guerrilla movement in Greece. This astonishing *volte face* was prompted by a meeting with Tsouderos on 17 December at which they discussed reports of very serious dis-

tress among the civilian population in the guerrilla held territories, caused by German obstruction of the distribution of
relief supplies. Tsouderos expressed approval for the proposed
appeal to the resistance groups but said that 'he was very uncertain about the continuance of the resistance movement at
all... He was inclined to think that unless His Majesty's
Government held strong views to the contrary, that it might be
better to urge the guerrillas to return to their villages, cultivate
the land and await future possibilities of action.' Before com-
mitting himself to such a withdrawal however he wanted to
consult with the Archbishop of Athens and other personalities
in Greece. Leeper however showed no such reservations and
wholeheartedly advocated such a policy, telegraphing to the
Foreign Office that 'the sooner we can make a justifiable withdrawal from Greece, the better it will be for the Greek people
and for our future relations with them...I suggest that we
should begin withdrawing B.L.O.s on a large scale,'[105] against
which Eden minuted 'Surely, we cannot do this. The war has
to be carried on.' Leeper amplified his views in a subsequent
telegram despatched on the same day, 18 December, after he
had consulted with the Commander-in-Chief Middle East. Both
agreed that the situation was getting out of British control and
that the Greeks must be left 'to settle their differences in their
own way'. Wilson, according to Leeper, believed that the
limited aircraft at his disposal should go to the Yugoslav Partisans and felt that 'it would be preferable to withdraw the
majority (of B.L.O.s) for proper military tasks, leaving a few at
key posts for intelligence purposes.' Leeper added that 'the task
of our officers in Greece has been rendered impossible by the
absence of outstanding patriotic leaders. Had they produced
anybody of the calibre of Tito, the results might have been very
different.' 'I have come to this conclusion', he continued, 'with
great reluctance but I feel that I must advise you in this sense
as I do not believe that further Greek resistance under present
conditions can help the war effort against the Germans, while
it will certainly inflict uncalled for hardship on a people who,
whatever their failures, have a warm affection for the British.'[106]

The Foreign Office was not impressed by Leeper's arguments. 'It is difficult', minuted Laskey on 20 December 1943,
'to see how we could do anything which would suit the German

better than to secure the break-up of the whole resistance
movement.' He also pointed out how unlikely it was, in any
case, that E.L.A.S. would heed any appeal to disband itself
voluntarily. Sargent shared Laskey's doubts, adding that

> I cannot understand the attitude of the C-in-C in all this.
> For a year past he has maintained that we must at all costs
> encourage the Greek guerrillas however politically undesirable
> they may be, however little direct contribution they made to
> the war effort, however little material support we could give
> them. We often felt that he overstated his case, but here he is
> going to the other extreme merely because the Germans have
> been more or less successful in preventing supplies from
> getting into the mountainous districts.'[107]

Cadogan, similarly disconcerted by the sudden *volte face*, concurred in Sargent's suggestion that Leeper should pursue his
original suggestion of an appeal by the Greek government for
an armistice. On 22 December Eden told Leeper that 'we do
not take the view that if we cannot bring the civil war to an end,
the bands should then go home. On the contrary we want
resistance to the enemy to continue....'[108] It was at this juncture that Sweet-Escott approached General Wilson to obtain a
message to be broadcast to the Greek guerrillas urging an end
to the civil war. 'The Greek peasant is a farmer', Wilson told
him, 'and his proper place at this stage of the war is on his farm,
not in the mountains.'[109]

In the event, Tsouderos broadcast his two appeals for a
cease-fire in late December, and the British, American and
Soviet governments issued public statements in support of his
appeal for unity, in the case of the Soviet government grudg-
ingly, although this reluctance seems to have been caused as
much by an almost total ignorance of the situation in Greece
as by willful obstruction. Following Tsouderos's appeal, a cease-
fire was eventually agreed to by E.L.A.S. and laborious negotiations began for the settlement of the protracted civil war.
While these negotiations were being carried out however Wilson
and the Chiefs of Staff were pushing hard for a policy of all-out
support for E.L.A.S. On 5 February, the very day that the
E.L.A.S. cease-fire came into effect, Wilson, reversing totally
his position of mid-December when he had backed Leeper in

the latter's advocacy of a policy of an almost complete withdrawal from Greece, cabled the Chiefs of Staff that he considered that the time had now come when political considerations should give way to the necessity of achieving British
objectives in retaining German divisions in the Balkans. To do
this it would be necessary to give every help to the E.L.A.S.
party in Greece, 'which is the only party in Greece which can
give us effective aid in killing Germans'. To obtain the best
results, he urged that the Foreign Office should reconsider 'their
ban on the return of Myers whose hold over E.L.A.S. leaders
produced such good co-operation last year'.[110] The Chiefs of
Staff supported Wilson's suggestion and proposed that the
British government resume full support 'for the E.A.M. faction
as being the most effective resistance movement in Greece'.[111]

Eden, in a minute of 10 February, argued strongly against the
proposals of Wilson and the Chiefs of Staff. He accepted that if
there were evidence that E.L.A.S. would be prepared to make
an all-out attack on the Germans, then there might be serious
grounds for considering whether or not the British government
should engage in a complete *volte face* and give all out support
for E.A.M./E.L.A.S. regardless of the political consequences.
He could see no grounds for such an expectation however and
considered E.A.M./E.L.A.S. 'a thoroughly unscrupulous gang
of communist fanatics, out solely for their own ends'.[112] He did
not advocate a break with E.A.M. but rather that existing
efforts to secure a military and political agreement should be
pursued. Churchill fully supported Eden's view and minuted on
14 February that 'we have not yet had any satisfaction from
E.L.A.S. for the murder of one of our officers.* They are more
hated by the countryside than the Germans. Obviously giving
them weapons will not increase their effort against the Germans
but only secure the domination of these base and treacherous
people after the war.'[113]

In a further minute to the Chiefs of Staff Committee on 24
February Churchill wrote:

> We must do our best to promote reconciliation between
> Zervas and the E.A.M.–E.L.A.S. bands. This will almost

* This is a reference to the killing of Lieutenant Arthur Hubbard the
previous November.

certainly prove impossible. We should suggest a British
Commander-in-Chief if no other agreement can be reached.
To effect this we should not hesitate to threaten and of course
if necessary to use the weapon of denunciation of E.A.M.–
E.L.A.S. for what it is worth. If in spite of all we can do the
negotiations break down, then we give no more support of
any kind to E.A.M.–E.L.A.S. but all possible support to
Zervas. No great results are anyhow to be expected from the
Greek guerrillas at the present time. The return of General
Myers cannot be allowed. . . There is no comparison between
them [E.A.M./E.L.A.S.] and the hands of Marshal Tito.
They are a mere scourge on the population, and are feared
by the Greek villagers even more than the Germans.[114]

At the end of February Colonel Woodhouse, after employing
such a threat of denunciation, was able to secure agreement for
a permanent armistice following the Merokovo conference. The
agreement was signed at Plaka on 29 February, an achievement
which Laskey considered was 'almost entirely due to Colonel
Woodhouse's tact and skill in handling the guerrilla delegates'.[115]
In retrospect it may appear that the conflict between short-
term military gain and long-term political advantage was
fundamentally an irresoluble one. Whatever direction British
policy had taken towards the resistance, the ultimate outcome
– the events of December 1944 – it may be argued, would have
been inevitable. None the less the overall impression left from a
study of the documents is that S.O.E. was generally more aware
of political realities and the balance of power within Greece
than was the Foreign Office. The Foreign Office's stubborn
rearguard action in defence of the King, with scant regard for
the wider interests of the Greek people, critically impeded its
scope for manoeuvre. It is only fair to re-emphasise though that
the Foreign Office could not really be regarded as a free agent
in this matter, given both the obduracy of King George and the
uninhibited support of Churchill for the cause of the monarchy
in Greece.[116] Eventually of course under the pressure of events,
the Foreign Office was forced to face up to the realities of the
situation in Greece and conceded what Brigadier Myers had
been urging from an early stage of the *Harling* mission, namely
that the King should not return before a plebiscite had been

held on the constitutional issue. Had such a concession been wrung out of the King in the spring of 1943 it might not have significantly hindered the wide control of the resistance in Greece which E.A.M./E.L.A.S. was able to build up, although it might have delayed that process. But, to put it at its lowest, an early and ungrudging adoption of this policy would have placed Britain in a stronger moral position when, in December 1944, she found herself engaged in bitter conflict with her former allies, E.A.M./E.L.A.S. The British government might then have escaped some of the obloquy heaped on it both in this country and in the United States, and the true direction of E.A.M./E.L.A.S.'s policies might have been brought home to public opinion rather earlier than it was.

NOTES

1. III (London, 1971) pp. 383–439.
2. Minute of 29 Jun 1941, FO 371/29840, R 6528.
3. Minute of 28 Dec 1941, FO 371/29842, R 10665.
4. FO 371/37196, R 3923. The Foreign Office seems never to have appreciated the depth of bitterness felt by the Greeks for the Metaxas dictatorship. Despite his experiences of war and post-war Greece, Sir Reginald Leeper was still able to write in his memoirs that 'it would be a mistake to imagine that the Metaxas régime aroused anything like the fierce hostility throughout the country that Greek politicians would have you think,' *When Greek meets Greek* (London, 1950) p. 10.
5. Minute of 18 Feb 1942, FO 371/33156, R 1240.
6. FO 371/29909, R 8996.
7. FO 371/29910, R 9987.
8. FO 371/33171, R 1018.
9. FO 371/37196, R 4117.
10. FO 371/33187, R 1836, R 1994.
11. FO 371/33187, R 2887.
12. FO 371/43684, R 5083.
13. FO 371/43684, R 5084.
14. 'Early British contacts with the Greek Resistance', *Balkan Studies*, XII. (1971) p. 354.
15. FO 371/33175, R 1793.
16. FO 371/33187, R 5354.
17. FO 371/33163, R 6961. I have been unable to trace a copy of Warner's actual report.
18. FO 371/33163, R 6961.
19. FO 371/33163, R 7640.
20. *La Résistance grecque 1940–1944* (Paris, 1966) p. 156, *The Kapetanios*

Partisans and Civil War in Greece, 1943–1949 (London, 1972) p. 22, *Griechenland zwischen Revolution und Konterrevolution (1936–1946)* (Frankfurt, 1973) p. 258.

21. Political Warfare Executive directives for 30 Oct to 5 Nov, 20 to 27 Nov, 27 Nov to 4 Dec, 4 to 11 Dec, 11 to 18 Dec.

22. Warner's emphasis. Minute of 5 Feb 1942, FO 371/33156, R 1269.

23. Minute of 31 Dec 1941, FO 371/2988, R 10898.

24. FO 371/37197, R 5657, Warner to Dixon, 20 Jun 1943, apropos S.O.E.'s proposal to spring the republican leader General Nikolaos Plastiras from the south of France, where he had been in exile since 1933. Warner added that he was horrified to learn that Ian Pirie 'reigns supreme in Greek affairs in Baker Street'.

25. FO 371/37208, R 11753.

26. FO 371/33163, R 7640.

27. FO 371/37199, R 8314; 371/37206, R 10553.

28. FO 371/37206, R 10553.

29. FO 371/43676, R 1127.

30. FO 371/37201, R 654. Emmanouil Tsouderos shared Sargent's low estimate of the value of the resistance effort in Greece: In a letter of 17 July 1943 he wrote to Leeper:

> Today all your expenses for the secret warfare of the guerrillas are in vain and still more so are our sacrifices in lives and material used for these secret operations.
>
> The profit you get out of these operations is small when compared to your enormous financial expenses for this type of warfare and to the reprisals taken by the enemy against us, by executions, expulsions, setting fire to villages and towns, rape of women etc. and all else that the enemy practices in revenge for the relatively unimportant acts of sabotage of the guerrilla groups.

Tsouderos Archive, file 10, Gennadeion Library, Athens.

31. FO 371/37201, R 2050.

32. FO 371/37201, R 2050.

33. FO 371/37194, R 2226.

34. FO 371/37201, R 2598.

35. Minute by Sir Alexander Cadogan, 6 Apr 1943, FO 371/37201 R 2636.

36. FO 371/37201, R 2636.

37. FO 371/37201, R 3348.

38. FO 371/33177, R 2657. See p. 121 above.

39. Minute of Dixon, 15 Jul 1943, FO 371/37203, R 5909.

40. FO 371/37203, R 5029.

41. Minute by D. S. Laskey, 16 Jun 1943, FO 371/37203, R 5192.

42. FO 371/37199, R 8314.

43. *When Greek meets Greek*, pp. 30–3, *Greek Entanglement* (London, 1955) pp. 228–65, *Eight Years Overseas, 1939–1947* (London, 1948) pp. 166–8. *O Doureios Ippos* (Athens, 1958) pp. 148–70. See also Chapter 6.

44. Harling to Cairo, No. 50, 21 Feb 1943. S.O.E. Records.

45. FO 371/37201, R 2050.
46. FO 371/37201, R 2702.
47. Cairo to Keelrow, 6 May 1943. S.O.E. Records.
48. FO 371/37196, R 4236.
49. FO 371/37202, R 4717.
50. FO 371/37196, R 3456.
51. FO 371/37203, R 6555.
52. FO 371/37202, R 4504.
53. FO 371/37197, R 6418.
54. Minute of 25 Feb 1944, FO 371/43680, R 3308.
55. FO 371/37202, R 4459.
56. FO 371/37202, R 4503.
57. *When Greek meets Greek*, p. 31.
58. FO 371/37204, R 7884.
59. FO 371/37204, R 7217.
60. *Baker Street Irregular* (London, 1965) p. 174.
61. FO 371/37204, R 7884. In his preliminary report on his mission, radioed from within Greece, Wallace made the point that during the course of his visit he had met only one genuine Royalist. FO 371/37204, R 8088.
62. *When Greek meets Greek*, p. 32.
63. FO 371/37204, R 7884.
64. FO 371/37198, R 7515.
65. FO 371/37198, R 7514.
66. ΓO 371/37198, R 7515.
67. FO 371/37198, R 7516.
68. FO 371/37204, R 7548.
69. *O Doureios Ippos*, pp. 154, 155. There is a discrepancy between the accounts of Pyromaglou and Leeper as to who was making the running over the constitutional issue in Cairo. According to Pyromaglou (op. cit., pp. 149–50, 160) it was the non-Communist delegates, i.e. Kartalis, Tsirimokos and himself, who were the most uncompromising (see p. 141 above). This was not, however, Leeper's reading of the situation. On 25 August he wrote to Sargent that Pyromaglou, whom he considered to be much the 'nicest' of the delegation, attached 'far more importance to weakening the influence of E.A.M. in Greece than trying to exclude the King from returning there. In fact he, like Zervas, will do anything we wish on this matter or on any other matters' (FO 371/37199, R 8314). One of the reasons why Leeper may have got this impression was because Pyromaglou, at his first meeting with Leeper, deliberately omitted any mention of the issue of the monarchy, as he had previously been told by Wallace that Leeper had been fully persuaded on the constitutional issue (Pyromaglou, 153). Leeper dismissed Kartalis, the E.K.K.A. representative, as 'a frivolous character educated at the London School of Economics' (371/4367, R 1860).
70. FO 371/37198, R 7758, R 7819.
71. FO 371/37231, R 7894.
72. *Greek Entanglement*, p. 254.
73. FO 371/37198, R 7950.
74. Minute of 24 Aug 1943, FO 371/37198, R 7950.

75. FO 371/37198, R 7950. The views put forward by Leeper and Churchill are a striking manifestation of the tendency, to which Colonel Woodhouse has drawn attention, of the British government authorities 'to under-rate the importance of what went on in Greece, so long as tranquillity was restored in exile', *Apple of Discord: A Survey of Recent Greek Politics in their International Setting* (London, 1948) p. 157.

76. FO 371/37204, R 7864, R 7884, R 8216.

77. FO 371/37204, R 7532. Pearson in his covering letter of 10 August wrote that Wallace's telegram had been delayed owing to corruptions in transmission. Further telegrams were forwarded on 11 August.

78. FO 371/37204, R 8088. Leeper, on learning from Wallace of the existence of the telegrams, was understandably furious, particularly as he discovered that some of them had been forwarded on to S.O.E. London, before he, in Cairo, had had sight of them. When he taxed Glenconner about the muddle, he was told that it was entirely due to a shortage of cipherers. Telegram of 16 Aug 1943, FO 371/37204, R 7754.

79. FO 371/37199, R 8314.

80. FO 371/37204, R 8216.

81. FO 371/37204, R 8048.

82. FO 371/37199, R 8314.

83. FO 371/37213, R 8419. This document was available to Sir Llewellyn Woodward in writing his official history of British foreign policy. According to Woodward the Foreign Office regarded the Wallace report as an extremely able piece of work. One of the recommendations contained in the Wallace report may have been that Myers should not return to Greece, for on 6 October Howard minuted that 'Mr Leeper has all along been against Brigadier Myers' return to Greece; so for that matter has Major Wallace. They base their objections on the fact that Myers is so committed to the guerilla cause (and in particular to the Communist E.A.M.) that nothing will change his views, and that even if he were convinced and wanted to change his policy, he would not now be able to do so.' FO 371/37205, R 9679.

84. FO 371/37199, R 8314.

85. FO 371/37198, R 7742.

86. FO 371/37199, R 8263.

87. FO 371/37199, R 8370.

88. FO 371/37199, R 8382.

89. FO 371/37205, R 9679.

90. FO 371/37205, R 9679. See note 83 above.

91. FO 371/37206, R 10831.

92. FO 371/37199, R 8314.

93. *Baker Street Irregular*, p. 173.

94. FO 371/37208, R 11753.

95. *Eight Years Overseas*, p. 169, *Baker Street Irregular*, p. 175. See also Sir Colin Gubbins, 'S.O.E. and the co-ordination of Regular and Irregular War', in M. Elliott-Bateman, *The Fourth Dimension of Warfare* (Manchester, 1970) pp. 94–5.

96. FO 371/37208, R 11753.

97. FO 371/37206, R 10553.
98. FO 371/37208, R 12295.
99. *Report on S.O.E. activities in Greece and the islands of the Aegean Sea*, Appendix III, 10.
100. FO 371/37205, R 9785.
101. FO 371/37207, R 11098.
102. FO 371/37207, R 11673.
103. FO 371/37209, R 12642.
104. FO 371/37209, R 13188.
105. FO 371/37209, R 13431.
106. FO 371/37209, R 13431.
107. FO 371/37209, R 1342.
108. FO 371/37209, R 13478.
109. *Baker Street Irregular*, p. 196.
110. FO 371/43677, R 1687.
111. FO 371/43678, R 1940.
112. FO 371/43678, R 1940.
113. FO 371/43678, R 1940.
114. FO 371/43680, R 3308. Cf. Churchill's minute of 6 February 1944: 'There seems to be no limit to the baseness and treachery of E.L.A.S. and we ought not to touch them with a barge pole,' FO 371/43678, R 1933.
115. FO 371/43681, R 3342.
116. Churchill, in a letter of 27 October 1941 to Tsouderos, referred to Greece's 'beloved constitutional monarchy', *Tsouderos Archive*, file 19, Gennadeion Library, Athens.

PART TWO

DISCUSSION

8 Following Sweet-Escott

Barker: May I ask a question about the information available to S.O.E. London or Cairo? You say that they did not have intercepts. But did they then rely entirely on reports from officers in the field? There was a lot of information other than intercepts, for instance reports from S.I.S. There were reports coming from exiled politicians such as Dr Miha Krek, the Slovene Clerical exiled leader, and the Croat Peasant Party exiled leader, Dr Juraj Krnjević, who were feeding in vast quantities of material all the time.

Gubbins: We were working of course directly with the emigré governments of the countries concerned in London and therefore we were dealing directly with the Prime Minister and the Foreign Secretary and those sort of people. We got their general information, which you had to check very carefully to be sure it was not biassed. But of course we did get a certain amount of information from our own sources, from the Foreign Office itself sometimes. And you see our Chief of Staff, General R. H. Barry, was almost a member of the Joint Planning Staff, under the Chiefs of Staff and also of the Joint Intelligence Committee. So General Barry was most frequently there at their meetings – they used to call him in and of course he got a lot of information from that. We did get a lot of local information from the field as well as on our own wireless transmissions.

Barker: On reading through the papers available in the Public Record Office it surprised me how much information there was available from the beginning of 1942 onwards from Croat and Slovene sources, through the Stockholm Press Reading Bureau, the Istanbul Press Reading Bureau and so on, which did throw quite a lot of light on the Partisans in Yugoslavia. I was wondering if this was available to S.O.E., whether they took it into account, or whether they relied very heavily on what their own officers were saying?

Sweet-Escott: I am not really competent to answer that, because

I was not there at the time, but I would have been very surprised to hear that we did not have this, at any rate through the
earlier part of 1942. But you must remember that from about
June 1942 (prior to the Battle of El Alamein) Cairo was a mass
of flames caused by the burning of government records, and the
whole of the intelligence system and the supply of intelligence
was disrupted through that.

Clissold: Could I ask a supplementary question to this? Another
source of information surely was the transmissions of Free
Yugoslavia, which was the radio station everybody knew was
set up somewhere in the Soviet Union and clearly the information coming over it was very biassed, but nevertheless from fairly
early in 1942 it was monitored and did in one way or another
provide a good deal of information.

Seton-Watson: There was a time in the winter of 1942–3 when
reports in the Soviet press reaching Cairo several months later
on operations in Yugoslavia or reported by the Free Yugoslavia
station, were quite useful sources of information. They indicated
that something was going on in parts of Bosnia. This is pretty
low grade information (from the intelligence point of view) but
it did in fact play its part in building up a certain picture.

Davidson: The country sections of S.O.E. were organised, as
Sweet-Escott has said, I think in August 1942. I was appointed
to the Yugoslav section – i.e. at the operational level – in
October, I think. My recollection on the intercepts is very clear
although I cannot put a date on it. I think that in early January
1943 we began to get intercepts and these arrived on my desk
probably at the beginning of January. These were very clearly
intercepts of the Sicherheitsdienst inside Yugoslavia, i.e., it was
extremely valuable information. Unfortunately I cannot specify
a date, but their arrival was a crucial factor because it marked
the beginning of a whole new concept. If it would ever be
possible it would be very interesting to know when that code
was actually broken. There is thus the interesting question –
how long had these intercepts been available and why did they
reach me, the lowly Major in, I think, January 1943? Why not
before or after and why in that case were they not available in
London? They were messages such as, for example, saying that
'Partisans at X or Y are moving to Z. We are calling up
Četniks against them.' A second factor of historical interest, in

my recollection, is that this information played a very considerable part in the persuasion of the Prime Minister, when he came to Cairo in February 1943 to initiate changes. I think these two factors refer back to what General Gubbins said at the beginning – why did it take so long for our masters to wake up to this situation and what happened to these intercepts? I think that if light could ever be thrown on those two factors we should get the third factor which is why our policy changed. There is one other thing I should like to say to Sweet-Escott – although the reviewer in the *Times Literary Supplement* may have been wrong, he was not being malicious. The general historical analysis put forward in that review was, and was probably intended to be controversial. It may be right or it may be wrong. It was certainly not malicious, and I know this because I wrote the review. I do not think it helps to call it malicious. I do not think that we shall get much further in elucidation of the general reconstruction of the history of that period unless we do take into account the general political trends which were dominant at the top.

Sweet-Escott: I forget exactly when I took over in London, but I was certainly in charge of the Balkan desk by the end of March. And I can say that I saw none of this. I think that part of the misunderstanding which there was between S.O.E. London and S.O.E. Cairo was due to the fact which is new to me today, that you in Cairo were seeing the intercepts and in London we were not.

Davidson: I am sure you were not but it would be very interesting to know why not.

Seton-Watson: There must have been a stage when someone, somehow began to release intercepts; because at various stages, one after the other, individuals were initiated into receiving them. The whole initiation ceremony was a very solemn occasion. The decision whether and when to allow someone to make use of this information was taken by a gentleman whom one had mixed feelings about, but I have always had a rather healthy respect for, the late Brigadier Keble. He was the man inside S.O.E. who, I think, had the right to decide which officers to reveal the information from the intercepts to. On the whole I think he judged it rather well. But there must have been a point at which he was allowed to have this information and then allowed to use his discretion. It would be very interesting to know at what stage somebody told S.I.S. to release it in Cairo. It might have had something to do with the views of the Commander-in-Chief Middle East.

Bailey: I think I can shed a little light on the question of when the intercepts first became available. It is negative evidence, but I think it has a bearing. When I became one of the victims of the 1941 Cairo purge, Taylor arranged for me to go to America. By the time I got there the Americans were in the war, so my activities were confined rather ironically to selecting half a dozen Canadian Croats who were the first to be dropped to contact the resistance forces in Bosnia–Hercegovina and Croatia – that is the Partisans. Later I was asked to return to Europe and go in myself to Mihailović to find out exactly what was going on there. I got to Cairo in August, promptly contracted malaria and did not start my parachute training until the end of September. I then hung about trying to get into Yugoslavia until Christmas Day 1942. At that time information was beginning to come in about the Partisans and other unidentified resistance groups active in Bosnia, Croatia and Slovenia. I have a very clear recollection of a wall map with areas mentioned marked in. When I asked what they were, Davidson replied, 'Those are groups that are coming to the fore,' but I do not think they were referred to as 'Partisans', but as guerrillas. I believe that supports the view that intercepts were not being made generally available, at any rate up to the time when I left for Mihailović's headquarters.

Davidson: I think it was after you left that we began to get information from intercepts.

Deakin: I quite agree with Bailey. I remember the same wall map. I do not think the information we are talking about started to come in until January 1943. I was in the Yugoslav section in London, perhaps the only one who had been, at the time, first in London and then in Cairo. I was literally at sea for nearly two months coming out by ship and therefore out of touch with information from either London or Cairo. I arrived in Cairo in December 1942. So from the point of view of the dates concerned, I think the memories of the three of us coincide, that these intercepts we are talking about really did not start to come into the Yugoslav section of S.O.E. Cairo of which Davidson was the head, until January 1943.

As to the nature of the intercepts, I do not think, although my recollection may be wrong, they were anything at all to do with the most top secret intercepts. I think they were at a fairly low level – military intercepts of military material, movements of German units inside the Balkans. They did not come from London. My recollection is that at a given moment, rather suddenly and mysteriously, Davidson and I were given these. I think they came at the insistence of the military in Cairo who had received all this from the Chiefs of Staff in London. The purpose was to prompt us and everybody by all means at our disposal to do something. As part of this general move, orders, or rather certain suggestions, came to us from inside General Headquarters Cairo. I think this is the nature of the intercepts we are talking about.

Davidson: They were Sicherheitsdienst intercepts? (S.D.s)

Deakin: They were S.D.s certainly.

Keble's name has been mentioned and this is a question of fitting the fact that we are discussing documents now in his report which he managed to hand personally to the Prime Minister. It is very interesting because it is the first time that there is any mention of anybody in Yugoslavia, apart from General Mihailović. This report is dated 20 February 1943. It was handed to the Prime Minister in Cairo on his way back from the Adana conference. He took it to London and passed it over to the Chiefs of Staff and to the Foreign Office. It was then distributed on a very limited circulation as a confidential print. This was the first time one gets a mention of the Slovene and Croat guerrillas – these mysterious bands that are very difficult to identify or even to analyse who they were; but this is where this first magic phrase appears.

Davidson: But this bears out Deakin's point that the intercepts might have been of local origin and that might explain why they did not get to London. This was intercepted German traffic. All I can say is that they were extremely correct and extremely detailed. So detailed – and I must have seen a hundred of them – that they made it possible to drop two teams blind and the first team got immediately to the headquarters of the Croat guerrillas or Partisans.

Taylor: I do think I can throw some light on the high level and the operational intercepts that Davidson was talking about.

There was a very definite distinction between them. I am quite sure we were not getting any sort of information in intercepts of either kind down to June or July 1942. I am also fairly certain that Barker's point about co-ordinated intelligence is right. We were not getting any sort of properly co-ordinated intelligence from various sources. Then, as far as the mystery of Cairo is concerned, I think that what happened was this – I can speak of this because in December 1942 I happened to be in Cairo as part of a general tour of S.O.E. missions. At that time Cairo and London had got into long and muddled arguments about whether the Partisans should be praised in the B.B.C. broadcasts. Quite a bit was known about the Partisans in general in December 1942. Cairo had themselves recommended to London that some effort should be made to contact the Partisans. Taking up this point London then accepted the suggestion of the Foreign Office, who were being pressed by the Russian Embassy, that the Partisans should be praised, or at least spoken of favourably in the B.B.C. broadcasts. Cairo came back and said that was not what they meant. They were very much in favour of contacting the Partisans, but in the meantime merely to praise the Partisans on the B.B.C. broadcasts was going to madden Mihailović and make him more obstinate and impossible than he was already without any compensatory benefit since no contact had yet been made with the Partisans. This argument went on back and forth. In the end I wrote out for Hambro a fifteen page detailed summary of every message we had received. The confusion was incredible. In the course of these exchanges it emerged in discussing the Partisans that Keble knew quite a lot about them and Cairo mentioned that he knew quite a lot about them because he had been receiving local operational intercepts in Cairo. The reason why he had been receiving these was nothing whatever to do with S.O.E., but because by pure good fortune, in his previous job, before he came to S.O.E., he was on the Middle East distribution list for the reception of operational intercepts and he remained on it after he left his previous post in intelligence. Nobody took him off, so he continued to get them. That, I think, explains why certain quite detailed operational intercepts came through to Keble in S.O.E., and he made use of them entirely at his own discretion. It is difficult to say now whether his discretion was wisely exercised or not. It is possible that he was so worried about the danger of being taken off the list that he did not make as much use of them as he ought to have, or as soon as he ought to have.

Barker: On this B.B.C. point – it was surely Hudson who was in favour of the B.B.C. mentioning the Partisans as a means of pressure on Mihailović, and at first he was very pleased.*

Taylor: He was, because at that time Hudson was wholly pre-occupied with the problem of having some leverage over Mihailović. As a matter of fact, the arguments that went on were incredibly confused. Both sides in the end completely changed their positions. So that in the end Cairo, who had been the first to raise the question of supporting the Partisans, were in the course of the argument moved to the position of not wanting them mentioned and appearing to take an anti-Partisan line and London who because of their relations with the Yugoslav government had been opposed to the idea of even contacting the Partisans, ended up by strongly supporting their mention on the B.B.C.

Bailey: This was still a problem at the end of 1942. And by that time Hudson had changed his mind. I think a lot of people were influenced – it was difficult not to be influenced – by local repercussions of propaganda for one side or the other. Sometimes it aroused the local population to fury, sometimes it produced entirely the opposite reaction. Moreover after several months in the field all of us who had been there on missions, with only very tenuous communications with the outside world, were affected. We became incapable of preserving our objectivity.

Taylor: I have no doubt that the ultimate attitude taken up in Cairo just before Christmas 1942 was in fact the right one. This was that it was tactically unwise to praise the Partisans over the B.B.C. at that particular moment and before contact had been made with them. It was essentially based on the idea that we were going to make contact with the Partisans and it was no good praising them and upsetting Mihailović before contact

* See telegram from Hudson (Bullseye 828) enclosed in letter of 1.11.42 from Peter Boughey (of S.O.E. London) to Elisabeth Barker (FO 371/33445) and Hudson's telegram of 15.11.42 in Boughey's letter of 27.11.42 to Dixon of the Foreign Office (FO 371/33473).

had been made and in a situation when we had no means whatever of influencing them or getting any results from them.

Barker: Was it also that Bailey was about to be dropped in and we did not want him to drop into a particularly unpleasant atmosphere?

Taylor: Yes; that is what gave the argument particular weight. The broadcasts by the B.B.C. on the lines proposed were bound to prejudice Bailey's project and make even more difficult his relations with Mihailović and they could not at that stage have done any practical good other than satisfying the Russian Embassy.

Myers: May I make one small point for the record in connection with the operations that were part of a cover plan to conceal the fact that the invasion was going to take place in Sicily. The greatest part of the success of the sabotage all over Greece for this operation, which went under the code name of *Animals,* was due to the efforts of the British and Greek personnel who were dropped in. This is quite true but if we had not had freedom of movement for these parties all over Greece they could not have achieved their job. Before we were in contact with large bands of andartes (guerrillas) we had to move extremely cautiously. The occupants of every village were petrified if we came anywhere near the village. Even Woodhouse on his way to find Zervas moved by night, as we did also on our way to evacuation (which never materialised) after we took part in the Gorgopotamos operation. Although we did come at night into the villages most of the time, sometimes we had to live out in the open. We did need these andartes for morale purposes as well as information about where the enemy were, where the security police were, who were paid by the occupying power and who would have betrayed us if we had not had these andartes to keep them quiet.

Stevens: If I could just pitch into the discussion of this formative period, I am afraid with a very fuzzy memory. I would certainly confirm that G.R. were recruited as soldiers, and relations with Ian Pirie (S.O.E. Cairo) for those of us who came into S.O.E. through G.R. were very distant and the reception was very cool. At least one felt that one was considered likely to blow somebody or something. This may have been the effect of the Antiparos operation. One was not encouraged to go up to that department, but you got occasional bits of paper which only really referred to Athens or to the general background. Then, when the headquarters reconstruction took place (August 1942), these bits of paper from Keble came. There was other intelligence coming in, but again mostly naval stuff, I seem to remember, about movements in the port of Piraeus, but nothing on the andartes or E.L.A.S. The point I want to make is that, looking back, it can be seen that we were at the mercy of the inevitably haphazard recruiting that had to be done. There were a limited number of people who knew Greece and who could speak Greek. There were a lot of volunteers who were ready to go and there were some people whom we were glad to see the back of. This much I can remember clearly – that just before I went into Greece in the spring of 1943 telegrams were coming from British officers, not far from each other, slanging each other personally, saying this man is now letting down the E.L.A.S. cause or that man has gone over to the Communists. It was this confusion and the fact that we had no background to check against in the form of information about guerrilla activity – we depended entirely on the field for taking decisions – which was one of the reasons why I was sent in to try and find out what was going on. I remember one man who was particularly brave but really knew nothing about Greece. I would add that when I arrived I could not conceive that Greeks would want to be fighting each other. Nobody had given me that idea but admittedly I was green about Greece. So I would just make the point that human material was very varied. Certainly up to April 1943 we were almost totally dependent on British Liaison Officers' reports about the situation in the mountains and they varied really wildly as to how they judged the loyalty, efficiency and reliability of the bands they were attached to, even in areas that were not very far apart.

Deakin: Did anyone ever see any intercepts regarding the movements of German troops in Greece?
Stevens: Yes, I was taken into Keble's room and shown the file. But they were on the whole confined to troop movements, mostly through the Piraeus. They did not refer to activities against andartes. But these were early days. At this time there really were no formed bodies which Germans were chasing

on any scale at all. I am talking of October 1942 to March 1943.

Woodhouse: At the beginning of that period it would only have been the Italians anyway. We hardly had any S.O.E. contact with the Germans until the *Animals* operation in the summer of 1943, because the majority of the garrison in the areas where we were operating then was Italian.

Stevens: I am clear in my mind of this, that we were relying on telegrams from Woodhouse and others. One particular one which we were questioning, because it was such an incredible thing, was to the effect that Woodhouse was under duress. Another point that I would like to raise is that at some point, certainly as regards Greece, the military view of S.O.E. took over from the political view. I think this is partly due to the point which Sweet-Escott made that the military value of Greece, to put it crudely, stopped much earlier than that of Yugoslavia. It stopped, or slowed down, whereas that of Yugoslavia accelerated. I came out of Greece before the end in 1944, and found that Colonel Vincent Budge, the head of the Greek section S.O.E. Cairo, had his game book in which he counted the amount of enemy heads that were chopped off; and he was nowhere nearer any feeling for what the underlying political problems were. I go back to the period we are talking about now – 1942–3 – when there was emerging the same problem as in Yugoslavia; two parties were beginning to appear and views were being held by rival British officers in the field about the respective merits of these two parties. And, I repeat, how highly unprepared were a number of the officers sent in with one or two notable exceptions here present. And I have the feeling that Keble and his successors had a much stronger military control over events in Greece and over judgements about Greek events than his political counterpart. But this was not the case as regards Yugoslavia. It may or may not have been, but this, I think, somehow warped judgements in Cairo.

Taylor: I can confirm in some more detail what Stevens was saying about the change in policy on Greece of General Head-quarters Middle East because this is all a matter of record. I think it is fair to say that the *Harling* mission was regarded as a relatively isolated military operation and you were all, with the exception of Woodhouse and one W/T operator, guaranteed that you would be brought out again when it was over. The success of the Gorgopotamos operation on 25 November 1942 obviously had a tremendous effect. On 1 January 1943 Keble wrote a memorandum to the Chiefs of Staff in Cairo trying to capitalise for S.O.E. on the success of the Gorgopotamos operation and saying that, in view of this and of the general strategic situation, would it not be sensible to retain the *Harling* mission in existence and try to organise in Greece, but more effectively than we had done in Yugoslavia, a general rising to fit in with the invasion of Sicily. Keble got his final approval for a definite plan in approximately March 1943; and Myers got a signal about twelve pages long, setting out in great detail what the strategic background was and what it was thought that S.O.E. might now do in Greece in the way of interfering with Germans. Now, as has already been pointed out, when General Headquarters Cairo finally adopted the new attitude of using S.O.E. for general resistance purposes, they really knew practically nothing about what the political section in Cairo had in fact been doing, and the information they had been accumulating literally for years. They had been getting quite a lot of information out through the W/T link with Prometheus II. But they never really succeeded in putting two and two together and at the time of Gorgopotamos, and even afterwards, when additional B.L.O.s were sent in to Myers, they were not, I think, ever as fully briefed as they ought to have been in the light of what the political section really knew. This was partly due to the old 'two sides of the house' situation in S.O.E. Cairo resulting from the fusion of G.R. with the remnant of the old S.O.E. personnel and the office reorganisation on 'functional' lines. Another factor was that the whole of the official planning of operations in Greece was supposed to be done with the Anglo-Greek Committee on which the Greek government sat and on which Kanellopoulos was the principal Greek representative. All of which was a complete myth in the sense that the Committee represented absolutely nothing. Everything that was being done by Pawson and other people was being done almost entirely behind the back of the Greek government, because if the Greek government had known about it they would have made the most frightful fuss; so that a muddle was inevitable.

Myers: Can we be quite precise about the date at which we got this general directive from General Headquarters? I think it was earlier than March.

Woodhouse: There were in fact four directives in the first four months of 1943. The first was on 2 January, the next two were in February and the decisive one, which lined up the *Animals* Operation and which contained the secret information that the target was Sicily and not Greece, was 29 May.

9 Statement by Brigadier Sir Fitzroy Maclean

In deciding what to try and talk about at this conference, I came to the conclusion that, having thirty years ago sent a large number of signals and reports to the government and military authorities and having since written two lengthy books, there would be little point in my giving this audience any further account of my mission to Tito during the eighteen months from September 1943 to March 1945. What I thought might be more useful would be for me to give for the first time some account of the circumstances which led up to my appointment as commander of the mission and to my eventual despatch to Yugoslavia. This may, I think, help fill in some of the gaps in Elisabeth Barker's paper, just as her paper helps to make clear to me a lot of things I had not known before.

In June 1943 I was commanding a detachment of the 1st S.A.S. which was then training near Haifa. We were due to go to Crete to attack an enemy airfield, but at the last moment the Germans moved their planes away and, much to our disgust, the operation was cancelled. It was then that it occurred to me that a permanent job in enemy-occupied Europe might perhaps be a better bet than occasional trips behind the lines, which were no longer anything like as easy to lay on as they had been in the heyday of the desert war.

I had naturally heard of the exploits of Myers, Woodhouse and others. I knew quite a lot of classical Greek and a few words of modern. And so, happening on a trip to General Headquarters Cairo to run across Rex Leeper, whom I knew from Foreign Office days, I asked him what he thought my chances were of getting a job in Greece. He said he thought rather good and promised to send a telegram to London to find out more. Feeling pleasantly elated, I went back to my unit and a few days later was summoned to Cairo to see the answer. This said that I was wanted, not for Greece, but for Yugoslavia and that I was to come back and report to the Prime Minister immediately.

On the assumption that I was destined to join General Mihailović, who at that time was the only Yugoslav resistance leader I had heard of, I accordingly climbed on to the next plane and flew home.

On reaching England I soon realised that the assignment was not what I had expected. Churchill explained to me that of late he had begun to have doubts about Mihailović's contribution to the war effort and wanted to know more about a shadowy figure called Tito whose Communist Partisans seemed from enemy intercepts to be operating on a considerable scale in Bosnia, Montenegro and elsewhere. He mentioned that Bill Deakin and some other B.L.O.s had been dropped in some weeks earlier and that heavy fighting seemed to be in progress. What he wanted me to do was to go in and find out who was killing most Germans and how we could best help them to kill more. Politics were to be a secondary consideration. He wished me to command the mission with the rank of Brigadier and also to be his own personal representative with the Partisan command. I could, he said, pick anyone in the whole Army as my second in command and the best available team of officers and N.C.O.s to go with us. What was important was that I should be dropped in as soon as possible. This would be done under the auspices of S.O.E. and he had given them instructions to afford me all possible assistance.

I accordingly went round to Baker Street to make my mark and ask them to get me on to the first plane to Cairo, which they undertook to do. A week or so later I rang up to ask when I was going and was told that, owing to bad weather, there had been no flying. A day or two after that I was sent for to No. 10 Downing Street to see the Prime Minister. He showed me a signal he had had from General Wilson, the Commander-in-Chief Middle East. This said that he considered me totally unsuitable for the job. I was somewhat pained at this as General Wilson happened to be an old friend from whom I had recently had any amount of help and encouragement in raising my detachment of S.A.S. Churchill then showed me the reply he had sent General Wilson over his private link. This said fairly abruptly that the Commander-in-Chief was to do what he was told and not argue. Meanwhile, S.O.E. continued to assure me that there were still no planes to Cairo.

Walking across the Horseguards Parade after leaving No. 10, I happened to meet a friend, who, in the course of conversation, told me that he was flying to Cairo next day. I accordingly went straight back with him to his office and rang up the Air Ministry direct. They had heard of me, but said they had been told by S.O.E. that I did not really want a passage. I said that on the contrary I wanted one very badly and they at once gave me one. I then went round to S.O.E., where I was as usual greeted with the news that the weather was not fit for flying. I said my information was otherwise and that I had my passage in my pocket. In that case, they said, I had better see Lord Selborne. I saw Lord Selborne, who was most agreeable, congratulated me on the trust which the Prime Minister had placed in me and suggested that I should take an oath of loyalty to S.O.E. I said I would rather not. At this he pointed to two little leather cases on his desk with the letters D.S.O. in gold. 'That', he said, 'is what we do for those who serve us loyally.' I almost said I would take one on account, but thought better of it. I was beginning to wonder about S.O.E.

On reaching Cairo a couple of days later, I was at once sent for by the Commander-in-Chief. His outer office was manned by two friends of mine. 'What', they asked 'has got into the Prime Minister? Jumbo [Wilson] has just had a personal signal from him about you in reply to nothing he ever sent, telling him to shut up and do as he's told.' We then exchanged notes and quickly came to the conclusion that someone must have drafted and sent a personal signal to the Prime Minister in the Commander-in-Chief's name, without bothering to tell the Commander-in-Chief.

After this enlightening interlude, I went in to see the Commander-in-Chief, who, rightly or wrongly, had never much liked S.O.E. He said that he intended to find out who had sent the signal in his name and take action accordingly. Meanwhile I was to get myself gazetted Brigadier and come back to him if I had any trouble over anything.

Having thus secured my base, I went round to Rustum Buildings to call on S.O.E. Cairo. Here I was taken to see Brigadier Keble, the Chief of Staff. His first question was why was I dressed as a Brigadier. I said because the Commander-in-Chief had told me to. He then asked me why I had been to see the Commander-in-Chief. I said because he had sent for me. He said that next time the Commander-in-Chief sent for me I was not to go. I said that, as a serving soldier, if sent for by the Commander-in-Chief, I would certainly go.

After this brisk exchange, Keble went on to say that I could take it from him that I would never go to Yugoslavia, whatever the Commander-in-Chief or the Prime Minister or anyone else might say. S.O.E. had opposed my appointment from the start and would see to it by one method or another that I never took it up. Meanwhile he had given strict instructions that I should be shown no files, signals or anything else concerning Yugoslavia. To this I replied, with, I hope, becoming dignity, that I saw no point in prolonging our conversation.

What now concerned me most was to ensure that my departure for Yugoslavia was not held up any longer than was absolutely necessary by S.O.E. or anybody else. I accordingly at once went to see the Commander-in-Chief.

When I arrived, his military assistant asked me if I would wait, as General Wilson was closeted with a Colonel P. C. Vellacott, whose job it was to spread carefully thought-out rumours and whispers, designed to cause confusion in the mind of the enemy and produce other no less desirable results. Meanwhile, said the military assistant, he would let the Commander-in-Chief know I was there.

After a few minutes the bell rang and I went in. 'Tell Fitzroy what you just told me,' the Commander-in-Chief said to Vellacott. At which Vellacott, a charming man and in real life a most distinguished academic, explained that he had received from S.O.E. a request to spread a whisper about me. This was to the effect that I was a hopeless drunk, an active homosexual and that during the whole of my time with David Stirling in the S.A.S. I had shown myself consistently cowardly and unreliable. This whisper was to be put round the bazaars, the bars of Shepheard's and the Continental, and of course G.H.Q. He was sure, said Colonel Vellacott, that S.O.E. had excellent reasons for wishing this impression of me to get around. But even so he had felt it wiser to get confirmation from General Wilson himself.

After Colonel Vellacott had taken his leave, with instructions to put a freeze on that particular rumour, the Commander-in-Chief asked me what I thought of that. I said that, after the conversation I had just had with Brigadier Keble, nothing surprised me. In fact I had come to ask him to send a signal to the Prime Minister on my behalf to tell him that I was not prepared to take the job on under existing circumstances. To this he replied that I need not worry. He had no intention whatever of letting this sort of thing go on in his command.

An urgent meeting was now called by General Wilson, which was attended by R. G. Casey, the Minister of State, Lord Glenconner, then head of S.O.E. Cairo, and myself, and in the course of which some hard things were said about S.O.E. As a result of this and the fiasco of the visit of the Greek guerrilla delegation there was the usual annual purge of S.O.E. and it was decided that on the military side I should be directly responsible to the Commander-in-Chief himself, as I was on the political side to the Prime Minister. In the absence of any other suitable set up S.O.E. would be temporarily responsible for my administration and communications until better arrangements could be made. I was not entirely happy about this, as my own experience hitherto had hardly been reassuring and various friends of mine who had been dropped into Greece and elsewhere had told me that large numbers of their most important signals had been either lost or deliberately suppressed. I accordingly took the precaution of arranging for an additional signal link, by which I could contact General Wilson or the Prime Minister. It was thus that later, when I found that Churchill was not receiving signals from me that had been duly despatched and acknowledged, I was fortunately able to repeat them to him in full by another channel. This, as can be imagined, soon put a stop to that particular nuisance and within a few months efficient alternative arrangements had been made.

Once it had finally been accepted by all concerned that I was really going to Yugoslavia, arrangements for my departure went ahead a good deal faster. I had asked Vivian Street, a regular soldier of the greatest experience and ability to come as my second in command and together we picked a team. My staff included John Henniker, Peter Moore and Michael Parker.

Only a few days now remained before we were to be dropped in, during which time we had somehow to get briefed and collect the neccessary supplies.

S.O.E. Cairo had now at long last reluctantly agreed to show me what they considered a suitable selection of files and signals. But, when it came to the point, there seemed to be very little recent stuff to see, which was perhaps not altogether surprising as we were told that there was a six weeks' delay on most signals – again not very reassuring. There were bits of what seemed to be an immensely long signal, six months old or more, from Bailey or Hudson or both, about the Četniks and there were some scraps of purely operational signals from Deakin, from which it appeared that there had been a lot of fighting. But there was nothing remotely resembling an up-to-date appreciation of the situation.

What there was however and what (for reasons at which I could only guess) was immediately handed to me by the junior officer who had been told to look after me, was a file which contained a number of signals and memoranda concerning my own appointment. This, I soon found, was full of references to a sinister organisation designated by two letters, let us say P.X. From these it appeared that P.X. was the real enemy and that P.X. must at all costs be outmanoeuvred and their knavish tricks frustrated. After a bit I came to the conclusion that it must be the Abwehr, or possibly something worse. Then I came on a signal which said that one reason why my appointment could on no account be countenanced was my own known connection with P.X. This was too much. I pinged my bell and my temporary assistant appeared. 'Tell me', I said, 'what does P.X. stand for?' 'Oh, P.X.', he said, 'that's the Foreign Office.' This revelation made things a little clearer, though scarcely any more reassuring, and I went off, pondering deeply, to be more than adequately briefed by Hugh Seton-Watson on the difference between Serbs and Croats and their respective historical backgrounds.

A week or so later we were dropped in and I can assure you that I did not take the first parachute that was offered me. A few days after that I met up with Deakin. From what he then told me and from what during the weeks and months that followed we all saw for ourselves, but quite frankly *not* from anything we had been told in London or Cairo before our departure, we soon formed a picture of a well-led nationwide resistance movement, which by its own unaided efforts had for a long time been containing anything between a dozen and twenty enemy divisions.

What I hope will emerge from this conference on wartime British Foreign Policy in the Balkans is some sort of answer to the following question:

Through Captain Hudson, S.O.E., who were supposed to be responsible for discovering and supporting resistance movements, first made contact with Tito and the Partisans in September 1941. By then they were already a considerable force, fighting hard and containing a number of enemy divisions. Hudson was to remain in Yugoslavia for almost three years after that and numerous other missions were to join him there, all of whom were at one time or another able to report back and, as we have heard, did report back. There were also, in every theatre of war, numerous order of battle experts, intelligence officers, cipher breakers, spies and so on, studying the enemy's every move.

Now the enemy, Hitler and Mussolini, knew all about Tito and the Partisans. They had learned the hard way and they knew exactly who all those divisions of theirs were fighting against. That is absolutely certain. How was it then that for about two years the biggest and by far the most effective resistance movement of World War II was to remain practically unheard of and quite certainly unhelped, while such help as we did give went to the Četniks, many of whom were actively collaborating with the enemy and very few, if any, of whom had done any fighting against the enemy since November 1941?

Clearly the blame cannot be laid at the door of any one department or of any one individual – though the published documents certainly reveal some pretty strange goings on. We all know that there were shortages, shortages of supplies and aircraft and cipher-clerks and disastrous failures of communication – some deliberate and some not. There was also a surprising lack of interest on the part of some of those concerned.

Much of this was a matter of priority and, once the Partisans got the priority they deserved, many of the difficulties disappeared. Certainly, on a cost-efficiency basis, the Partisans deserved a high priority, because rifle for rifle and round for round, hand-grenade for hand-grenade and even sortie for sortie – they were probably producing better results cheaper than any Allied troops.

What is more disturbing is that for almost two years a number of people should have been able, for reasons of their own and by the sort of methods I have described, to suppress vital information and so prevent action from being taken and that it should in the end have taken the vigorous personal intervention of Churchill himself to break this conspiracy of silence.

10   Statement by
George Taylor

I should like to try and throw a little extra light on the development of S.O.E.'s ideas of what the policy should be towards Mihailović and the Partisans during the period from about the end of November 1942 to about March/April 1943. This really amounts to adding something to the picture which emerges from Elisabeth Barker's paper, summarising the story as it emerges from the Foreign Office files. I hope it will do something to remind us of, and to explain, the impression that utter confusion reigned and that a dialogue of the deaf seemed to be going on between S.O.E. and the Foreign Office. All the initiative in the development of S.O.E.'s Yugoslav policy or S.O.E.'s idea of what the policy to Yugoslavia should be, came from the Cairo end. London was really in the position of always being a bit behind and being briefed by Cairo and having the situation explained to them by Cairo. The result was that distance and poor communications produced all the problems that arise between headquarters and somewhat distant operating missions. Thus there was never a complete understanding, and the picture which S.O.E. London from time to time gave in its communications with the departments, particularly with the Foreign Office, was a very much over-simplified and rather misleading picture, as compared with what S.O.E. Cairo were really thinking.

I am in a position to talk about this because I was in Cairo at the time, arriving there at the end of a tour, coming not directly from London, but having spent twenty-six weeks in West Africa. I arrived at the end of November 1942 with the primary purpose of trying to bring Cairo and London more into line, because they had already got out of step in their assessment and description of the situation in Yugoslavia. To do this of course the first and obvious thing was to find out what Cairo really thought. I remember because I wrote it all down at the time and so it is a matter of reliable record. All I propose to do now is to tell you what Cairo thought the policy towards Mihailović and the Partisans should be, and to explain incidentally how this led to some confusion in London because S.O.E. London did not quite understand what Cairo were trying to say.

As far as Mihailović himself and the Četnik movement were concerned, I found that Cairo had already arrived at a clear and pretty accurate concept of what they amounted to. It was a very different picture from what had been presented through propaganda to the public, by everyone in London including the Yugoslav government. By November 1942 it was fully realised by S.O.E. Cairo, that in fact Mihailović's primary concern, his over-riding, overwhelming concern, was not with carrying on the war against the Germans and Italians, but with what the ultimate power situation in Yugoslavia would be when the war came to an end. He was primarily concerned with ensuring that his Serbs should be in a dominant position at the end of the war; and whilst, of course, he hated the Germans and wanted to see them go, and despised the Italians and was quite sure they would go very soon, it was not his intention, nor in his interest to achieve this end himself. He thought that the Allies would sooner or later do that and he mainly aimed at establishing a position for himself and the Serbs against the time when the Germans and Italians had withdrawn from Yugoslavia and the internal problems had become the immediate ones. This Cairo understood fully and they realised that this made Mihailović of very limited use in the short term. It rather suited the British government's policy in relation to the Balkans, but was not much military use in the short term. They understood that it was no good at all trying to make Mihailović do things that were completely at variance with his real aims – which were quite justified from his own point of view but not from ours; and that therefore the way to use Mihailović on a rather medium and long-term basis was to try and establish a position of influence over him and reach a working agreement with him by which he would do some of those things which we, including the military, wanted him to do and which he did not want to do and would not be pushed into doing. That was how S.O.E. thought Mihailović should be used. I think that was quite realistic. It was the only way in which Mihailović could be used. If the British mission, the British Liaison Officers, could have developed a really effective influence over Mihailović and worked out a practical compromise about what he should do and what he should not do, this would in fact have been the ideal outcome. That remained the S.O.E. Cairo attitude and really the basis of all directives given to Colonel Bailey when he went in. It is what he set out to do – i.e. to achieve enough influence over Mihailović to reach a working agreement on these lines. Secondly, S.O.E. Cairo were convinced that Mihailović was the only possible effective instrument we could use in Serbia proper. Again I think that was quite right, that that corresponded to the facts. The Partisans did not have any organisation or any influence in that part of Serbia and so S.O.E. felt that the immediate policy should be one of support for Mihailović on the basis that I have just described.

As far as the Partisans were concerned, S.O.E. knew quite a lot about what was happening in the rest of Yugoslavia, that is outside Serbia, though not as much perhaps as they ought to have known, or at any rate ideally should have known. I would say that there were two main weaknesses in the S.O.E. picture of the Partisans. One, they did not realise at that stage the extent to which the Partisan movement was an organised movement with a central headquarters, with Tito in command. Secondly, they certainly did not realise the full potential of the Partisans in Bosnia, Montenegro and the Sandzak. They were very much influenced by what they did know about the German intention to wipe out the Partisans and indeed also with the efforts which Mihailović had made in the same direction. But they did feel that there was an important resistance movement completely irreconcilable with Mihailović and the Četnik movement in some areas outside Serbia and that contact should be made direct with the Partisans primarily in Croatia.

This policy had certain implications. The most important was that the understanding of Mihailović's true attitude and potentialities as I described them, caused S.O.E. Cairo not to worry too much about the collaborationist activities of Mihailović or Mihailović's people because this was all quite understandable; and although it was undesirable, it was so logical and opportunistic from Mihailović's own point of view that it would have

been foolish to get excited about it. It did not represent anything in the nature of a genuine, real support for, or any sympathy whatever with the Axis powers. This led to further confusion in London because I think S.O.E. London were more
concerned with this aspect and did on the whole tend to tone
down reports, or at least not draw attention to perfectly genuine
reports of the collaborationist activities of quite a number of
Mihailović's people and of Mihailović himself – particularly
with the Italians and to some extent with Nedić; his rather
passive attitude to the Germans, and his preoccupation with
fighting the Partisans. Another cause of confusion which comes
out over and over again in the texts of memoranda and in
comments in telexes and signals – examples of which are given
in Barker's paper – was the complete contradiction between
S.O.E. Cairo's quite realistic view of what Mihailović was, what
he was trying to do and what his intentions were and how he
could possibly be used, and the picture of Mihailović which had
been built up outside Yugoslavia over the preceding year and a
half, as a great national leader and someone under whom the
entire Yugoslav resistance could be organised. That had no
reality at all, and S.O.E. Cairo knew that it had no reality, but
London never quite got round to this, at any rate, did not realise
it as quickly as they should.

That explains in effect the policy which S.O.E. Cairo was
recommending to London – that we should concentrate primarily on aid to Mihailović with the object of getting sufficient
influence and control over him to reach a working agreement
about activities in favour of the Allies which did not too
flagrantly run against his own objectives. And at the same time
parallel with that policy, to make contact with the Partisans and
see what could be done with them; but to run these two horses
quite separately. This led quickly and logically to the idea of
actually dividing the country into geographical divisions. Thus
Mihailović should be supported in Serbia where he was thought
to be strong, and the Partisans would be supported over the rest
of the area. This remained S.O.E.'s idea, an idea which they
continued to put forward, certainly until the end of 1943. It
had some other consequences. One was that though S.O.E.
Cairo were in no way opposed in principle to propaganda
encouragement of the Partisans, and were in fact determined to

achieve contact with them, they had not so far achieved this.
As they were going to send Colonel Bailey to Mihailović in an
effort to carry out the policy which I have just described, they
were very much opposed to what to them seemed quite pointless encouragement of the Partisans through B.B.C. broadcasts,
or indeed in any other way, because it could not have any good
effect for us and must alienate Mihailović. We had not any
contact with the Partisans at that stage; pro-Partisan propaganda on the B.B.C. was bound to make Bailey's mission much
more difficult, to infuriate Mihailović and push him more than
ever in the direction in which he was going already and make
the reaching of a working agreement with him more and more
unlikely. So S.O.E. Cairo were opposed to the public support
of the Partisans at all until contact had been made with them
and we could devise a policy for co-operation with the Partisans. I think that covers the main points of Cairo's policy
towards Yugoslavia and which Glenconner and myself then put
back jointly to London over and over and over again both by
signals and by mail. I do not think it ever completely got across
in its complexity. Attitudes which London took up on particular
issues, especially in their discussions with the Foreign Office,
resulted in a dangerous over-simplification of the whole picture;
so that they seemed to be trying to maintain the old and quite
erroneous picture of Mihailović as the great national leader of
resistance in Yugoslavia instead of simply a limited instrument
for our purposes in Serbia; and equally to be discouraging any
sort of support for the Partisans at all. Neither of which was, of
course, Cairo's idea.

The only other thing I would like to add to that as, in a sense,
a bit of background to Bailey's story, is that the vital element in
the S.O.E. Cairo policy towards Mihailović, the attempt to
reach a working agreement, proved completely impossible for
one simple reason, that unless he had some leverage there was
no way in which Bailey or anybody else could possibly achieve
effective influence over Mihailović and be in a position to
negotiate a working agreement on the lines I have described.
The only leverage that he possibly could have had was supplies.
The only way in which Mihajlović could have been seriously
influenced and made to fit into the S.O.E. programme was if he
had received substantial support and Bailey could have said,

'If you do not do so and so the support will stop.' But it was quite useless to say support would stop if support had never arrived. Bailey had no cards in his hand at all. And that was why a perfectly sensible, rational policy on the part of S.O.E. did in fact come to absolutely nothing.

The only other point I would like to make is in regard to the attitude of the military side – the Chiefs of Staff in London and General Headquarters Cairo. By and large I found that for the last couple of months of 1942 and perhaps the beginning of 1943, the general view on the military side, both in Cairo and in London, was much the same as S.O.E.'s because they were taking essentially a medium and long-term view of the situation. They were not ready for anything in the nature of an invasion of the Balkans and they did not want such resources as were available for resistance to be wasted on premature uprisings. But in 1943 the general strategic situation in the war changed fairly rapidly and the military side became extremely interested in the possibilities of intensified resistance activities in the Balkans in support of military operations in the Mediterranean theatre; it was quite obvious that if early and effective fighting of Germans and Italians in Yugoslavia was to be secured, the Partisans were a very much better bet than Mihailović. Thus the switch of interest in Cairo led to military opinion moving over to supporting the Partisans – and this for perfectly obvious, legitimate military reasons. So much so that by the middle of 1943, S.O.E. Cairo were more or less adopting the same attitude of mind and becoming much more interested in the Partisans than they were in Mihailović. London, being as usual several steps behind Cairo, was still inclined to favour an attempt to keep Mihailović as an instrument in Serbia. Under certain conditions this could perhaps have been done; but it could never be done without putting our representative with Mihailović in a decent bargaining position by giving him some leverage. That was never achieved in the early stages because, in 1942 and early 1943 when Bailey first went in, the aircraft and supplies were simply not available. It was not achieved later when they were available, because by that time, for perfectly legitimate military reasons, British support was concentrated on the Partisans. I think that is really all I can add to this picture.

Following Barker, Bailey
Maclean and Taylor

Seton-Watson: We must, I think, distinguish between 1943, when
at last there was a lot of information coming in, and 1942, the
worst year of the war, the year of Singapore and Stalingrad and
Rommel's threat to Egypt – when not much attention was or
could be spared for the Balkans. I wonder whether there was
really very much material coming in in 1942 – material that was
or was not made available. There was certainly some after
Bailey had arrived. It was then – that is to say early in 1943 –
that the long, extremely interesting account by Hudson of his
earlier experience was in fact sent by Bailey in signal form. It
had not in fact been received until then, and he thought that,
although it was out of date, it was so good that it should come
to us.

Bailey: Hudson had, to put it bluntly, been superseded. I was
obliged to tell him that I must take over the day to day business
with Mihailović and his staff although I should want him
[Hudson] with me on many occasions. One of the reasons why
I was sent there was because there had been gaps in his communications and his telegrams were so sketchy and cast in such
language that it was thought he might be acting under duress.
Also he had not included in his telegrams the special groups
intended to convey that he was not acting under duress.
Having confirmed on my arrival that our fears were unfounded,
I invited him to write the telegrams which founded the *PLOZ*
series. He sent 200 or more of these telegrams over a period
of perhaps six weeks starting about 15 January 1943. The
original intention had been to evacuate Hudson as soon as
possible after my arrival. For technical reasons, this proved to
be impossible. The *PLOZ* series was sent over whichever of the
two or three links we had with Cairo happened to be on the air
and with no other messages to send. I saw the text of all these

telegrams before despatch, but purely for information. Very occasionally I commented on one or two of them over my own personal wire, but all such comments were shown to Hudson by way of courtesy, before they went off.

Maclean: I saw one rather battered signal from Bailey transmitting a long message from Hudson which must have been sent off in about February 1943, about six months before I went in. But already in July 1942 we find Glenconner writing to the Southern Department as follows: 'As we know, any activities in Yugoslavia should really be attributed to the Partisans. But for public consumption we can see no harm in a certain amount of this going to the credit of Mihailović.' That means that in July 1942, long before Bailey went in, S.O.E. Cairo already knew that the Partisans were doing all the fighting.

Bolsover: As an outsider this is puzzling me a great deal. From what Davidson said yesterday, the intercepts of the Sicherheitsdienst began to become available to him and presumably to other people in S.O.E. Cairo in early January 1943. As I understood, Keble had been receiving these intercepts because he had been on the circulating lists in another incarnation. Who else in Cairo had been receiving these and for how long had they been receiving them? If from these intercepts you could get some indication of the trouble the Partisans were causing to the Germans why did the other people receiving the intercepts not understand the importance of the Partisans?

Davidson: There is, I think, no means at all of knowing this.

Maclean: In any case it should not really have been necessary to depend on intercepts. When it is a question of the whereabouts of twenty or thirty enemy divisions over a period of a couple of years an adequate Director of Military Intelligence ought to have been able to find that out in other ways.

Davidson: I would just like to say that at the operational level, at least in September/October 1942, there was absolutely no information available to us on the Partisans. Nothing. And the orders were that we should concern ourselves uniquely with such support as could be given to the Mihailović forces and no effort of any sort was to be made to find out anything about the Partisans who, for all that we were concerned, might not have existed. Although, obviously, we knew that they existed from public sources such as Free Yugoslavia, press reports and that sort of thing. Then suddenly it changed. When these intercepts began to come in – I think early in January 1943 – about three weeks before Keble wrote his famous memorandum to the Prime Minister – Keble clearly was concerned to run his policy to make contact with the Partisans and exploit it. He made sundry efforts to find a senior officer who would go in, as his nominee and the Army's senior representative. All this went on and it certainly changed about this time. I think that the question which you posed is really the extremely interesting one – what happened in the second half of 1942, now that we know that people at the top knew that the Partisans were important, because you have just quoted this July 1942 statement. What happened in the second half of 1942: (a) to prevent intelligent interest in this situation, or (b) to start it up at some point towards the end of 1942?

Maclean: Somebody in Military Intelligence in London must have known. If the Chiefs of Staff knew that there were twenty or thirty German or Italian divisions doing something in one small country in the Balkans, you would think they would have been certain to follow it up and discover the reason. That is what is so mysterious about it all. The moment Churchill got on to it of course things began to happen.

Barker: But was not that because the right strategic moment had come? As has been said, the military were not really interested until February/March 1943 and therefore they just let the whole thing lie. I found in the files what appeared to be a War Office Most Secret Report of April 1943 by Major Michael Maclagan which was an extremely detailed and very long account of Partisan operations from 1941 onwards.* This means that some-body must have been following the situation in Yugoslavia all this time because they could not just have produced it out of the blue. Somebody in the Military Intelligence Department of the War Office had had full information; but I think they were not interested until it became actual. It seems to me that it was not just a question of S.O.E. withholding information, but that the Foreign Office obviously knew perfectly well during 1942 what was going on. There were masses of information on the Parti-sans from one source or another. And S.I.S. must also have had quite a lot of information.

* FO 371/37586.

Taylor: Yes. I am sure this is the case. You quoted in your paper and Maclean has just repeated a reference to Glenconner's memorandum of July 1942. When Glenconner wrote that memorandum he was not in Cairo; he was in London. He was head of the Balkans Section in London and I do not think there is any doubt that by July 1942, and probably somewhat earlier, everybody in London, S.O.E., the Foreign Office and Chiefs of Staff, all knew that practically all the fighting that was going on in Yugoslavia was being done by the Partisans. But everybody concerned in S.O.E. was still working under a very clear directive, which was in fact very much the view of the Foreign Office: that the policy of His Majesty's Government was support of the Royal Yugoslav Government and Mihailović as its Minister of War. That was why S.O.E. London paid no attention at all to the Partisans. This I can confirm from my own recollection. We *did* know. I was in London until about May or June 1942 and in a position to see everything that went through then. There is no doubt that we knew a lot about the activities of the Partisans. We knew perfectly well that what was being attributed to Mihailović was not Mihailović at all but we were still working under a very definite directive, that all support was to go to Mihailović. It was Glenconner, after he went to Cairo in the middle of 1942, who began to get the idea in about October/November of that year that we ought to make contact with the Partisans as well as with Mihailović. But when he first made even a hint of this suggestion to London (though I was not there at the time, I saw these signals afterwards in Cairo), he got hit on the head from S.O.E. London; or rather the hitting on the head came from the Foreign Office through S.O.E. Glenconner's original proposal was to send in someone to make contact in Croatia because at that time that region was regarded as the heart and headquarters. We did not know that Tito was in fact commander of the whole lot and that there was an organisation with a general staff built up around Tito. It was believed that Croatia was a natural centre for the most active Partisans. Then between November 1942 and January 1943 the idea developed in Cairo of backing both horses – of continuing to support Mihailović in his limited area and in the only way in which he would be of any use to us, but making contact with the Partisans and finding out what could be done with them. This, though discouraged from London at the beginning, was finally approved.

Maclean: That was still the idea right until the end of 1943. I got instructions to which I cannot say I paid all that much attention, to impress on Tito the advisability of coming to terms with Mihailović. Just as Bailey got the same parallel, complementary instructions to do the same the other way round. But we both came to the conclusion the policy was inoperable.

Taylor: I think what happened is pretty clear. When early in 1943 Cairo, on Glenconner's initiative, finally received permission to make contact with the Partisans, Keble decided that this was going to be an important development and it was something he was going to hang on to for S.O.E. And he used every conceivable means to keep his hand on it. So that when Deakin had gone in there were all the beginnings of an association with the Partisans. Later when you personally came on to the scene I am quite sure, knowing Keble as I did, that he simply made up his mind to stop your entry. He was determined to keep the whole project under his hand in S.O.E.

Deakin: One or two views seem to have been put forward. One is that certain people in S.O.E. knew about the Partisans in 1942. We have Glenconner's minute of July 1942. It could also be said that the only people who knew were the War Office which was not interested because it was not of any strategic importance at that particular moment. But in a sense we cannot have it both ways; either S.O.E. did know in 1942 at a certain level, or they did not. Or the War Office knew and did not communicate.

Seton-Watson: I would suggest a partial reconciliation of the contradiction. There was information – there must have been some information because of Glenconner's statement – but that information was probably rather scanty and it was largely from press reports. As Barker said, there was a lot of information which built up to a not very clear picture. There was known to be a lot of resistance not under Mihailović's control. That came basically from press reports plus occasional travellers' stories, plus the odd S.I.S. reports. I remember myself there were one or two in that winter [1942–3], not very high grade information but the overall picture was fairly clear. It was that what fighting there was, was Partisan. It was not any direct information: and it was not intercepts. These came later.

Taylor: The fundamental thing was the policy laid down with the full support and on the initiative of the Foreign Office. As far as S.O.E. were concerned it should concentrate on support of Mihailović. The exact wording of Glenconner's minute is interesting because it makes quite clear that he took it for granted that not only he knew, but also the Foreign Office knew that all the fighting that had gone on in Yugoslavia had in fact been done by the Partisans and not by Mihailović. There was no illusion about that. Nevertheless, in spite of that being known, it was the policy of His Majesty's Government to support Mihailović and S.O.E. were restricted to doing that and told to get on with it.

Deakin: Information available to S.O.E. in 1942 when Glenconner wrote that minute was simply based on monitoring of the Free Yugoslavia radio and on the Swiss and neutral press. This was surely not enough to convince Glenconner to write that minute.

Taylor: There was probably a lack of co-ordination. There was a certain amount of fairly high quality intelligence available but unknown to S.O.E. Therefore S.O.E.'s knowledge, as revealed by implication from Glenconner's memorandum, was not of a very high quality. It was enough to make S.O.E. quite certain that it was the Partisans who were active and not Mihailović, but it did not reflect as much detailed information as was in fact available from other sources, mainly intercepts.

Woodhouse: On the issue of suppression of information or failure of information to reach its destination, I think there is no question that Keble was substantially to blame, because he was, as has been said, a very strange character. We all know that he was an extraordinary man, but I think there is another factor, bearing on this, to add to the one which Seton-Watson has mentioned as operative in 1942 which certainly was a very difficult year. It came out very clearly in Sweet-Escott's paper about the peculiar structure of S.O.E. in Cairo at that time. As he explained, it was changed from time to time, but during 1942 the structure was functional and not geographical. There was the strange situation in which there were departments performing different functions which each had within them a

Yugoslav section, a Greek section and an Albanian section, which apparently were not communicating with the corresponding section – Yugoslav, Greek and Albanian – in another functional department of S.O.E. in Cairo. If you want proof of this, I published it in a paper* last year on the briefing of Myers and myself for the *Gorgopotamos* Operation. I published the actual text of our Operation Order, a long document full of so-called intelligence, which never even mentions E.A.M. or the K.K.E. or (with one exception) any of the people whom in fact we were going to co-operate with; although it is perfectly clear from the documents Clogg has been examining that the existence of E.A.M. and the role of the K.K.E. were perfectly well known already in the Foreign Office and in the War Office, in General Headquarters Cairo and in the other departments of S.O.E.

Maclean: I should like to refer to Barker's quotation from the Foreign Office paper of 7 June 1944: 'If anyone is to blame for the present situation in which the Communist-led movements are the most powerful elements in Yugoslavia and Greece, it is we ourselves. The Russians have merely sat back and watched us doing their work for them.' My comment on this would be that the Russians, by sitting back and letting the British help Tito, produced the opposite effect from that which they intended. By not helping the Partisans they did their own cause no good while we, by supporting the Partisans, ultimately won their friendship.

Seton-Watson: The idea that King Peter if he had gone to Tito would somehow have held him back seems to me an extraordinary one.

Maclean: Yes, but Churchill being at heart a romantic liked the idea of the young king joining his embattled people. On his instructions I sounded Tito out about this as early as October 1943 and Tito did not seem entirely against it. Of course it could have helped him in Serbia and he may have realised King Peter was not a very strong character.

Barker: But why did Tito in 1944 put up such a very strong resistance to meeting King Peter?

Maclean: By 1944 the whole situation had changed. By then the

---

* C. M. Woodhouse, 'Early British Contacts with the Greek Resistance in 1942', *Balkan Studies*, XII (1972) 347–63.

Partisans were stronger in Serbia. Indeed their whole position was much stronger and they did not need to make those sort of concessions. Of course we now know that Stalin was urging him to take King Peter in order to please us and then have him assassinated.* Rather typical of Stalin.

Barker: One thing I had not time to go into about the summer of 1944, was the way in which Churchill switched around even before he had met Tito. Once Tito was on the island of Vis, Churchill immediately started to say, 'let us send the King to Vis at once, he has got just as good a right to be there as Tito has. Now we can bring them together.' It was Eden who said, 'No we cannot do this.' It was extraordinary the way Churchill at that point said words to the effect of 'Ah, now we have got him.' – meaning Tito.†

Maclean: That is interesting to me, because it throws light on what happened when Tito was coming out of Vis. We had fixed up for him to come out in order to see General Wilson. This was in July 1944. And the day before the aeroplane came over to pick him up – you could land by Dakota in Vis then – at the very last moment Tito came and had lunch in my mess. After lunch he said, 'There's something I want to talk to you about.' I took him up to my room upstairs in the little house I was living in and he said, 'I cannot go tomorrow to see the Commander-in-Chief.' I was naturally not at all pleased and said, 'You will do yourself nothing but harm by being rude to the Supreme Allied Commander.' To which he replied, 'It is more complicated than that.' Of course I had no idea that there was any question of his being confronted with King Peter and would have strongly opposed the suggestion, had I known of it.

Barker: At the beginning of 1943 there was yet another re-shuffle in the Yugoslav government and Jovanović who was then Prime Minister must have had some idea of the way things were moving. He more or less formally asked our ambassador, George Rendel, whether we were still maintaining our support

---

* V. Dedijer, *Tito Speaks* (London, 1953) p. 234.

† See Prime Minister's Personal Minute to the Foreign Secretary (serial number H.685/4) of 5.6.44 (FO 371/44291) and Eden's answering Minute to the Prime Minister of 7.6.44 (FO 371/44291), also letter from Prime Minister to General Wilson and H. Macmillan (T.O.O. 2220Z) of 10.6.44 (*ibid.*).

for Mihailović, because he could not keep him in his government if we were thinking of changing our policy. Rendel said 'no change'. And so Jovanović kept Mihailović in the government. We could at least have said that we had doubts about him. But of course I suppose the Foreign Office did not want to reveal what they were thinking until they had contacted the Partisans.*

Bailey: On the question of Mihailović's collaboration with the enemy, it was officially condoned, I think, as early as July 1942, in the belief that when the crunch came, all the Italian arms, perhaps even some Italian troops in Montenegro, could be brought over to our side.

* See note by Rendel on conversation with Jovanović of 31.12.42 (FO 371/37578); also minute by E. M. Rose of 1.1.43 on discussion between Rendel, Sargent and Howard at which it was agreed to have the formula that no change in our policy had taken place but not to commit ourselves to *continue* to support Mihailović (*ibid.*).

12   Following Deakin

Woodhouse: May I comment particularly on Bill Deakin's argument, which obviously is quite correct, that the importance of
this imaginary plan for invading the Balkans lies in its effect on
(a) the enemy, and (b) our Allies. Now exactly the same is true
in Greece. The Communist leadership in Greece was equally
deceived into thinking that there was about to be an Allied
landing in Greece, or somewhere on the Balkan coast. Brigadier
Myers was the only person to be told in Greece that the landings
were going to take place in Sicily. He confided in me, but in
nobody else, and therefore the guerrillas in Greece were all
launched upon what we called Operation *Animals*, in ignorance
of what they were really doing. But inevitably they leapt to the
conclusion, as the Germans did, that this must be a preliminary
to an Allied landing in Greece. Now even after the landings in
Sicily, which revealed that in fact Greece was not the target,
both the Germans and the Greek Communist leaders continued
to be deceived and continued to expect landings in Greece. I am
entirely persuaded, though I cannot produce evidence of this
from the Greek Communist side, that it was because they were
convinced that Allied landings were about to come that they
launched in September 1943 what is known in Greek history as
the first round of the civil war. Their object was to try and wipe
out all the rival resistance forces and be the only ones in control
when we landed. So that successful though this deception was, it
carried very grave and unforeseen consequences as well.
Deakin: I suppose that there must be a connection, too, in the
fact that the First Mountain Division which was sent in to
smash Yugoslav resistance in anticipation of a landing was
switched back to Greece when they thought the landing was
coming in Greece and had not come in Yugoslavia.
Myers: It might be relevant to mention here that when in May
I received this highly secret and most important signal about the
Allies' future plans, my first action was to destroy it and all

evidence of it. Almost my next was to signal Cairo, pointing out that, as a result of their latest instructions, we would be aiming to bring the resistance forces up to a peak of efficiency and activity in two months' time and asking when Greece's turn would be coming. For I knew that unless I could keep E.L.A.S. fully occupied in one way or another, they would be at Zervas's throat again, or worse. In due course the answer came back that Greece would not be liberated until the end of 1943 anyhow and probably not until the spring of 1944. But I need not worry, because the enemy would be fearing invasion all this time as a result of Allied deception measures. I was greatly concerned by this news. S.O.E. Cairo did not seem to realise what I had got on my hands. I could not keep the resistance forces idle for long. I had to continue building them up morally and qualitatively even if not numerically. After discussing my problems with Woodhouse, I signalled back that I considered it essential to come out and explain them personally to my superiors.

Bailey: May I ask you a question? At this moment of the Italian surrender Deakin said that he had no warning and you said you had no warning too. I want to fix your mind on what happened at Mihailović's headquarters, in connection with my original flaming row. Mihailović heard about it only over the radio as we did, and sent for me and asked for an explanation. At the same time the first signal to come through from Cairo was not a record of the announcement of surrender – we had heard that over the open radio – but a suggestion that the British mission should take charge of all the Italian weapons. Did you have this in Greece?

Woodhouse: Yes. We were already in negotiations with the commander of the Pinerolo Division in Thessaly, whose name was Infante. He had got a D.S.O. in the First World War and had long realised that he was on the wrong side. Even before Mussolini fell he was negotiating with us to surrender his division. And this he did when we got orders to accept a surrender, and we got about 14,000 Italians as one organised formation. A lot of others came in in dribs and drabs in other parts of the country, but we had one complete Italian division with all its equipment. Obviously, I could not personally take command of all this, so I turned General Infante and his division into a co-belligerent and told them to keep all their weapons and fight on our side. This for a bit they did, but in order to get the thing properly tied up, because we had a Joint General Headquarters at that time, I had to get all the guerrilla leaders to join in the armistice. So we all signed the armistice together, but it was quite obvious that E.L.A.S. was going to get hold of all these weapons just as quickly as they could. They had their contacts through party cadres in the division already, and they started working on the Italians. Eventually they got them completely demoralised and divided up into small pockets here and there and finally disarmed them and ended up as a result 14,000 arms the richer, with mountain artillery and aircraft and an enormous accretion of strength. This was really one of the most painful and difficult dilemmas I have ever faced, because General Infante would only sign an armistice with me. He regarded my signature as guaranteeing that it was all above board. Of course from the E.L.A.S. point of view it was never above board at all and the only alternative I could have chosen would have been to let all this armament go to the Germans. I still do not know whether I did the right thing. Anyway, I did what I was told. It was a very awkward dilemma. If only the Pinerolo division had been on the other side of the Pindus Mountains, how different things would have been.

Maclean: Tito was naturally furious when he first heard about the fifty–fifty agreement between Churchill and Stalin in October 1944. I myself just heard about it by signal in Belgrade. I got to Belgrade on 20 October, which was the day when Belgrade fell. And I hardly had time to look round before I got a top secret signal from the Foreign Office to say that they had reached this agreement. I must say I was amazed and I also thought that when Tito finds out about this it is going to be very awkward. But as far as I know he did not find out about it until after the war, did he?

Deakin: He was, in fact, told of it at the time by Churchill. Here is the text of a telegram from Churchill to Maclean, dated 3 December 1944.

Please convey the following message to Marshal Tito from me. I am sending a copy of this telegram to Marshal Stalin. As you know, we have made an arrangement with the Marshal and the Soviet Government to pursue as far as possible a joint policy towards Yugoslavia, so that our influence there should be held on equal basis. But you seem to be treating us in an increasingly invidious fashion. It may be that you have fears that your ambitions about occupying Italian territories of the north Adriatic lead you to view with suspicion and dislike every military operation on your coast we make against the Germans. I have already assured you that all territorial questions will be reserved for the Peace Conference. And they will be judged irrespective of wartime occupation. And certainly such issues ought not to hamper military operations now.

Maclean: There had been some unfortunate incidents in Dalmatia.

Deakin: This story is completed by the fact that Churchill sent to Stalin a copy of this telegram to Tito, and the telegram to Stalin starts: 'In view of our agreement about our joint policy in regard to Yugoslavia, I am sending you a copy of a telegram which I have been forced with much regret to send to Tito. I should be very ready to hear your views.' Stalin's reply is preserved in a Foreign Office minute. Stalin replied he wished to consult Tito before observing on it. And I presume he did so before Tito sent his reply. Tito's reply which is not quoted here, came through Maclean to the Foreign Office but it refers to each point in Churchill's telegram to him, except the part about fifty–fifty which he ignores.

Maclean: Of course to say equal joint policies towards a country is not quite the same as saying, 'We are going to split you up fifty–fifty.' The first time I discussed this awkward subject with Tito after the war, I did my best to explain it on the grounds that of course it did not mean anything like spheres of influence and that it seemed to me pretty silly anyway.

Barker: Did it not mean, in fact, at the start, that the Russians were to be left to run their land forces, if we were going to equip their air forces?

Deakin: But Churchill's own explanation of this, and I think it is borne out by the subsequent evidence, is still very controversial. Certainly his intention was merely to try and get something out of Stalin, to provoke Stalin into giving him some idea where the Russian Army was going to end up. And this was simply a balloon, put across the table. After dinner, Churchill scribbled out in his own hand a series of percentages, but this was not in any sense meant to be an agreement. In fact he sent a telegram to Roosevelt that this would be limited to three months. What he was really after was to see where the Red Armies were going. He was not trying to divide up the Balkans. Maybe he gave the wrong impression; but all I can be sure of is what he thought he had done.

Maclean: He gave me the wrong impression all right.

Barker: The negotiations with the Russians had been going on from the previous April.

Woodhouse: It is true that the discussions had been going on for four or five months before that. But they were not discussions aimed at arriving at percentages.

Maclean: I suppose the Partisans must have heard of the idea that was still current right up to the end of 1943, of a division of Yugoslavia into spheres of influence between the Četniks and the Partisans, which in a way would have amounted to the same thing.

Deakin: They got hold of this very simply. Bailey mentioned the Ibar telegram earlier. I think this telegram did not originate with S.O.E. Cairo at all, but within the Middle East Command. I think this was originally a military telegram. It was sent to Bailey in Yugoslavia after our mission had left for Montenegro, so we had no knowledge of this and no briefing about it. But the idea did get around, though certainly not from our mission, that we had some idea of a division of Yugoslavia into 'spheres'.

Bailey: The Ibar proposal was that put forward by Hudson and myself shortly after I went in, but it had obviously been floating round for some time; I do not think it surprising that it should have gained a certain amount of credibility. I would like to make one or two very minor points. It is true that like Woodhouse in Greece, I had no prior warning of the Italian capitulation. Indeed the news came in most unfortunate circumstances. We had been on the move the whole day. As we had not had a supply drop for about four weeks, I was in the doghouse which meant that instead of being invited to ride with the general, I was at the back end of the baggage train. About nine o'clock it was almost dark and I was summoned to join the general. I cannot say he was white with rage because it was too dark to see, but he could hardly speak. He said, 'We have just heard over the B.B.C. about the capitulation of Italy. Why have you not informed me?' I replied, 'For the very simple reason that I have not been informed myself.' He did not actually call me a liar, and I managed to calm him down by pointing out that we had been moving since 6 a.m., that it was already between 8 and 9 p.m., and that I had no chance of contacting Cairo. Sure enough, the first message I got the following morning gave the news. This put me in an even worse position, for Mihailović could not bring himself to believe I did not know. To him it was quite incredible that I should have been left in the dark. He thought that I had obviously had the message and had concealed it from him for my own purposes.

Glen: Bailey and I had the good fortune to know Mihailović in better days. My memory is of an interesting man – I would say an academic rather than a soldier; a tense man. He was not a narrow man at that time. He had this withdrawn remoteness, but there were inner tensions in him too. In the 1914–18 war Serbia, with a population of six million, lost a million and three-quarters of her people. The problem of the loss of human life was something desperately important to Mihailović, both for its own sake and as a factor in the Yugoslav state. There were also the other forces, Communist or otherwise, as well as his fears about the survival of Serbia as well as of the monarchy and everything else that he held dear. I think one would guess that he might be a bad chooser of people. I do not believe he was a narrow Pan-Serb at that time. On the other hand I just wonder how any of us would have stood up to the kind of forces of loneliness, solitariness or of hopelessness that were imposed on that man. I think he was a terrible human tragedy.

Bailey: I would add one thing to the facts arising out of the First World War. Mihailović repeatedly related to me the story of the 16,000 boys of military age who in the winter of 1915–16 marched out through Serbia, Bosnia–Hercegovina down to Corfu. Owing to cold, typhus and other afflictions their numbers were reduced to under 4000 by the time they reached safety. That had made a lasting impression on him because he was a young officer himself at that time. He was deeply affected even at that long remove by Serbia's sufferings in the 1914–18 war. This made him even more determined in the Second World War to pursue his policy of passive resistance until what he deemed to be the right moment.

Henniker: But he was extremely secretive with you, was he not? I would have thought Glen's description was right – lonely.

Bailey: This depended largely upon the supply situation. If we had received two drops within two weeks everything in the garden was lovely and I enjoyed his confidence. But if we then got nothing more for three or four weeks I was again relegated to the end of the baggage train or put in a billet very close to the point at which the Germans might attack us. This happened more than once. Then things would go a little better. The B.B.C. would say something complimentary about him and I would be invited to dinner.

Barker: I did come across one or two rather uncomplimentary remarks, both by you and by Brigadier Armstrong, about Mihailović's capacity either as a military commander or as an organiser.

Bailey: It was not for me to judge his capacity as a military commander, but I was, I think, entitled to criticise his absolute obsession with military administration. There was discussion earlier* about intercepts and the Germans cracking Mihailović's ciphers, particularly his internal ciphers. What they made of them I simply cannot think. A typical example of the bulk of them might read, 'Lance-Corporal XYZ is appointed Acting Unpaid Sergeant with effect from...', etc. I am not exaggerating. Hundreds of such messages were sent off during my stay with Mihailović. I was not particularly worried about the risks involved as he did not often issue operational instructions. Perhaps he realised his codes had been cracked. The alternative then would have been to have sent a courier who might have taken fifteen days to reach his destination, by which time the local British Liaison Officers had got fed up with the delay and the project had had to be called off.

The situation about the supplies we actually sent is another thing which should be investigated. He once received a drop of 500 left-footed boots! Deakin had the same experience. On another occasion he received a consignment of size 6 boots.

* See pp. 210–14 above.

Yugoslavs generally are big people but fortunately we were able to give the small boots to children, so we got some propaganda value out of them. Another tragi-comic example was when Cairo sent several hundred hand-grenades and quite properly put the grenades themselves in one container, the fuses and detonators in another. Unfortunately no instructions were issued from Mihailović's headquarters nor could have been because we had not been told the contents of the drop. So there was a row on the spot between two local commanders and in the end one went off proudly carrying the six hundred hand-grenades and the other chap took the detonators and fuses. Examples like that can be multiplied.

Maclean: A whole lot of detonators once came in to us loose with our mail.

Hornsby-Smith: I do not think enough weight has been given to the very firm political convictions and the depth of public support over this difficult period; this, I think, was admirably brought out in Barker's paper which showed what appeared to be terrible delays and vacillations. The gallant young King had arrived in London; the euphoria over this young man and other royalty who escaped to Britain was very real and in the circumstances of the time synonymous with Mihailović. He was built up as defender of the monarchy. In the early days of course Russia was not our ally and the political scene was set with the idea that we were going to maintain a monarchy in Yugoslavia. We would go back and help a new young king whom we had trained – and indeed very intense efforts were made to see that this idle young man should be trained, inspired by George VI and advised by Churchill. This training, King Peter did not always follow.

There was at the same time a very deep fear of Communist influence in the Balkans and in the Mediterranean, which was very obvious in the minutes exchanged between Lord Selborne and the Foreign Office. But then came the change in the direction, which I am sure was Churchill's alone, and his deliberate intervention by personally appointing Maclean to go into Yugoslavia. I do not think we have given enough weight to the depth of the reaction there would have been publicly – certainly in the earlier years – had we thrown over a monarch who had come to us as a free ally.

Maclean: Could I just add something to that? I had spent 1937 to 1939 in the Soviet Union in the embassy in Moscow, and 1937 to 1939 was when Stalinism was at its height, so I was very conscious of what was involved; indeed I think also it is one of the reasons why Sargent, who was an old friend, pressed for me to go to Yugoslavia. As soon as I heard that I was not going to Mihailović but that I was going to somebody called Tito and that Tito was thought to be a Communist, the first question I put to the Prime Minister was, 'Have you thought out the implications of backing a Communist-inspired movement bound to be responsible to the Russians? He replied, 'Yes, we have,' and that was when he said, 'What we are concerned with is who kills most Germans and how we can help them, and political considerations are secondary.' Later, when I wrote my first long despatch in November 1943, and when I subsequently saw both Eden and Churchill, I made it clear that in my view Tito would undoubtedly end up on top and would undoubtedly set up a Communist regime. After the war there was some question about what I had reported, but in fact I made it absolutely clear that the future regime of Yugoslavia would certainly be a Communist one. That was when Churchill said to me, 'Are you going to live there?' And I said, 'No.' And he said, 'Neither am I, so had we not better leave the Yugoslavs themselves to work out what sort of system they are going to have?' That seemed to me a perfectly clear directive, and that was the basis I went on throughout. On the other hand, as soon as I got there I was much struck by the difference between Tito and the Communists I had encountered in Moscow and elsewhere. That was why I wrote in this same despatch of November 1943, 'Much will depend on Tito and whether he still sees himself in his former role of Comintern agent, or as the future ruler of an independent Yugoslavia.' I also put this very question to Tito the first time I met him. I said, 'Are you going to make this country into a Soviet colony?' This provoked the fairly sharp retort of which he has reminded me once or twice since.

Henniker: One factor in some people's mind was also the memory of us supporting Serbia in previous wars and also a pro-Serb feeling.

Maclean: And we had built up Mihailović into something which he never remotely thought he was himself.

Johnstone: Mihailović had the great misfortune of having to compete with a military and political leader of the stature of Tito who also had a new programme to offer, which, whether you believe it to be realised or not, had immense attractions for the Yugoslavs, not merely some Serbs, but the other nations of Yugoslavia too. Against these handicaps Mihailović simply could not compete.

Hornsby-Smith: Of course Mihailović was quite unrealistic about the demands he made upon us and our limited supplies. He always worked on the basis that he would ultimately have all the supplies he demanded and be the great conqueror. I can remember day in and day out the battle we had with 'Bomber' Harris and other Air Force leaders to get aircraft and often we had to wait weeks before they would divert one single machine for a major mission.

Davidson: The difficulties under which S.O.E. laboured were really enormous, and up to at least April 1943 it is true that there were only four Liberators available for all the operations from Egypt. But there never really were four Liberators available. There were at most three, sometimes two and very often one. That one aircraft had to do Greece, Yugoslavia and other missions. I think one has to bear in mind this terrible shortage of the means of supply which went on right up through April/May 1943 and even beyond; in fact it was not mastered until early 1944.

Barker: As far as British public opinion went, surely Mihailović's collaboration was a serious embarrassment. This seems to be something that Eden was seriously embarrassed about and certainly Sargent was in December 1943 when information was coming in, and with Radio Free Yugoslavia being more and more taken up not only by the B.B.C. but also by the press and news. This made it extraordinarily difficult for the British government to go on presenting the Mihailović case to the world.

Hornsby-Smith: They thought long and perhaps too hard about what to them was a major constitutional decision – whether to abandon the King and the exiled government.

Maclean: Of course they carried the King and the new exiled government with them ultimately and it did not make the slightest difference. It just put everybody in a rather false position.

Woodhouse: I have been a little surprised by what has been said about the availability of aircraft. Of course I do realise that Greece was much nearer to Egypt than Yugoslavia, therefore presumably it did not need the bigger aircraft so much until Italy was invaded and available for a base. But certainly in the middle summer of 1943, in the run up to the *Animals* operation, we in Greece were extremely well off for aircraft. We were getting something like eighty sorties a month.

Sweet-Escott: There were ten Halifaxes after April 1943 because in February or March the Chiefs of Staff agreed to make ten Halifaxes available for S.O.E. in Cairo. But it took a long time for them to become available. They had to be got from several points of the world and had to be altered.

Henniker: I do not think Yugoslavia began to have many aircraft until about the beginning of 1944.

Woodhouse: The point I am making here is that in the middle of 1943 Mihailović was in the doghouse and was therefore not being allowed any aircraft, and Tito had not yet become the rising star.

Maclean: In principle we ought to have got them in the winter of 1943–4 – it had been agreed that we should and Churchill was backing it, but the weather was very bad then.

Henniker: But by the spring of 1944 we were getting a lot.

Sweet-Escott: In the second half of 1943 we were dropping 150 tons a month on the average. As I recollect, it was 900 tons for the six months and I should say it was 300 tons to Greece and 600 tons to Yugoslavia.

Glen: Woodhouse is right. There were curious brackets of range with these aircraft which were very decisive indeed. I think you probably had quite a few Wellingtons over and above short range.

Woodhouse: We did not have Wellingtons in Greece. We did our parachute training in Wellingtons, but we were told we had to go in Liberators to drop in Greece. So presumably Wellingtons were not available, or had not the necessary range.

Davidson: There were only four Liberators available until about April 1943, of which normally one and at the most two were serviceable. Then came the Halifaxes. Not just ten straight away, but one and two and three, until finally towards May, more were available.

Sweet-Escott: The ten Halifaxes were not all there by June 1943. I think that is right.

Maclean: We went by Halifax in September 1943, leaving from Protville in Tunisia. And then the second time I was dropped in, I went from Bari in a Dakota.

Sweet-Escott: I wonder if, in the context of Allied landings, you could tell us something about the dispersal of American controlled landing craft in the Mediterranean at the time of the Italian surrender. What puzzles me is something told me just after the war by Lord Killearn. He told me that at the time of the Cairo Conference in 1943 Churchill was very worried about the Dodecanese failure and he had asked Killearn to lay on a party with the King of Greece to explain what went wrong. According to Killearn, Churchill said something like this: that there were only a certain amount of landing craft in the Mediteranean at that time, and General Eisenhower had command of them. They had priority for his use. But if Salerno had gone off like a bomb, Eisenhower had agreed that some of these landing craft might be available to General Wilson. At the critical moment Salerno had gone wrong. So there were no landing craft available for the Dodecanese operation, except for a certain number of vessels which, I think in accordance with the Quebec Conference, had to be sent to Arakan. I think that Churchill subsequently wrote that the exchange of telegrams between himself and Eisenhower at the time was so bitter that it was the most painful episode in his relations with Eisenhower throughout the war. What was the truth of that? I have never been able to find out. Were any of Eisenhower's landing craft made available for the Dodecanese? Were the landing craft which were sent to Arakan sent by some minor official in pursuance of the Quebec Conference decision, or what?

Deakin: I must confess that I am not very competent to give you a factual answer in detail. I think that there are two other issues apart from the ones you raise. Your hypothesis about Salerno is fascinating. I did not realise that there was any suggestion that if Salerno had been a quick and a successful operation then Eisenhower would have agreed to release landing craft. There are two issues which throw some light on what you say. One is of course that it was not only a question of reinforcing the landing craft in the British Isles for *Overlord*. The agreement that we made with the American Chiefs of Staff was that as compensation for their agreement to operation *Husky* we said we would not be difficult about landing craft. We would not make too many demands in the eastern Mediterranean. We agreed with the American Chiefs of Staff reluctantly that they should be released for Normandy, not for anywhere else. At the same time the person who benefitted by this row, and the row was certainly a very bitter one, was Admiral King sitting in Washington, who promptly switched all he could get hold of in the shipyards in the United States to the Pacific. But I cannot answer your question with any figures. I do not think that at any stage any landing craft were moved in the eastern Mediterranean for the Aegean operation. I think that was carried out with existing resources. But the Americans were particularly cross with us because they thought they had some reason to think that we were being rather disingenuous. They thought they had made an overall deal with us that we should not make these demands, if they agreed to Sicily. That is why the bitterness crept into it.

Sweet-Escott: And hence the telegram from Churchill to Wilson telling him that he must 'improvise and dare'. Killearn said to me that at the dinner party he had arranged Churchill said to the King of Greece, 'So he improvose and dore.'

Clissold: Could I ask something on an issue which I do not think has been ventilated yet. It relates to the invasion of Yugoslavia and my question is this: Did we attempt at any time to use as a lever of pressure the offer of territorial concessions to Yugoslavia after the war either on an official level in approaching the Yugoslav government – Prince Paul – or else on a clandestine level? There was a certain amount of clandestine contact going on in those years (1939–41), particularly with the organisations of Slovenes in Istria and Venezia Giulia and I remember rumours that various things were being promised to these people in order to step up their opposition and I wondered whether you had come across any evidence from the files?

Barker: There was a formal government offer as regards Istria at the beginning of 1940. It did not specifically mention Trieste. When Eden saw Stalin in December 1941 I think he mentioned to him our assurance given about Istria and Stalin said he agreed that the Yugoslavs should be extended to that area. That was why Dixon wrote a famous minute afterwards saying that Stalin favoured an extended Yugoslavia, but we thought he was aiming at Italy.

Deakin: We have talked a number of times about intercepts and interpretation of the Yugoslav ones and the value of them and we know that the Germans were intercepting Mihailović's messages. This convinced the Germans even further that we were going to land in the Balkans because they were reading Mihailović's messages saying that he was sure of it, and they were certain that he was right because what he had been saying about our analysis of Mihailović and the monarchy in 1940 and 1941 was precisely the same as Hitler's analysis. Hitler never conceived we were going to support Tito. He was thinking in terms of the First World War, too, and therefore he thought that Mihailović was far more dangerous than the Communist Partisans in Serbia. That was Hitler's personal attitude. Also as an Austrian he was anti-Serb. This comes out of the intercepts. The Germans picked this up and passed it on to Berlin and said in effect: Mihailović says that the British are going to land and Mihailović is the bright boy of the British, therefore they are going to land.

The second consequence of the intercepts is even more odd. This comes to light because after the war there was a so-called indictment which was a trial – Case Seven – of the German generals in the south-east, including the ones in Greece. The evidence of this trial disclosed how Mihailović's telegrams were intercepted – there was a special intercept station in Belgrade, run by a German technician of south-west African origin. He was brought to give evidence because the defence lawyer of one of the generals was very taken aback when he discovered that the Mihailović intercepts by the Germans were used to write a report for General Gehlen and they were taken textually from Mihailović's messages giving his impression of how strong his organisation was. Gehlen, in order to curry favour with Hitler – because there were also people who were anti-Mihailović and pro-Mihailović at German Headquarters – literally took these deciphered messages and built a whole order of battle for Mihailović – which is based entirely on Mihailović's own signals to and from his commanders. This was put in as evidence in that trial to show that Mihailović was a far worse danger than Tito.

So that is the second use of intercepts, in this particular context.

Bailey: I hope Gehlen cut the figures by about 50 per cent.

Deakin: He knew what he was doing. Gehlen did it on purpose. Because he wanted Hitler to believe this.

Maclean: Of course the Soviet attitude towards Mihailović was quite interesting too. They upset Tito very much because they showed some interest in the Četniks in the early days and Eden also told me that Molotov had expressed interest in sending a Soviet mission to Mihailović presumably because he thought we were on to something rather good and they did not want to be left out. That of course annoyed Tito more than ever.

Deakin: Therefore in the first period the interpretation of the Russians and the Germans was identical.

13 Following Woodhouse, Myers and Clogg

Johnstone: There are one or two points which were raised in my mind after Clogg's paper. One rises out of a remark he made about the history of Leeper's relations with S.O.E. before the events he was describing. They are relevant and should be borne in mind throughout this discussion. The dispute between Leeper and S.O.E. and his personal feelings about S.O.E. dated from long before his appointment as ambassador to the Greek government-in-exile – indeed from the earlier days of the war when Leeper was a director of P.W.E. Both P.W.E. and S.O.E. were answerable to the same Minister, and for various reasons, some of them highly personal, the two organisations had already got across each other. These dissensions were perfectly well known to the Foreign Office when they appointed Leeper as their liaison with the Greek government. Knowing what his attitude was, they nevertheless appointed him, and what thereafter might have been expected to occur, duly occurred.

After having heard previously in this conference some of the things about P.X.* and other mishandlings of relations between the two organisations, the antagonism which prevailed between them and which developed between the Foreign Office and S.O.E. is understandable though still deplorable. But, leaving out personal animosities, the Foreign Office came to believe, rightly or wrongly, that they had only two alternatives before them. Either the mission – as it then was in Greece, a small mission – must have a political adviser, directly approved and sent out by them, or they must find someone who could combine the mission's two fields of action, the military and the political. The first alternative was tried and ended, as we know, tragically.

* See p. 226 above.

It then, by greater good fortune than perhaps the Foreign Office deserved, proved possible to implement the second alternative, and thereafter that worked with great smoothness and effect. That, in general outline, is how I see it. I saw it very much from the fringes, though with some experience of the actors and their problems.

For about forty years of my life, from 1928 until his death, I was a friend and at various times a subordinate of Leeper, so I can claim to have known his character, and his reactions, fairly well. At the time we are discussing in this conference I was not serving under him either in Egypt or subsequently in Greece, though I naturally saw him from time to time. On the Myers episode, although I shall always retain the warmest memories of Leeper, and deep gratitude to him, I should be happy to see Myers justified publicly and I have no use at all for the kind of petulant abuse contained in the Foreign Office papers and quoted in Clogg's paper. I think it can fairly be attributed to strain and ill health. I do not know whether, in order to make the valid point that there was personal animus, sometimes unjust, on Leeper's part towards Myers, it is necessary to quote verbatim. I can only remind those present that of the parties to this dispute, one is alive here and happily with us today and the other is dead and unable to defend his action. I would hope therefore that the kind of severity which Clogg has rightly shown in his paper towards Leeper's attitude at this juncture might be expressed with the minimum of personal denigration, first because I do not think this really does much good to either party, and secondly because I believe that when Clogg reads further in the recently opened documents he will discover a more constructive attitude on Leeper's part from the Lebanon conference onwards showing that, when all the personal bitterness had subsided, some of the lessons which had been learnt first of all from Myers, and later from his successors, sank in and affected policy, in the embassy certainly, and I think in the Foreign Office too.

Clogg: I am sure Johnstone is right in that a study of Leeper's handling of the Lebanon conference and especially the December 1944 crisis would go some way at least to redressing the balance of the perhaps rather one-sided picture that emerged in my paper of his handling of the mission of the six Greeks to

Cairo in August 1943.* Moreover the fact that while the Foreign Office papers have been opened, those of S.O.E. remain closed, apparently for the indefinite future, inevitably contributes to a somewhat one-sided view of the relations between the Foreign Office and S.O.E.

Taylor: May I add two points to the picture that has been provided by the two papers linked together, one in a rather introductory fashion that refers to events in the years preceding Gorgopotamos, and the other a word on the epilogue; that is to say the way in which the crisis which occurred mainly as a result of the Greek imbroglio in Cairo, and also to some extent the crisis resulting from the Mihailović/Partisan rivalry, developed and was finally resolved in London in September/October 1943. I would like to say first of all that as far as Woodhouse's paper is concerned, there is absolutely nothing in my memory and nothing in the records which I have which is in any way inconsistent with the picture that he has given. It is exactly the picture as I saw it. I think it is a fair and accurate statement of the position. I must also tell you the basic source of my information about certain facts relating to the early period – which throw light on the accounts given in the two Greek papers. In 1945 when it was clear that the war was coming to an end and it was known that S.O.E. would very soon cease to function, all sections were instructed to compile fairly extensive records which were intended to be the sources for the comprehensive history of S.O.E. which W. J. M. Mackenzie was going to write.† The complete and detailed record of everything that had been done by the S.O.E. Greek section from the time it was set up in Athens in early 1940 until the Gorgopotamos operation in November 1942 was written by Ian Pirie. He was the first person to be put in charge in Athens (by me in 1940), and he remained in the Greek section in Cairo and Istanbul until he was reluctantly recalled under pressure from the Foreign Office. This record is essentially a record of fact from which certain conclusions can be drawn. The main one is represented by the picture built up as a result of the information which came out of Greece to the S.O.E. Greek section through signals from the Prometheus II W/T link in Athens, reports from emissaries sent

* Subsequent reading in the later documents confirms this view. R.C.
† See M. Howard, *Grand Strategy*, IV (London, 1972) p. 481.

into Greece, and couriers or escapees who came across, mostly to Izmir. I think it is fair to say, as a sort of summary conclusion, that this information built up a picture which showed that in the total field of resistance in Greece, in the mountains and in Athens and other cities, there was an absolutely unanimous attitude of hostility and distrust of the Royal Hellenic Government and of the King. It was quite unmistakable. This information compiled and circulated in Cairo was made available to everybody mainly by the system devised by E. G. Sebastian, who had been consul in Greece and had been appointed to the Minister of State's staff as a liaison between the Minister of State's office and his old friend Tsouderos, although he remained in close touch with Pirie. This picture was repeatedly conveyed to the Greek government, to General Headquarters, to everybody concerned, and of course to the Foreign Office. It is quite clear from this record that this picture was one that the Foreign Office and the Greek government refused to accept and did its best to suppress. As far as the Greek government was concerned it went even further and endeavoured to break and remove from any position of influence or even presence in the Middle East the principal individuals concerned in disseminating information from Greece, that is Sebastian and Pirie himself. The record shows the gradual process by which Prime Minister Tsouderos began to turn on his friend Sebastian because he neither liked, nor was prepared to accept, the picture that Sebastian was giving him of the situation inside Greece. It also shows quite clearly that the Foreign Office also refused to accept this picture; because, if accepted, it would have made nonsense of its fundamental policy of unlimited and unquestioned support of the Royal Hellenic Government and the return of the King. So, not only did they refuse to accept the picture, but, and this is not to exaggerate, they persecuted the perfectly honest and reliable people who were presenting it with the best motives. In conclusion I would like Woodhouse's view as to whether it is fair to say that the whole picture of the character, attitude and political views of every element of the resistance in Greece, which were fully known and readily available in the work of the political section of S.O.E., was as Woodhouse and Myers found it, by bitter experience, when they got there.

Woodhouse: This is true, but of course there is the important difference that we were not told anything about the situation before we went in.

Taylor: That you should have been sent in without this briefing is most extraordinary. There are three elements in the explanation. The first is that the Gorgopotamos operation was originally intended as a single military operation and you were almost all coming out again. So there was some pretext or excuse for not giving the sort of full political briefing which would have been possible. The second explanation, as has already been revealed in the discussion, is that the Greek side of the political section in Cairo, as a result of the attitudes and pressures of the Greek government and the Foreign Office, was kept in a sort of quarantine and more or less not allowed to talk to anybody. It was understandable that, unless it was absolutely necessary from a military point of view for them to brief you, there might be a certain reluctance to invite trouble by having the briefing. The third explanation of course is to be found in the very unfortunate organisation set up by Terence Maxwell by which the operational side was completely divorced from the political side. One must remember that the Greek section of S.O.E. was kept in quarantine, because S.O.E., and for that matter General Headquarters, could not afford to broadcast its conclusions without being involved in terrible rows with the Greek government and the Foreign Office. Moreover a ridiculous system of a sort of double life about operations, one real and one entirely imaginary, was being carried on. In theory all work back to the resistance in Greece was to be carried on under the supervision of the Anglo-Greek Committee. The Anglo-Greek Committee consisted of representatives of the Greek government, the Foreign Office, S.O.E., P.W.E. and General Headquarters.This Committee usually met about once a month and it was a complete farce because in order not to provoke tremendous trouble from the Greek government, the Committee only discussed plans in Greece which were acceptable to the Greek government and mostly discussed quite mythical Royalist organisations, such as the Six Colonels in Athens, which never had any real substance at all. The real operations of S.O.E., mostly conducted from Istanbul and Izmir into Greece, were never mentioned at all. The whole thing was kept completely separate and this to a large extent explains why the *Harling* party were never briefed at all on the political background, though they could have had the fullest possible picture leading to exactly the same conclusions as they arrived at for themselves, very painfully, when they got there.

Woodhouse: May I argue one or two of the points which Taylor has made? I think the argument that it was not really necessary to brief us on the political situation, that we were going to blow up a bridge, is perfectly true as far as Myers is concerned, but it was not true as far as I was concerned because from the beginning the intention was that I should stay there. A second point which I think is worth mentioning concerns the membership of the Anglo-Greek Committee. I think it was on Kanellopoulos's insistence that the Anglo-Greek Committee was originally set up because he was a victim of the Antiparos operation.

Taylor: I think it was actually set up before Kanellopoulos became a member of the government – but when he became a member of the government he was a usual attender.

Woodhouse: I am sure it is true as you say that important things were steered away from the Anglo-Greek Committee. I knew nothing of this. Indeed I never heard of the Anglo-Greek Committee until well after the war but there was no reason why I should. But I think I must have had a kind of instinct that not everything was above board about the *Harling* operation because I do recall that I insisted on seeing Kanellopoulos before we went in. I was not sure whether what we were going to do was something that fitted in with the Greek government's notion of things. I did insist on seeing Kanellopoulos and I had a very interesting talk with him though he, like everybody else, told me nothing about E.A.M. or the K.K.E. I cannot help wondering whether even Kanellopoulos would have been told about the *Harling* operation if I had not insisted upon seeing him.

Taylor: I do not think he was told officially.

Woodhouse: No, he was not until I saw him and told him what I was going to do. The last point I should like to make is of a more general character, although there is no doubt about where my sympathies lie. I can understand the point of view of the Greek establishment outside Greece, the King and his court and government. I can understand, even if I do not share, their view that the reason why the British, and in particular S.O.E., were getting all this mass of information hostile to the King was because, in the nature of things, all their agents were republicans. The reason was simple: the republicans were available for recruitment because they had been pushed out of the armed forces and other employment under the Metaxas dictatorship, whereas loyal monarchists were fully employed and not available. Mind you I think the republicans were right, but I can see why the King's circle were angry about it.

Pawson: I can confirm that, because I handled nearly all that traffic and everybody who came out. I was in Turkey from before the end of 1941 to September 1943. During this time I personally handled all the traffic that came over the Prometheus II link, and no one else had a code. I would not trust anyone else with a code knowing what was going on in Cairo and when I received a telegram to send the book we were using I said quite truthfully that I had left it in Crete. I had to get out of Crete in a hurry and we left the signal plans and the code behind. When Prometheus sent a courier to me in Cairo I sent him back with new crystals, signal plans and the new book. The only books we could get were two paperbacked Turkish books. So when I received a very peremptory telegram saying I was to provide the code, I was able to give the name of the book but I said I could not get a copy in Turkey, which was perfectly true; but that if he tried, perhaps he could. So no one had the code except me and I decoded all the messages myself. As far as anybody knows I might have made the whole lot up, whereas in fact I assure you that I did not. I can bear witness to everything that Taylor has said, that everything that came out from our agents over the wireless link and through couriers and through the escapees I talked to, was to the effect that if we were going to impose the King on them they would not fight the enemy. I remember writing this in a memorandum as early as the end of 1941. I finished up by saying that unless we could persuade the King to say that he would hold a plebiscite before he went back to Greece we should not get any results. I know that that memorandum got as far as Pearson in London. Whether it got any further I do not know. So the accusation levelled at Myers was inaccurate. A plebiscite had been thought of long before Myers was accused of advocating it.

Taylor: I do not think anybody could fail to be shocked by the revelations contained in the paper based on the Foreign Office files, shocked by the comments and the attitude of the Foreign Secretary himself and of the senior members of the Foreign Office. It needs an explanation and the explanation is this. The Foreign Office simply could not afford to accept the S.O.E. picture as it was coming out of Greece without completely stultifying their policy of complete, total support of the Royal Hellenic Government. Therefore the attempts to suppress and rebut this picture turned into an attack on S.O.E., which was its source; this poison, as it were, just grew and grew in London and Cairo. They had to discredit the picture because once they accepted it the whole basis of their policy would have been removed and it would have been shown to be non-viable. The epilogue to the Cairo conference links up to some extent with the extraordinary story which Maclean has told us on the Yugoslav side. I refer to the crisis which occurred in Cairo as a result of the delegation from the andartes coming out and the conference blowing up in Leeper's face. The consequence of that crisis was in the end the preparation of a General Head-quarters paper which was brought to London by Brigadier Davey. This made the point, but not very offensively, that S.O.E. must be brought under closer control and that S.O.E.'s activities in Greece and elsewhere had political implications about which other departments, particularly the Foreign Office, had a right to be consulted. That paper arrived in London at the very moment when the Foreign Secretary was about to launch his second major campaign against S.O.E., on the broadest possible basis, virtually aiming at completely strangling it. The result was a tremendous row in London, in which Selborne and Gubbins, who had just been appointed the new chief of S.O.E., waged a tremendous battle in which Selborne fought like a tiger mainly against the Foreign Secretary, using all of his personal influence with the Prime Minister to defend S.O.E. and rebut the Foreign Office proposals, which would in fact have practically abolished S.O.E. The outcome of that was a memorandum from the Prime Minister which was somewhat soothing in character. It was intended to satisfy Middle East, to give some satisfaction to Eden but under no circumstances to humiliate Selborne, and as a result it was somewhat ambiguous.

Sweet-Escott: I was very foxed about this move of Middle East when I was writing my present contribution and I wrote to Gubbins about it. I myself was sick with malaria during the month of September 1943. He replied to me in effect that it was not just operational control within their own theatre that the Middle East paper was asking for – this they already had but had not got down to exercising it: what they were proposing was the actual dismemberment of S.O.E. in the Middle East and its links with London, to be replaced by something of their own creation entirely within their own hands. Their paper to the Chiefs of Staff, brought to London from Cairo by Brigadier Davey of General Wilson's staff, was passed by the Chiefs of Staff to S.O.E. with a request for S.O.E.'s reply to it within three or four days; this was done.

I asked Gubbins when this was and he replied that he has entries in his appointment book (then kept by his secretary) of two days away from his office, 11 and 12 September 1943, to write the paper which was handed in to the Chiefs of Staff on 13 September; of an appointment in his office with Brigadier Davey at 5.45 p.m. and with Lord Selborne at 6.30 p.m. on 13 September; of being called to the Chiefs of Staff Committee at 11.30 a.m. on Tuesday 14 September, and at 5.30 p.m. the same day, with Lord Selborne, to the Defence Committee of the War Cabinet. At this Chiefs of Staff meeting, the S.O.E. rebuttal of the Middle East proposals was accepted in all main features with the recommendation that S.O.E. should retain its autonomy.

I would add that Gubbins shortly after this went to Cairo to establish closer links with General Headquarters and to review the S.O.E. organisation there in the light of the changed strategic situation *vis-à-vis* the Balkans, created by the Allied occupation of Southern Italy which offered a far superior base than Cairo for all S.O.E. operations on the Balkan mainland. Gubbins was given all possible help and co-operation by General Wilson and his staff, including General Scobie and Brigadier Davey. Wilson and Gubbins agreed between them on the name of a suitable person to be appointed to the vacant post of Commander of S.O.E. Middle East, i.e. Major-General W. A. M. Stawell who took up that post immediately: the incident of the Middle East paper was already dead and

forgotten as far as General Headquarters Middle East and
S.O.E. were concerned.

Taylor: That is completely in line with my records also. On 9
October I wrote a memorandum briefly summarising what had
been happening in which I said amongst other things, that the
Middle East Defence Committee paper, in the none too friendly
hands of the Foreign Secretary, was made the occasion of
raising much wider issues than I believed had been in the minds
of its compilers. I think that is certainly true of Wilson anyhow.
This battle ensued and as a result the Chiefs of Staff wrote a
paper based upon the Prime Minister's memorandum, applying, so far as they could, the decisions it contained. It was
agreed that Gubbins should go out to Cairo and discuss the
implementation of the paper with the Commander-in-Chief.
He went out sometime just after 9 October. This whole battle
on several fronts resulted in the end in a compromise – in which
the attempt by the Foreign Office virtually to abolish S.O.E.
was rebutted, the independence of S.O.E. in relation both to the
Foreign Office and to all local supreme Allied commanders was
very much reduced, and Selborne was obliged most reluctantly,
but inevitably, to sacrifice Glenconner. Keble was returned to
the army and Tamplin promptly died. At that stage nothing
was decided about Myers and I certainly wrote on 6 October a
memorandum in which it was still assumed that he was going
back to Greece. Then for some reason of which I have no
record it was finally decided that he would not go back to
Greece.

Clogg: That Myers was not sent back was a direct consequence
of the outbreak of civil war in Greece in early October and
particularly the death of Lieutenant Hubbard in rather mysterious circumstances. It was held that to send Myers back at
that particular juncture might imply some approval of E.L.A.S.

Maclean: Did Wallace go into Greece as your political adviser
or did he go in to report? What I would really like to know is
did he have his own ciphers?

Myers: The answer to the last question – no. He was Eden's
personal representative and my political adviser or words to that
effect.

Woodhouse: Wilson's memoirs slightly confuse the issue here by
describing him as Myers's second in command which of course

he was not and was never intended to be. He was Eden's personal representative but he had no cipher.

Maclean: I took an S.I.S. cipher because I had heard stories that signals had never reached their destination and I was going to see Menzies,* who again was an old friend of mine; I asked him to fix up for me to take another set, which I did.

Woodhouse: I think the really unfortunate thing was simply that W/T communications were so overloaded at that time, S.O.E. was not capable of handling the traffic. It should have prepared itself for this because, after all, Wallace was dropped in at the end of June, though he did not actually come on the air until late in July, by which time S.O.E. Cairo really should have been ready to handle the traffic. There was a backlog of traffic then, not merely Wallace's signals, but everything in the field which went back certainly many days, probably in some cases even a week or two.

Taylor: That I can confirm. I came through Cairo for twenty-four hours on my way back from India to London in the beginning of September and the backlog was quite appalling.

Woodhouse: This was something Leeper could not believe, and in a way one can understand that. He believed it was all being held up deliberately; but I am perfectly certain it was not.

Barker: On the other hand Clogg made the point that the Foreign Office in London got the first Wallace telegram from S.O.E. London on 10 August.

Woodhouse: If there is any significance in this curious point, and I think this does need careful analysis, then it is that S.O.E. was concealing things from Leeper which it was prepared to tell the Foreign Office. This is very odd.

Taylor: I am bound to say I do not think it impossible given the character of the man in question.

Myers: Having seen what went wrong, the answer possibly is a simple one – that there was a different group of cipher girls sending traffic on to London than there was for local distribution within Cairo.

Maclean: I think this is as possible as anything.

Taylor: That is a good point. It does make it a possibility that the delay occurred in separate sections on the distribution side.

Myers: Although either Woodhouse or I put *DDD* (immediate

* Sir Stuart Menzies, head of M.I.6 (S.I.S.).

priority) at the top of our signals, at this period we were not getting a reply within a fortnight and it had to be really top priority to get a quicker reply.

Woodhouse: Wallace landed in the last week of June and came out with Myers on 9 August, so he was in Greece for about five or six weeks.

Myers: During the first two or three weeks the only signal he sent concerned some missing kit. The first fortnight or three weeks he sent no operational, no Foreign Office signals at all. He was building up his picture, very sensibly, very thoroughly, and then he sent off a salvo of more than half a dozen telegrams, one after the other.

Woodhouse: But as Clogg pointed out in his paper, this really did not matter, because after all he was back in Cairo by 10 August and could say all those things that were in these missing signals.

Taylor: It does not absolve Leeper in any way.

Maclean: And until he had seen Leeper he was saying the same as you were saying.

Taylor: All the evidence seems to point to the fact that until he was brainwashed he was in complete agreement with Myers.

Woodhouse: I think this picture of brainwashing is not convincing. I did not know Wallace all that well. But I do not think he was susceptible to brainwashing. I think that one must remember that almost everything one knows not only about Leeper's opinions but about Wallace's opinions came from Leeper.

Taylor: It is fairly clear, is it not, that Wallace actually killed both the telegrams and his initial analysis? He came back from Greece substantially with the same picture as Myers and as a result of discussions with Leeper, on Leeper's own evidence in the documents, he changed his view. That seems to be clear.

Woodhouse: But we really only have Leeper's own word for it.

Johnstone: I wonder whether anyone who saw him after he had seen Leeper found that his view was substantially altered from what you say it was.

Myers: I can throw a little light on that because I met him on several occasions. On no occasion did he indicate to me that he had been brainwashed in the way that Leeper's account suggests. But he was a very embarrassed man in my company when talking about the subjects about which we had previously agreed. I would put a more generous interpretation on it, as has been suggested by Woodhouse just now, that he was torn between two loyalties, one to me, who had been his temporary commander in the mountains, and secondly to his actual bosses in Cairo. When Leeper changed his mind Wallace was placed in a very invidious position as regards me. This was my general impression. I never got any further advice from Wallace from the day we arrived in Cairo. He was not my officer and he made it quite clear that he was Leeper's and he must play it that way. He was never disloyal to me, but he was highly embarrassed, which indicates, as I say, that he might have gone along with Leeper to the extent of saying: 'Well, you are older and more experienced than I am. I suppose you could be right. Anyhow I can see your point of view.' But this is surmise.

Taylor: But this much is quite clear, that the man who was sent to report on the position on the spot came back and accepted the view of the man in Cairo.

Woodhouse: Of course it was not the first time this had happened. You will remember a brief intervention of Stevens when he indicated that he was sent in because such contradictory reports were emerging from us in the field. I think he said at one point that one of my reports had led him to think I had gone mad – or words to that effect. Now Stevens ended up, I should say, almost the most fanatically anti-E.A.M. officer we ever had – having been originally sent in to strike a balance and sort us all out.

Taylor: It seems odd to me that the somebody from the spot could have his opinion changed by the views of somebody who had never been there.

Clogg: This is odd, though there is that remark of Leeper's about Woodhouse's report of 19 October from Pertouli* – to the effect that had Woodhouse realised the trend of opinion in the Foreign Office, that it had moved towards a total break with E.L.A.S., he would have been far more critical of E.L.A.S. than he was. One would have thought that what Leeper wanted was Woodhouse's assessment of the situation as it was, not as it might have been or as Leeper might like it to be, and the Foreign Office might like it to be.

---

* FO 371/37207, R 11673.

Mrs Pamela Pawson: I worked with Wallace for a short time in Athens and I thought he was very young, very uncertain of himself, very easily influenced.

Hammond: Did he not go back to London and report to Eden?

Clogg: Yes, but his final considered report is not available for consultation.* This would presumably provide more conclusive evidence of the way in which he did change his ground and along what lines, if in fact he did. But certainly Leeper, in the latter part of August, was saying, for instance, that he had not realised, until he learned it from Wallace, the extent to which, as he put it, Zervas had been browbeaten into adhering to the andartes Joint General Headquarters agreement. This appears to be one way in which Wallace changed his mind because this view was not apparent in his initial report from within Greece, the one which was delayed in transmission or whatever did happen to it.

Davidson: Was Wallace an expert on Greek affairs, did he know the Greek language, did he have much experience, was he the kind of man who within a month or two could have formed an opinion about the situation?

Woodhouse: He was not a novice. He had been in Greece at the time the war broke out and he was taken on temporarily then in the press attaché's office for a time – I do not know for how long. So he had been there some time and he had some knowledge. But neither Myers nor I would have found any fault with what he was saying when he was in Greece. It was all exactly what we had been saying.

Davidson: It seems a little strange the Foreign Secretary should have appointed somebody who was not in fact highly qualified to form a judgement.

Woodhouse: He was as qualified as any of us were when we first arrived.

Johnstone: You left him to try to form his own impressions for himself and when they were formed and communicated to you within a short time they appeared sensible. This does show a certain ability to recognise what sort of things were happening.

Woodhouse: This is perfectly true. And, speaking for myself, I made no attempt to influence him at all. I actually declined to

* FO 371/37213, R 8419.

talk to him in private before he had gone around and formed his own view. I think Myers and I were so convinced that any-body who came with his eyes open must see the same things that we had seen that there was no reason to take any other attitude towards him.

Clogg: As Myers said before Wallace was parachuted in, he would lay a hundred to one bet that Wallace would agree with him over the constitutional issue; this is precisely what did happen.

Johnstone: I think that the views of those within Greece did in fact sink in, though the initial reaction was one of resistance on Leeper's part.

Clogg: Leeper, to be fair, was always more aware of the impor-tance of the constitutional issue in Greece than the Foreign Office itself. I think aspects of his perhaps rather erratic be-haviour in August are also explained by the fact that he was quite seriously ill. Some of the quotations that I gave in my paper were written in the period after about 20 August, the very peak of this illness. This is certainly a factor which cannot be left out of account.

Johnstone: On a wider view, surely as the war developed and especially after *Animals* and the collapse of Italy, the political aspect of resistance both in Yugoslavia and in Greece was bound gradually to overshadow the military – because every one was taking up their positions for the coming post-liberation phase. Liberation was beginning to appear as a possibility, although it was not to be by a full-scale Allied invasion of the Balkans, and everyone was taking position accordingly. Those in control of the political side of things therefore tended to demand more of a say in the assessment and handling of the situation than they had had when the purely military aspects were dominant.

Maclean: I think that at the beginning of 1945 the Yugoslavs thought it was conceivable that we might try to restore King Peter by force of arms.

Barker: I think that Woodhouse, in making the point in his paper about Churchill saying that in one place we supported a Communist and in another place a King, was rather implying that some efforts should have been made to co-ordinate the two policies. But surely in a sense, the fact that we were doing one thing in the one case and the other in the other case made the two policies possible because you appease right-wing opinion by backing the King in Greece, and left-wing opinion and the Russians by backing the Partisans in Yugoslavia. I do not think this was consciously thought out but it was surely a very convenient way of handling the matter.

Woodhouse: This may be so; the point I was trying to make was not exactly that. For all I know it may well have been right to pursue these opposite policies in the two countries. What I was saying was that as far as I could discover nobody at the time had ever thought about the implications of what was being done in one country in relation to the other. I may be wrong about this but I can find no evidence of it. The two countries might have been on Mars and Venus for all the connection that was seen between them.

Barker: I have a feeling that certainly in June 1944, but I think earlier, one comes across the comment that really E.A.M. and the Partisans were just as bad as each other except that the Partisans did actually fight the Germans.*

Maclean: That was what certainly decided the issue in Yugoslavia. It was put to me quite clearly by the Prime Minister more than once. The first time I saw him after I came out, he said the same thing, that what mattered was who was fighting the Germans and that politics were a secondary consideration. That was made absolutely clear.

Hammond: The Greek campaign, and what the Greek army achieved in Albania, I think, had a tremendous effect upon the attitude in England towards the Greek monarch and his government. It was very much harder to shake that off than we perhaps now think and this affected the Foreign Office more than it affected S.O.E.

Clogg: This feeling of a personal debt of loyalty to the King who had stood by us in this very dark hour is quite explicit in the documents. He stood by us – we cannot let him down.

Maclean: This argument was also made in the Yugoslav connection – the fact that King Peter had been concerned with the March 1941 coup.

Clogg: Was there ever any explicit mention in the documents that Greece was, as Sargent cabled to Eden during the August

* See Howard minute of 15.2.44, FO 371/44247.

1943 crisis, a vital British interest? Is there any indication that Yugoslavia was not regarded as a vital British interest in the sense that Greece was?

Barker: Obviously it was regarded in a different category but there was some talk at some stage as to whether we could maintain our influence in Serbia as a sort of buffer state protecting Greece. But this never got beyond loose talk in minutes.*

Sweet-Escott: But surely there was this difference in 1943–4, that Greece was supposed to be essential because it guarded the route to India. Our pre-war policy, or policy in 1941, in Yugoslavia – was expendable, more expendable than it was in Greece.

Barker: Quite obviously they would have liked to keep their hold on Yugoslavia as an optimum objective but I do not think they said it was vital.

Maclean: What would be interesting would be to know the attitude in the Foreign Office about how essential it was to keep Yugoslavia united.

Barker: This I find mysterious. Formally we were committed to the restoration of a united Yugoslavia. And during 1942 there were a number of attempts made to get a joint declaration by the Serb and Croat politicians in London on the future of Serbo-Croat relations; but they all completely broke down. The Foreign Office then went off on the idea of having separate Serbian, Croat and Slovene units in a wider Balkan federation, of which the Greek–Yugoslav Pact of 1941 was to be the sort of nucleus. That all fizzled out because of Soviet opposition, and then quite late on Sargent or somebody else said in a minute that we might perhaps just maintain our interest in Serbia, detach Serbia from Yugoslavia.† This was more or less instantly dismissed and I suppose this was because the Russians had come down in favour of a united Yugoslavia.

Maclean: The Russians had had different attitudes on that particular subject over the last thirty years. There was a time, prior to 1934, when Soviet policy was to split up Yugoslavia and there were other times when it favoured a united Yugoslavia.

* See, for example, minutes by E. M. Rose and Sir Orme Sargent of 17.11.43, FO 371/37615.
† But when President Roosevelt suggested detaching Serbia in a message to Churchill on 19.5.44, the Foreign Office reaction was chilly. FO 371/44290.

Barker: But when Eden saw Stalin in December 1941 Stalin came down in favour of a united and enlarged Yugoslavia. I do not think he ever subsequently changed from that.

Seton-Watson: I should like to try and clarify this issue of different policies towards Serbia and the rest of Yugoslavia. It was widely believed in London that Serbia was for Mihailović, and from this the conclusion was drawn that through Mihailović we could gain the support of the Serbs. Now in my opinion this sort of reasoning was based on no more than a half-truth. It is true that there were more Royalists in Serbia than in the rest of Yugoslavia, because the dynasty was a Serbian dynasty. But that the Serbs were more or less pro-Communist or more or less infectable by Communism than the Croats, seems to me a very doubtful proposition. The truth was that those people who were pro-Communist or likely to be pro-Communist were to be found in all parts of the country. And those people who were likely to be anti-Communist again were found in all parts of the country. There was a higher proportion of Serbs than of Croats or Slovenes among regular officers, simply because historically the army had been a Serbian creation. On the other hand the intellectuals and semi-intellectuals and disaffected peasants (sometimes, incidentally, quite rich peasants, because rich peasants had more time to think) were more amenable to political argument than poor peasants. Those social elements who were accessible to Communism or to sympathy for Communism were probably more numerous in the Serbian lands than they were in the rest of the country. The idea that there was an association between Serbs and conservatism and between Croats and Communism was quite wrong. There were of course Croats who were Communists, but other Croats had a different kind of conservatism, their own Catholic kind. Also, it seems to me that devotion to the Yugoslav monarchy was not a very important factor on the British policy side – not in the same class as the corresponding factor in Greece. The devotion of the British government to the Greek monarchy seems to have been an immensely deeply rooted dogma and not to have applied to the same extent to the Serbian monarchy. Of course, it could be explained partly by geography, i.e. Greece was geographically nearer to regions of strategic importance to Britain than was Yugoslavia. But I wonder whether we

should not also look for the explanation again in personalities –
whether there were not individual personalities, perhaps even
Churchill himself and others, who happened to feel strongly
about the Greek monarchy. These personal links might have
been quite an important factor in explaining the difference
between the two situations.

Woodhouse: Then of course there was the dynastic connection.
It was much closer in the case of Greece as well. King George
was a much more serious character than Peter, was he not?

Maclean: What is quite certain, although I doubt if it was
obvious to the Foreign Office at the time, is that the Communists were the only people who were likely to produce a
united Yugoslavia. They are having quite a struggle to manage
it thirty years after – but still I think that if King Peter and
Mihailović had been put back on the throne in 1945 there
would have been a Serbo-Croatian civil war. But there were
also rumours that the Foreign Office was run entirely by
Roman Catholics and that they were all violently prejudiced in
favour of the Croats. Whether that was George Rendel or not
I do not know but there was that story.

Barker: I never saw any trace of that in the papers. I am sure
that it was put round by the Serbs in London; but they also
thought that S.O.E. had plotted with the Croats to get rid of
Simović or other Serbian leaders.*

Bailey: To take up Seton-Watson's point, with which I largely
agree, about Communism in Serbia, especially the Orthodox
area of Yugoslavia – I agree that intellectuals, semi-intellectuals and so on were much more prone to Communism, but I
think there was a good reason for it. When Yugoslavia was
created it was still the kingdom of the Serbs, Croats and
Slovenes. In 1918, there was an immediate rush for higher
education among many sections of the population. In particular
almost every peasant wished to see one member of his family
given a university education. Unfortunately, no policy was ever
adopted of selecting candidates and channelling them into
definite disciplines with the result that, of the intake of Belgrade
University, 80 per cent was either in the legal or in the medical
faculties, whereas there was a crying need in the country for

* See, for instance, Rendel to the Foreign Office 18.12.42, FO 371/33443.

engineers of all classes and other technicians. The further consequence of this was that many of these students took seven or eight years or even longer, to qualify. Owing to this hyperproduction of intellectuals in these two professions, when they did qualify and had completed a two-year obligatory period of military service they very frequently found that there was no job for them. Of course the academic staff of Belgrade University was extremely left-wing. That does have a bearing on many things that transpired afterwards.

To revert to the Greek situation. In January 1943, shortly after I reached Mihailović's headquarters, he raised the question of establishing some sort of liaison with the Agrarians in Bulgaria and especially with Zervas in Greece. This again was a manifestation of this Pan-Balkan movement by which there would be Balkan federation extending from the Adriatic to the Bosphoros and from the Danube to the Mediterranean. I think Mihailović must have heard the B.B.C. broadcast about the Gorgopotamos exploit. He was an avid listener to the B.B.C. Very often there was nothing else to do on our mountain top. I reported this to Cairo who must have decided that this offered a perpetual goad with which to prod Mihailović into activity because towards the end of February I received a number of messages from the 'Senior British Liaison Officer with the National Army of Liberation in Greece'. Among them was one from Zervas which I was instructed to hand to Mihailović. It was of an exhortative and complimentary nature, and quite innocuous. Mihailović never asked us to send a reply back to Zervas *via* Cairo but I learnt from a member of his staff that he had in fact sent off a courier with a very long letter for Zervas. I doubt whether the courier got through, after all it was a matter of several hundred kilometres, mostly on foot. There were no further developments, and the matter passed from my mind until Mihailović was brought to trial in 1946 in Belgrade. There the public prosecutor read out Zervas's letter which had been found in Mihailović's archives at the time of his capture and proceeded grossly to exaggerate its importance and to read the most sinister implications into it. These were to the effect that, at the instigation of the British government, Zervas had suggested to Mihailović that they should collaborate, so far as supplies, topography and communications permitted, in the liquidation of the rapidly developing Partisan forces. There was no truth whatsoever in this charge. I had read the message myself. But unfortunately at the time there was little we could do to rebut the charge. It would be interesting to hear if either Myers or Woodhouse had any knowledge of this. I am struck by the fact that the situations in Greece and Yugoslavia were identical but in reverse. I had similar experience to Myers when I had an audience with the monarch, except in my case the question was King Peter's impending marriage. The only clue I got to King George VI's opinion on Balkan affairs was that as I left he said there are too many of these Balkan states with their bloody intrigues and he was related by marriage to all of them. The whole thread that runs through what has been said at this conference has one underlying cause in my opinion and that is inadequacy. First of all inadequacy of communications, of which we have heard a lot. There were not enough people to decode messages, with consequent delay, then inadequacy of supplies due to lack of aircraft and in this case I am bound to say from the supply angle the unfortunate Mihailović was by far the worst off. He was in the centre of the peninsula and at the time when we might have persuaded him by giving him adequate supplies to carry out some active operations. But of course there were not the aircraft that could get to him. Above all, the sheer human inadequacy for anyone, whether they were in the field or at General Headquarters, to absorb regularly and consistently, to say nothing about analysing and synthesising, the enormous mass of information, frequently conflicting, frequently biased, with which they were constantly confronted. S.O.E. in particular never recovered from the initial mistake made by Laurence Grand.* He asked for everything he wanted and by and large he got most of it. But there was one essential factor he failed to ask for and that was time. S.O.E. from the outset, and I can talk with some authority about this because I came in October 1939, when it was still D section, was expected to run not merely before it could walk but before it was out of the cradle and, in my opinion, that affliction remained with us, at any rate as long as I was with the organisation. All this of course has a perfectly adequate explanation – from June 1940

* See above p. 4.

until December 1941 the British were virtually alone. Our resources were totally inadequate, yet after June 1941 we tried even to help the Russians with what little material and other supplies we had. The outcome of all this was delayed strain and a situation which was so urgent that no one really had the time or the detailed and qualified information to plan adequately for more than one or two months ahead. Plans were made for post-war Europe but they were not properly thought out and, in my view, could not be properly thought out. Hence I think it not unfair to say that our heroic defence of our own country and of the free world during that period of eighteen months (in 1940 and 1941) must, if viewed from the angle of our post-war political interests and economic interests in south-eastern Europe, eastern Europe and the Middle East, be regarded as a Pyrrhic victory.

Woodhouse: May I comment on the communication between Zervas and Mihailović? This is extremely interesting to me and I am sure to Myers, because we never knew the other end of this story before. It is true that Zervas sent a message through our wireless destined for Mihailović at our suggestion, at that date, which was December 1942; and Bailey received it I gather in January 1943 or a little later. We did at that time think it desirable to bring together what seemed to be essentially similar types of resistance movement. You must remember these were very early days before we knew either the realities of Mihailović or the realities of E.A.M. This message was sent but we got no reply. We were slightly hurt and I am interested to hear that Mihailović sent a courier in our direction because we sent a courier in his direction of whom also we never heard anything more. We certainly never received a courier from Mihailović, at least I do not think we did. If Zervas did he never told us. But perhaps more interesting, a few months later, probably in March or even April 1943, Zervas took this idea of liaison with Mihailović sufficiently seriously to send to his own second in command, Komninos Pyromaglou, northwards to try and get through to Serbia and make contact with Mihailović, which clearly showed that he regarded it as a matter of very great importance. But Pyromaglou was unable to get through and returned a few weeks later. I never heard the full story from him of how far he got or why he was unable to get through but no direct contact of any kind was ever established between Zervas and Mihailović. Of course in retrospect that is a great relief. For if we had succeeded in forging this contact it would have been very difficult indeed to exculpate Zervas from the same kind of accusations that were being levelled against Mihailović. Even as things were strenuous efforts were made by the Communists in Greece certainly, and I have no doubt in Yugoslavia, too, to link Zervas and Mihailović as two scoundrels of the same kind. During Mihailović's trial the Greek Communist papers were full not only of accounts of the trial but of detailed analyses of the parallel between Mihailović and Zervas. For years and years, not merely during the trial but before and after it, the Greek Communists were trying to represent Zervas, as they put it, literally as the Greek Mihailović. This would have been a much more serious matter if we had succeeded in creating the liaison which we originally adumbrated with the best intentions. The other point that I would like to comment on arises from what Bailey said yesterday about the character and personality of Mihailović. I was tremendously impressed with this because of the attempts at representing Mihailović and Zervas as two of a kind. You really could not have had a description of anyone more totally unlike Zervas than the account of Mihailović, absolutely totally. If you reversed every feature of the portrait you have just about got Zervas instead.

Afterword: Thirty Years After

G. H. N. SETON-WATSON

The picture which emerges from the main contributions to this book, and from the discussion, is one of confusion. It is right that this should be so, because the reality was confused. There remain also some unexplained contradictions and some un-reconciled differences of opinion. These too were, for the parti-cipants, part of the reality, and must remain so for the his-torian. It would be not only presumptuous but silly to try to iron out the contradictions, or to provide any final conclusions. All that this last chapter can do is to add some personal observa-tions and comments, based not so much on documents as on my own very fallible memory, as well as on a sustained interest in the subsequent fate of Yugoslavia and Greece, which I have both observed from afar and revisited at irregular intervals.

Any discussion of British relations with the resistance move-ments must start from an awareness of the war situation in 1942. The defence of Britain itself and the maintenance of the position in Cyrenaica absorbed most of the resources available. Then came the disasters in Malaya and the East Indies, and the Japanese threat to India through Burma. In the summer of 1942 Rommel nearly got to Cairo, and on the Russian front the Germans reached Stalingrad and the Caucasus. It was not until the autumn that the tide turned, and the invasion of southern Europe from Africa became something to be seriously planned. During 1941 and most of 1942 aircraft and supplies were simply not available for help to Balkan resistance on the scale that was needed. The Chiefs of Staff had to be convinced that it was worth diverting any resources at all to the Balkans. It was S.O.E. Cairo's job to convince them.

S.O.E. was an upstart organisation, inevitably viewed with

suspicion and jealousy by all existing departments. From the beginning it was given impossibly ambitious tasks and denied the resources for them. When the tasks were not achieved, it was easier to blame the upstarts than to find remedies. That S.O.E. survived, and in the end achieved some important results (though not precisely those originally assigned to it), testifies to the toughness and devotion of its leaders, whatever their other faults.

The first recruits to S.O.E., in 1939 and 1940, were a mixture of widely different types from different places. There were bankers and tycoons from the City of London; businessmen, mining engineers and journalists from the Balkans, some of whom had worked for many years in these countries and knew well the local language and customs; and younger men, able and eager to learn, who had more enthusiasm than experience. These were later joined, in the Cairo period, by volunteers from the armed forces, some impelled by special knowledge of, and special concern for, Greece and Yugoslavia, others looking for a more individual and adventurous kind of service. Nearly all the earlier recruits lacked the habit of subordination to a regular hierarchy; were disciplined by no mandarin ethos; and were impatient or even contemptuous of the bureaucratic conventions of the diplomatic service and its auxiliaries. To the diplomats they often appeared brash, ignorant of things which diplomats were trained to regard as important, and at times a positive menace. Some S.O.E. members knew far more about Yugoslavia or Greece, in which they had worked for a long time past and made great numbers of personal friendships and connections, than diplomats whose career sent them there for a year or two. Often neither side made much attempt to understand the other. The loose framework of the early S.O.E., which could only horrify persons accustomed to correct civil service procedure, had some compensations. Some of those who held responsible positions in S.O.E., and who themselves were often younger than their diplomatic counterparts of similar responsibility, had the gift of understanding, encouraging and getting the best out of the younger recruits, who were eager to give of their best without reserve. The S.O.E. of 1941 in the Balkans had something of the quality of a band of brothers, which was even enhanced by its apparent pariah status.

After the German conquest of the Balkans, most of them, at least by the end of 1941, found themselves in Cairo or Istanbul. Having been plunged in Balkan politics in 1940 and 1941, whether they had wished it or not, they brought their political attitudes to their new task of finding ways to get back into the Balkans to stimulate and help resistance.

The predominant attitude among S.O.E. members who had worked in Yugoslavia was sympathy for the Serbs, especially for the Serbian democratic parties. The Serbs had been allies from 1914 to 1918, incurring fantastically high casualties. British and Serbs had fought together on the Salonika front, and these memories had been vigorously maintained by veterans of both countries. The Serbian military tradition was greatly admired, as was the individualistic outlook and passion for political liberty of most Serbs, peasants as well as urban middle classes. Prince Paul and his circle, with whom of course British diplomats were obliged to have close relations, were regarded by most politically conscious Serbs and their British friends at best as weak defenders of the Serbian tradition and at worst as liable to surrender to the German enemies of Serbia and of human freedom. The fact that Prince Paul personally was a convinced friend of Britain, and was liked by those British people who knew him, counted little against these widespread beliefs. The surrender in fact came on 25 March 1941, but it was followed by the action of 27 March. The role of S.O.E. in that event was perhaps overestimated at the time by S.O.E. members. It was true that Djonović and to a lesser extent the Agrarian party, with whom S.O.E. had close relations, were involved at least on the periphery of the conspiracy, but the decisive action was undertaken by a few officers of the Yugoslav Air Force. However, the events confirmed the affection and admiration for Serbia, and the feeling that Britain owed a debt of honour to liberate these brave people. This was strongly felt by all S.O.E. members who had served in Yugoslavia. The news of resistance by Mihailović was therefore received with great enthusiasm. Mihailović was personally known to at least two S.O.E. members, Alexander Glen and Julian Amery, and he had an excellent professional reputation. He thus became a symbol of all the qualities that S.O.E. members admired in the Serbs and a symbol of the Anglo-Serbian friendship in war which they had tried to further during their service in Yugoslavia in 1939–41.

There had also been S.O.E. members in Zagreb, who had a good understanding of the Croatian point of view, and respected the very strong democratic convictions of most members of the powerful Croatian Peasant Party. However during the interval between the *coup d'état* of 27 March 1941 and the German invasion of 6 April, the attitude of the Croatian leaders was hesitant, and during the invasion Croatian fascist (*Ustaša*) supporters quickly appeared to help or to greet the invaders. The Croats were represented in the exiled government by Dr Juraj Krnjević, a true friend of the British cause but at the same time a super-sensitive and pugnacious champion of Croatian interests not only in great matters but in small details. The quarrels between Serbian and Croatian members of the exiled government made things difficult for the British officials concerned with Yugoslavia. There was a scarcity of British specialists informed on Croatian affairs, especially in S.O.E.: of the two main S.O.E. members from Zagreb, one became a prisoner in Germany from 1941, and the other was transferred to other duties outside S.O.E., so that their advice was not available to S.O.E. There were however some specialists on Croatia in other organisations in Cairo dealing with Yugoslavia.

It was to be expected that S.O.E. members should have little sympathy for the Communists, not only because S.O.E. contained bankers and businessmen but perhaps still more because during the period of alliance between the Soviet Union and the Third Reich the Yugoslav Communists had directed their main hatred against Britain. There were however some S.O.E. members who had Communist friends in Belgrade, and who knew how strong was the sympathy both for Soviet Russia and for social revolution among young educated Serbs. When news came of Communist resistance in the autumn of 1941 they urged their chiefs not to underrate this movement – not with much success at first. As the S.O.E. office in Cairo was enlarged during 1942, and became more representative of general feeling among the armed forces at that time, admiration for the Soviet war effort at least diminished hostility to Communists, and even favoured the growth of a 'Popular Front' state of mind. There was one member of the Communist Party of Great Britain at

S.O.E. headquarters. As already stated in other published works,* this was James Klugman, who was in fact a quite exceptionally efficient staff officer.

The range of attitudes to Yugoslavia in the Foreign Office was probably not very different from those in S.O.E., though their relative weight was different. Up till 25 March 1941 there had been a tendency to trust Prince Paul. It had of course been the duty of the diplomats to keep in touch with him and his circle, and it is unjust to blame them for sympathising with him in his painful political predicament (though at the time S.O.E. members did – inevitably – blame them for this). The contradiction between a diplomat's two functions – to get on well with the government to which he is accredited and to inform his own government of all important aspects of the country's affairs – is inherent in the nature of the diplomatic profession, and there is no infallible solution to it. The action of 27 March 1941 was of course welcomed by the Foreign Office, and admiration for the Serbs as allies and as fighters was not less than in S.O.E. Foreign Office officials made great efforts to be fair to both Serbs and Croats. They, still more than S.O.E. members, because they were more constantly faced with it, disliked the endless squabbling between the exiled politicians, the efforts of some Serbian exiles to increase their own prestige by inflating the numbers of Bosnian Serbs massacred by Croatian fascists, and the zealous defence of Croatian honour on every occasion and at every pretext by the Croatian exiles. In the Foreign Office there was little sympathy for Communists, but a genuine desire to co-ordinate with the Soviet Union a policy towards resistance in Yugoslavia, leading to several sincere, patient but fruitless attempts to enlist Soviet support in reconciling Tito and Mihailović. In general Foreign Office people had the merit of greater detachment than the rather passionate S.O.E. members, but they had the disadvantage of less insight into Yugoslav minds. Their basic point of departure was also different, since it was their duty to concern themselves with long-term British interests; not only with winning the war. They therefore judged the warring factions by criteria different from those of S.O.E.

---

* Bickham Sweet-Escott, *Baker Street Irregular* (London, 1965), p. 172 and Walter R. Roberts, *Tito, Mihailović and the Allies 1941–1945* (New Brunswick, N.J., 1973) p. 89.

or of the Chiefs of Staff. The conflicts which from time to time emerged between short-term military and long-term political needs were as painful for them as for others, and it was unfair to blame them for the fact that conflicts arose.

In Greece before the German invasion the people with whom S.O.E. had the best relations were liberal Venizelists. Such persons were predominant in the Greek professional classes, or at least among that section of them which preferred Britain to Germany. The Anglophile attitude of Venizelists and the pro-Venizelist feeling of British residents in Greece went back to the events of 1917, to the Salonika Front in the First World War, and indeed further still. This tradition can be compared with the similar tradition with regard to Serbia. The regime of General Metaxas was hardly to be considered pro-British. It is of course oversimplifying to identify dictatorship with support of Hitler, or the eloquent profession of democratic convictions with effective ability to help the British cause. It is true that the government of Metaxas received a guarantee from Britain and France in 1939, and that when Mussolini presented impossible demands in October 1940, Metaxas said 'No'. But it is also true that most supporters of Metaxas were lukewarm or even hostile towards Britain, and that it was in the ranks of their opponents that S.O.E. members could expect to find allies. This inevitably was less true of the diplomats. Their duties brought them into contact with the government and the royal family. At the very top of the regime, in the person of King George II, Britain had a true friend. Of this the S.O.E. officials might be vaguely aware, but it was not a fact of life brought daily to their attention in their work. George II played a part of the greatest importance in the crisis of March/April 1941, when his government had to decide whether Greece, which had successfully resisted Italian attack, should engage in a hopeless struggle with Germany as well. Metaxas was now dead, and his successors were understandably hesitant. It was largely because of the firm attitude of the King, who believed in Britain's ultimate victory, that the decision to defy Hitler was taken.

The S.O.E. Greek experts, David Pawson and Ian Pirie, moved respectively to Turkey and to Cairo, and re-established contact with Greece. Information received by S.O.E.'s wireless link and from Greeks who reached Cairo by neutral Turkey, either by crossing the land border legally or by escaping by sea, showed that preparations for resistance, or acts of resistance, were the work of the Left, of Venizelists or of Communists. Before 1941 the Communists had been a small but not insignificant party (with fifteen seats in the last elected parliament of 1936). They enjoyed less general sympathy than in Serbia, but they had an organised following in the working class of Piraeus, Salonika and Kavalla. All reports stressed disillusionment with the monarchy, and there was a growing demand that the King should declare that he would not return to Greece until there had been a plebiscite for or against the continuation of the monarchy. This state of mind did not surprise the S.O.E. Greek specialists, and it confirmed the expectations of many British businessmen or consular officials who had long lived in Greece and were now in the Middle East. However the demand was quite unacceptable to the King, and his refusal was fully supported by Mr Churchill and his government, and so became binding on the Foreign Office. Apart from this, it is perhaps arguable that there survived in the Foreign Office a remnant of the Palmerstonian belief that constitutional monarchy is the only form of government that is good for Balkan peoples – that it alone can bring stability in place of their natural turbulence. Whatever the origins of the Foreign Office belief, there certainly soon arose a direct contradiction between the views of the Foreign Office and of S.O.E. already in the winter of 1941–2, long before the Communist Party had forged E.A.M. into an effective force or put the E.L.A.S. units into the field.

Sweet-Escott has referred to the annual purges of S.O.E. Cairo. The purge of 1941 got rid of several prominent S.O.E. Yugoslav experts, but did not much affect the Greek side. One of its effects was to bring into S.O.E. a considerable number of soldiers, including a high proportion of regular officers. The G.R. section of General Headquarters Middle East was fused with S.O.E. It is obvious in retrospect, though it was not quite so obvious at the time, that any organisation located in Cairo must come more and more under military control, and that it must serve the needs of the military command. The original S.O.E. component within the Cairo office became relatively less influential, and the link between the office and S.O.E. headquarters in London became less important than its subordination

to the Commander-in-Chief Middle East. Inevitably also, the
soldiers in General Headquarters, and still more the soldiers
in S.O.E. Cairo, were forced to have attitudes, and to take
decisions, of a political character. The reluctance of S.O.E.
London to give up its leadership, and the desire of General
Headquarters to 'keep out of politics' could not prevail against
the facts of wartime life. These things were obscured for a time
by the military crisis of July 1942, when Cairo seemed about to
fall to Rommel, S.O.E. archives were largely destroyed in panic
haste, S.O.E. personnel were scattered to the ends of the earth,
and General Headquarters were understandably so preoccupied
with saving the situation in the desert that they lost all interest
in S.O.E. or in the Balkans.

When things were once more stabilised in the late summer of
1942, the man who took effective charge of S.O.E. operations in
Cairo, under its civilian head, Lord Glenconner, was Colonel
Keble, a most resolute and ambitious man. Keble devoted himself to the task of getting some active resistance going in the
Balkans and to persuading General Headquarters that the Balkans was strategically important. From this point of view the
brilliant success of the Gorgopotamos operation, on 25 November 1942, was a turning-point. After Gorgopotamos the case for
greater efforts in Greece became convincing to the military
layman, and opportunities in Yugoslavia became interesting.

Great hopes were still entertained of Mihailović, but events
offered little justification for them. The events of 1941, and the
misfortunes of Hudson, have been briefly described in Bailey's
contribution to this book, and at greater length in Deakin's
The Embattled Mountain. When Hudson resumed contact with
Cairo in the autumn of 1942, he made it clear that Mihailović
was entirely passive in the face of the enemy, and was approving
of collaboration by several of his local commanders with the
Italian forces. Meanwhile information about the Communist-
led Partisans had been increasing. Much of it came from the
enemy and neutral press, and from the broadcasts of the *Free
Yugoslavia* radio station, located on Soviet territory and repeating information supplied by Tito. This information was more
readily available, and was better collated, in London than in
Cairo. Probably the B.B.C. were in fact better informed at this
time on Yugoslavia than any department of the British govern-

ment. Only scraps of this were known to S.O.E. Cairo, which did however receive a certain number of intelligence reports which mentioned resistance groups in Croatia. These were then believed – wrongly, as was later shown – to be organised by the Croatian Peasant Party. There was however another much better source, in the form of intercepts of local *Sicherheitsdienst* wireless communications. These, as George Taylor has shown, were seen by Keble in his earlier job in General Headquarters, and he continued to receive them when he was posted to S.O.E. They do not appear to have gone to S.O.E. London, but certainly must have reached some quarters in London, including some members of the Foreign Office, in the summer or autumn of 1942.

The fact that already in the summer of 1942 S.O.E. and the Foreign Office knew (though not from exactly the same sources) that the Partisans were fighting and Mihailović was not, and that they still supported Mihailović and did not help the Partisans, is not so sinister as a reader may at first suppose. In the first place, the fighting that was going on in the summer of 1942 was not on a very large scale. Secondly, in the crisis before and after the first Battle of El-Alamein, there was no possibility of giving any help to any one in the Balkans. Thirdly, Mihailović was believed to be husbanding his strength for a time when he could attack an enemy forced on to the defensive, with real effect, and the time for this was clearly not yet. To denounce a man who was a Minister in an allied government-in-exile and had been praised as a great Allied hero, and to make statements of admiration for the Communists which could not be followed up by practical help, would have done no one much good. The situation changed after Montgomery's victory in the desert and after Gorgopotamos. Now it was immediate action against the enemy in southern Europe, not vague promises of an all-out assault in an indefinite future, that General Headquarters Middle East wanted. This Keble understood, and he made his plans accordingly.

The differences in attitude between S.O.E. Cairo and London at this time have been clearly explained by George Taylor. They were not due to ideological disagreements, though it is probably true that the emotional commitment to Mihailović as a symbol of the spirit of 27 March 1941 was still a potent force in S.O.E. London but had virtually disappeared in S.O.E. Cairo, as a result of changes of personnel at both places. The decision to make contact with the Partisans was not rejected by S.O.E. London, but the initiative for it, and the planning at the decisive level, came from Keble. It is he who deserves the credit for making General Headquarters aware of the Balkans as a theatre of war. Unfortunately Keble was an unlovable man, driven by ambition and apparently determined to build up his own little empire and to let no one into it who was not directly under his orders. This is most clearly seen in his extraordinary treatment of Fitzroy Maclean, described above.* The discovery of the intrigues to which he had resorted, combined with the odium cast on S.O.E. by the fiasco of the Greek resistance delegates' visit to Cairo in August 1943, brought about Keble's fall.

By now however the decisions had been taken, and subsequent events flowed from them. The Communists won in Yugoslavia and were defeated in Greece.

The attempt to divide Yugoslavia into a sphere of interest each for Tito and for Mihailović was bound to fail, as at least several S.O.E. members realised from the very beginning. Mutual hatred between Mihailović and Tito was irreconcilable. The Partisans had become a hardened and efficient fighting force, while Mihailović's army existed only on paper. The notion that the Partisans were a 'Croatian' force, or that their supporters were to be found only west of the Drina, or even of the Ibar, was a fallacy. It is true that there were more Royalists in Serbia than anywhere else, but it is also true that there were proportionately more Serbs than Croats among the Communists and that this applied to Serbs from the kingdom as well as from Croatia and Bosnia. Allied support for Tito was bound to lead to abandonment of Mihailović. On the other hand the attempt to subordinate all Greek resistance forces to General Headquarters in Cairo was also bound to fail, for the Communists had other and more distant loyalties, which were bound to make them reject British authority sooner or later. The attempt did however have the important effect of separating republicans from Communists. By the end of 1944 fear of coming under Communist rule moved Greek republican democrats more powerfully than reluctance to see the King return.

* pp. 221–8.

The question raised by Woodhouse which is the crucial issue emerging from our discussions, namely why the British government took opposite decisions in Yugoslavia and Greece, cannot be answered with complete certainty, but there are some relevant points that can be enumerated.

Greece was always seen to be geographically more important, and physically more controllable, than Yugoslavia. Greece in hostile hands would undermine British security in the eastern Mediterranean; and conversely, British naval power would make it possible for Britain to hope to impose its will on Greece, at least on the assumption that Britain was going to remain a Great Power. Neither of these things were true of Yugoslavia, even though it was undoubtedly desirable that Yugoslavia should be in friendly hands.

The commitment of the British government to the Greek monarchy was stronger than to the Yugoslav. King Peter was a symbol of Serbian defiance of Hitler, but the action of 27 March 1941 was the work not of the King but of a few brave officers of his air force. King George had played a personal and vital part in keeping his country on Britain's side in the face of German threats. Whether these facts, or some deeper and unknown factors, account for the exceptional strength of Churchill's devotion to the King of Greece, we do not know today.

The military achievements, strength and ambitions of the resistance movements in the two countries were also different. Tito's Liberation Army was a far more effective force than E.L.A.S., and fought several long, bitter and large-scale campaigns against the Germans, whereas E.L.A.S. only carried out a number of rather small unconnected actions. On the other hand Mihailović persistently rejected Allied requests, and stood on his dignity as War Minister of a sovereign government, whereas Zervas readily agreed to do what was asked of him — even if he did not always carry it out.

The reactions of British Liaison Officers to the Partisans and to E.L.A.S. differed. It is true that relations differed from place to place: both Myers and Woodhouse had an understandable respect and liking for Tzimas, and Sheppard admired E.L.A.S.'s efforts; while in Yugoslavia Tempo and Kosta Nadj were much liked by their British contacts, but Arso Jovanović and Peko Dapčević were usually unpleasant. But in general B.L.O.s got on well with Yugoslav Partisans and disliked E.L.A.S. This different attitude may have had some influence on British policy.

Another important point is the independent status of the British mission to Tito's headquarters, as opposed to those with Mihailović or with any Greek resistance groups. Deakin was sent by Keble and General Headquarters, but the coincidence that he had a personal relationship to Churchill became an important factor, greatly increased of course by his exceptionally brilliant record in the field. Maclean also had the direct and personal blessing of Churchill, and had his own reasons for emancipating himself from control by S.O.E., most convincingly explained in his contribution to this book. Maclean quickly formed his own judgement, that Tito's forces were a substantial army, and that Tito must be treated as an ally and an equal. This judgement was accepted by Churchill, and it paid off, at least until Tito's surprise flight from Vis to Moscow in September 1944. Bailey was subordinated to General Headquarters Middle East, and was at the mercy of those who decided priorities for supply drops. The missions to Greece were closely controlled by headquarters, behind whom stood a profoundly suspicious Foreign Office; and they were supposed to dictate to their Greek hosts and to treat them, too, as subordinate to General Headquarters Middle East.

Contributors to this book have done their best to set down the truth, as they have discovered it from the documents or as they remember it from their own experience, or from both these sources. They realise that their story will produce different types of reaction in different types of readers, depending on their nationality, their age, their own life experience and their political preferences.

Yugoslav or Greek readers may be shocked at the crude calculus of British politicians, generals or officials of 'who is killing most Germans'; at the thought that Yugoslav and Greek lives were treated as mere commodities, expendable according to British military interests. Yet this should not really cause shock or surprise. Men's lives are the currency of war, and in this war the survival of Britain was at stake. Britain's leaders had to be ruthless. So also did the resistance leaders. The lives of Russian soldiers killed on the Volga and of British soldiers killed in the western desert formed part of Tito's calculations too.

British readers will probably find the story of conflict between government departments, and within S.O.E., unedifying. Yet this too is part of war. There were unedifying quarrels between State Department, O.S.S., F.B.I. and other American agencies; and between *Abwehr, Sicherheitsdienst*, S.S. and regular army within the German war machine. Both these sets of rivalries are amply documented. That there were no less bitter rivalries between M.V.D./M.G.B., Communist Party hierarchy, Red Army Intelligence and other branches of the Soviet government can hardly be doubted, though the refusal of the Soviet authorities to release Soviet archives for unregimented research makes this impossible to document.

British officials were well aware at the time of potential or certain contradictions between Britain's long-term interests in the Balkans and short-term military advantage. In a desperate war, inevitably the latter prevailed. It may be obvious in 1974 that the war would have been won even without any Balkan resistance effort, but this was not obvious between 1941 and 1944. The argument as to whether it would have been possible, by a major attack through the Ljubljana Gap, to enter the Danube valley before the Red Army, and so to produce a completely different political map of Europe from that which has existed since 1945, can never be definitely settled. It is fairly certain that the superiority of the effective military might of the Western Powers over that of the Soviet Union in 1945 was such that they could have forced the Soviet leaders to give up their conquests if they had been willing to treat the Soviet Union as an enemy. It is equally certain that the overwhelming majority of the people, and of the politicians, of the Western Allied states did not in 1945 regard the Soviet Union as an enemy, and would have rejected such a policy.

The question whether the policies adopted by the British government towards Yugoslavia and Greece (which essentially were decided by the end of 1943) promoted British interests, is difficult to answer from the perspective of 1974. It is difficult to see how Mihailović could have been brought to power: if he had been, there would have been another round of Serb-Croat massacres, probably little if at all less bloody than those of

1941–2, and Yugoslavia would have fallen apart. If E.A.M./ E.L.A.S. had been allowed to take over the whole of Greece, that country would have been placed under a totalitarian regime such as was established in Albania and Bulgaria. Whether this would have lasted unmodified up to 1974, is of course more doubtful; but even if there had been eventual liberalisation or revolution, it seems certain that for a good many years the Greeks would have suffered horrors much greater even than those which befell them during the civil war of 1946–9. Nevertheless, the fighting in Athens in December 1944 and the execution of Mihailović in June 1946 leave a sour taste behind. In both cases men who had fought on the same side as Britain, who had once been praised by the British as heroes, were abandoned to their enemies or were shot down by British troops.

Did Marshal Tito's Yugoslavia or the Greek monarchy prove to be long-term friends of Britain? This question too looks different from the two perspectives of 1945 and 1974. Official British doctrine in 1945 was that Britain was still one of three Great Powers, even if weaker both economically and militarily than the United States and militarily than Soviet Russia. As a Great Power, Britain would continue to have important interests all over the world, especially in the Mediterranean. The situation in the Balkans would therefore matter to the British. It was not foreseen in 1945 that Britain would decline in the 1960s to the status of a middle-rank Power, and would follow in the 1970s a course that seemed likely to reduce her to a still lower status, amid the growing indifference of the British public to any of those things which were traditionally subsumed under the words 'national interest'. The question posed above can therefore simply not be answered.

It is perhaps just worth stating that in 1974 relations between many thousands of British people and many thousands of Yugoslavs and Greeks were closer and warmer than they had ever been. The 'special relationship' between Greece and Britain was weakened by the Cyprus conflict and by the passions unleashed or stifled by the Colonels' regime; but the memory of Eddie Myers, Monty Woodhouse, David Pawson and other British friends of Greece, and their continuing contacts with Greeks, are still something to be reckoned with. It is also not inappropriate to speak of a 'special relationship' with Yugoslavia, not so old as that with Greece, but going pack to the exploits of the Scottish nurses in the retreat through Albania in 1915 and the comradeship of the Salonika Front in 1917–18, growing between the wars and still more during the years of resistance. The comradeship of 1943–4 was not obliterated by the hostility of 1945–8 but revived again rather rapidly. The special relationship included a special bitterness as well as a special mutual affection, and both sentiments affect both Serbs and Croats. I can do no more than assert my personal belief that the affection is stronger than the bitterness, and that the credit for this belongs, in different ways, to Bill Deakin, Fitzroy Maclean, Bill Bailey and some scores of others who can remain nameless.

This book then is a piece of micro-history. It is an attempt by some of us who took part in these events, or were witnesses of the process of decision, to make our small contributions to a small sector of history *wie es eigentlich gewesen*. Readers born after these events will not see them as we saw them, but they would do well to reflect, before they proclaim that *theirs* is the *correct* viewpoint, that their own children in due course will certainly see it all differently again.

Select Bibliography

Alexander, A. R. L. G. (Field-Marshal, 1st Earl), *The Alexander Memoirs 1940–1945*, ed. J. North (London, 1962).
Amery, J., *Sons of the Eagle* (London, 1948).
Auty, P., *Tito: a biography* (London, 1970).
Avon, Earl of (Anthony Eden), Memoirs Part II, *Facing the Dictators* (London, 1962).
Butler, J. R. M. (ed.), *Grand Strategy*, v, vi (London, 1956).
Byford-Jones, W., *The Greek Trilogy. Resistance–Liberation–Revolution* (London, 1945).
Četniks, The (A.F.H.Q. Handbook, 1944).
Churchill, W. S., *The Second World War*, 6 vols (London, 1948–55) esp. v, *Closing the Ring* and vi, *Triumph and Tragedy*.
Clissold, S., *Whirlwind: The Story of Marshal Tito's Rise to Power* (London, 1949).
Davidson, B., *Partisan Picture* (Bedford, 1946).
Deakin, F. W., *The Embattled Mountain* (London, 1972).
Dedijer, V., *Tito Speaks* (London, 1953).
——, *With Tito through the War, 1941–1944* (London, 1951).
Djilas, M., *Conversations with Stalin* (London, 1962).
Fielding, Xan, *Hide and Seek, The Story of a War-Time Agent* (London, 1954).
Fotich, C., *The War We Lost. Yugoslavia's Tragedy and Failure in the West* (New York, 1948).
Gubbins, Sir Colin, 'Resistance Movements in the War', *Journal of the Royal United Service Institution*, xliii (1948).
Hamson, Denys, *We Fell Among Greeks* (London, 1946).
Hoptner, J. B., *Yugoslavia in Crisis 1934–41* (Columbia, 1962).
Jones, W. *Twelve months into Tito's Partisans* (Bedford, 1946).
Jordan, William, *Conquest without Victory* (London, 1969).
Knezevitch, Z. L., *Why the Allies Abandoned the Yugoslav Army of General Mihailovitch: With Official Memoranda and Documents* (Washington, 1945).
Lawrence, C., *Irregular Adventure* (London, 1947).

Leeper, Sir Reginald, *When Greek meets Greek* (London, 1950).

Leverkuehn, P., *German Military Intelligence* (New York, 1954).

Lincoln, John, *Achilles and the Tortoise. An Eastern Aegean Exploit* (London, 1958).

Maclean, F. *Eastern Approaches* (London, 1950).

——, *Disputed Barricade* (London, 1957).

Macmillan, H., *The Blast of War* (London, 1967).

Moss, W. Stanley, *Ill met by Moonlight* (London, 1950).

——, *A War of Shadows* (London, 1952).

Mulgan, John, *Report on Experience* (London, 1947).

Myers, E. C. W., *Greek Entanglement* (London, 1955).

National Liberation Movement of Yugoslavia (A.F.H.Q. Handbook, 1943).

Peter II (King of Yugoslavia), *A King's Heritage* (London, 1956).

Rendel, A. M., *Appointment in Crete. The Story of a British Agent* (London, 1953).

Rendel, G., *The Sword and the Olive* (London, 1957).

Rootham, J., *Miss Fire* (London, 1946).

Sweet-Escott, Bickham, *Baker Street Irregular* (London, 1965).

Wilson, Field-Marshal, Lord, *Eight Years Overseas 1939–1947* (London, 1948).

Woodhouse, C. M., *Apple of Discord. A Survey of Recent Greek Politics in their International Setting* (London, 1948).

Woodhouse, C. M., *The Struggle for Greece, 1941–1949* (London, 1975).

'Zür Geschichte der Resistance in Griechenland', *Vierteljahreshefte für Zeitgeschichte*, II (1958).

'Early British Contacts with the Greek Resistance', *Balkan Studies*, XII (1971).

Index

BISHOP'S UNIVERSITY
LIBRARY
LENNOXVILLE